NEW LIFE FOR OLD SUBURBS

New Life for Old Suburbs

Post-war Land Use and Housing
in the Australian Inner City

HAL KENDIG
Urban Research Unit
Australian National University

SYDNEY
GEORGE ALLEN & UNWIN
LONDON   BOSTON

First published in 1979 by
George Allen & Unwin Australia Pty Ltd
8 Napier Street
North Sydney NSW 2060

National Library of Australia
Cataloguing-in-Publication entry

Kendig, Hal, 1948-
  New life for old suburbs.

  Index
  Bibliography
  ISBN 0 86861 392 4
  ISBN 0 86861 001 1 Paperback

  1. Urban renewal — Australia. 1. Title.

711.59'0994

Library of Congress Catalog Card Number: 78-74190

Set in 10 on 12 point Times by G.T. Setters , Sydney
Printed in Hong Kong

To Wendy

Contents

FIGURES

TABLES

MAPS

Preface

This study has demonstrated the wisdom of the saying that the best way to learn a subject is to write a book about it. Because the inner suburbs have such varied land uses and strong pressures for change, studying these areas is especially valuable for understanding interrelationships between different aspects of urban development that usually are considered separately. Three themes in particular have been emphasised. First, inner-suburban development — or the development of any one part of the metropolis — is heavily influenced by developments elsewhere in the metropolis and by broader economic and social changes. Second, urban growth and change have important social consequences that should be taken into account in policy formation. Third, Australian cities are significantly different from those of other countries; better urban management in Australia demands a better understanding of these differences. This study measures inner-suburban features and change in ways that may prove useful to students learning about urban change and to professionals who influence policy and practice.

Hal Kendig
Canberra, July 1978.

Acknowledgements

As a relative newcomer to Australia, I have had considerable assistance in conducting this study. Most of all, I must thank Peter Harrison and Max Neutze for their guidance and encouragement. This study draws heavily from their experience and insights. Jenny Norman's research assistance and June Harries' translation of the manuscript have been invaluable. Richard Davis helped with some of the programming and Pauline McDonough helped with the data collection. I am also indebted to Lyn Smith for typing and Leo Pancino for the maps and figures. All the other members of the Urban Research Unit, but especially Ian Manning and Owen Donald, have helped in one way or another.

Many other people have provided data, criticism, or otherwise contributed to the effort. In Sydney, Joan Masterman, Brenda Humble, Colin Menzies and Margaret Barry proved to be excellent guides to sources of information; comments from John Roseth and Rod Jensen substantially improved the last two chapters. Paul Madden, Tony Dalton and Andrew Burbidge in Melbourne, and David Lewis in Adelaide, kept me informed of developments in their cities and provided helpful advice on parts of my rough draft. Comments from Don Beattie and Terry Henderson also improved the last two chapters. Essential data on non-residential incursion was provided by Mr Lacey of the New South Wales Department of Main Roads, Mr Acason of the New South Wales Department of Education, and the property officers or superintendents of hospitals and tertiary education institutions in inner Sydney.

Finally, I am grateful for the rare opportunity for undertaking the research made possible by a fellowship in the Research School of Social Sciences of the Australian National University.

CHAPTER 1

Introduction

Urban and social change have profoundly influenced the inner suburbs at each stage of metropolitan development. Australia's first penal colony in Port Jackson has been transformed into the Central Business District in Sydney. The inner residential areas were nearly all developed by the early twentieth century and have been reshaped by a wide variety of evolving needs. They were designed for transport on foot and by horse but have adapted to the widespread use of motor vehicles. They have traditionally catered for the poor, especially during times of depression, and they have served as the main reception area for the immigration that has created the nation. All urban growth, even in outer areas, continues to have an impact on them. Despite the onslaughts of urban change, the inner suburbs have vestiges of nearly every past stage of urban development and remain under pressures of continuing change as every new stage emerges.

This book aims to explain the major residential developments in the inner suburbs of Sydney, Melbourne and Adelaide during the post-war years. These include non-residential incursion, the building of flats and, most importantly, the improvement and changing occupancy of the existing stock of housing. At the same time, there have been large population losses, and stable, working-class communities have evolved into diverse mixes of population which also include, relatively, more old people, non-British migrant families and affluent young adults. These developments are considered in the context of changes throughout the metropolitan areas and particular attention is paid to the effect of the developments on the availability of low-cost housing near jobs and urban attractions.

The inner suburbs have long been at the centre of the policy debate on equity and urban development. A traditional view, emphasised since the turn of the century and in many post-war policies on urban development, is that inner-city residential areas are on the decline, suffering from deteriorating housing and losses of jobs and of all but the poorest people. This diagnosis suggests that redevelopment by government and by the private sector is needed to improve inner-area housing and bring back investment, jobs, and residents of all income groups. An alternative view, put forward increasingly frequently since the mid 1960s, is that the inner areas have, in some respects, had too much investment and improvement. Redevelopment and rising housing costs, proponents of this view argue, have forced the poor from familiar and formerly cheap housing out to the barren urban fringe. These alternative diagnoses — 'slums and blight' versus 'over-centralisation and gentrification' — underlie many of the policy-relevant questions that this study attempts to answer.

The Overseas Experience

In London, Paris, New York and hundreds of other Western cities, older areas near the city centre have lost both housing and people, while there has been rapid residential expansion on the urban fringe. The reasons behind these inner-area losses, and the changes among the types of inner-area residents, have varied considerably between countries and individual cities. The translation of British and American experience to the Australian situation can be misleading. The differences between the inner suburbs of Australian, British and American cities call for caution in transplanting to Australia policies developed overseas. The overseas situations of today do not necessarily offer clues for tomorrow's Australian; Australian policies should be based on analyses of Australian cities.

There are many differences between the inner suburbs of cities in Britain and in Australia. First, the inner areas of most British cities were built in the early nineteenth century, whereas there was little urban development in Australia before 1870. Most housing in the British inner suburbs was of poor quality, amenities in the neighbourhoods were usually limited and the streets were suitable only for travel by horse or on foot. Home ownership in Britain has been limited mainly to the rich, by house prices that are high relative to incomes; suburbanisation has been less rapid because of low car-ownership rates, as well as the expense of the new dwellings.

Partly as a result of the Blitz and a greater acceptance of the ensuing public intervention, the British post-war rehousing programme of 1955 to 1967 demolished or closed over a million houses and subsidised improvements to an additional one and a half million (Cullingworth, 1974: 263). By the early 1970s, municipal public housing comprised a third of the total British housing stock and about half of the new dwellings. The persistence of stringent rent controls and the taxation advantages of owner-occupation have forced many landlords to sell to occupants and has severely constrained new building for private rental. The British concern in recent years for the movement outwards from the inner areas of unskilled jobs (Department of the Environment, UK, 1977) has, for reasons discussed in Chapter 9, much less relevance for Australia.

Despite the country's strong British heritage, Australian cities are less like British and more like American cities, especially the newer ones on the west coast of the United States and Canada. [1] Very little of the existing housing in either Australia or North America dates before the mid-nineteenth century. Australia has slightly higher rates of home ownership, while the United States has higher incomes and car-ownership rates. American urban densities are slightly lower: in 1970, 1349 persons per square kilometre compared to 1550 in Australia (Harrison, 1977: 16).

Notwithstanding these similarities, post-war urban development in Australia and America has differed considerably. Inner-city areas in America have generally had more rapid residential and non-residential suburbanisation, less public housing, large losses of jobs, little investment, and falling real property values. While in Australia the inner-suburban housing has been improving in almost all respects, in the United States it has deteriorated until there have emerged 'grey areas' where nobody invested (Frieden, 1964) and housing was abandoned (Sternlieb & Burchell, 1973). The stagnation of non-residential development in most American inner-city areas is all the more marked considering that the Americans spent tens of billions of dollars subsidising commercial redevelopment in the city centres and building freeways for commuters to the new housing on the fringe. By the mid 1960s the construction programmes of the Urban Renewal and National Highway Acts had displaced well over two million inner-city residents, with little compensation for tenants. Why have the patterns of urban development gone in opposite directions?

There are many possible explanations and it is hard to evaluate their relative importance. In America inner-city areas have fewer advantages for commercial and industrial activities than do inner-city areas in Australia; fast-growing American cities have less centralised structures. Most American cities are inland, and goods largely travel by truck along the highly developed network of freeways between and within cities. Ports and railway terminals are less important and, in any event, have often been moved away from the city centres. The old industrial cities of the northeast, which were traditionally more centralised like Australian cities, have been declining (Sternlieb & Hughes, 1975). Much of the remaining industrial and commercial activity has moved from the inner areas, which have more antiquated and run-down infrastructure than in Australia, to the urban fringes, which generally have better road and other infrastructure than in Australia. The production techniques of American firms are often more advanced, need more space and can be more economically located in outer areas. With larger plants and head offices, more American firms are less dependent on the central-city services that attract smaller firms to inner areas. Few major American cities are state capitals and hence few have benefited from the sustained growth of the public sector. Finally, American firms have been following the more extensive movement of the labourforce to the suburbs.

The residential location of American populations has decentralised farther and faster, partly because of the greater job decentralisation, better freeways and higher car-ownership rates. High-income American whites, with the help of federally subsidised mortgages and tax deductions for new homes, could easily afford to leave racially troubled and deteriorating inner areas. On the other hand, few black migrants from rural areas could afford to buy homes or pay enough rent for properly maintained dwellings. Australia has avoided major income disparities and racial discrimination on a large scale. In Australia, the post-war, non-British migrants, unlike American blacks, have been largely assimilated economically and their arrival in Australia strengthened the demand for inner-suburban housing. The cheap, wooden, walk-up tenements that served the immigrants to America around the turn of the century left a difficult legacy. Unlike Australian brick terrace houses, these units do not lend themselves to renovation or sale to occupants.

The greater financial responsibility of American local governments has aggravated inner-city problems. Local councils in America have to impose high property taxes in order to finance many education, welfare and other services which, in Australia, are provided by state governments (although financed mainly from federal income taxes). American firms and individuals can avoid contributing to the costs of public services for poor, inner-area residents by moving into another municipality, thereby extending its tax base and thus lowering its rates. Inner-city municipalities in America have fallen into a vicious cycle of declining property values, contracting tax bases, rising tax rates and declining quality of public services.

Inner suburbs of Australian cities

Change in the inner suburbs of Australian cities has been the greatest in the older, larger and more concentrated metropolises. Accordingly, this study focuses on the inner suburbs of Sydney, Melbourne and Adelaide. These cities, in contrast to most American cities of their size, are all state capitals on the coast; they are the largest cities, the primary ports and the financial and governmental centres of the nation. Brisbane and Perth, the only other urban areas with populations of over half a million, also dominate their states; but the growth of these two cities has generally been more recent and their development more dispersed; in general, they have also experienced less inner-area change — except for concentrated office building.[2] Yet even in these cities and smaller cities still, such as Newcastle, there is concern about issues in inner-area development.[3]

The metropolitan areas have differences that are largely explained by the accessibility to inner city employment and the general constraints of their geographical sites. In Sydney, where jobs are most centralised and access to the city centre is physically more difficult, people have adjusted to the poorer accessibility by living at a higher urban density (1918 people per square kilometre) than that of Melbourne (1811) and much higher than that of Adelaide (1459) (Harrison, 1977:16). As is shown in Table 1.3, the Sydney metropolitan area has the highest proportion of flats. Although higher densities mean reduced distances from home to work, the proportion of workers commuting long distances (over one and a half hours daily) still is higher in Sydney (28 per cent) than in Melbourne (21 per cent) or in Adelaide (9 per cent) (Harrison, 1977:22). The demand for inner-suburban housing to provide access to jobs is greatest in Sydney and least in Adelaide.

The inner suburbs discussed in this study are those local government areas

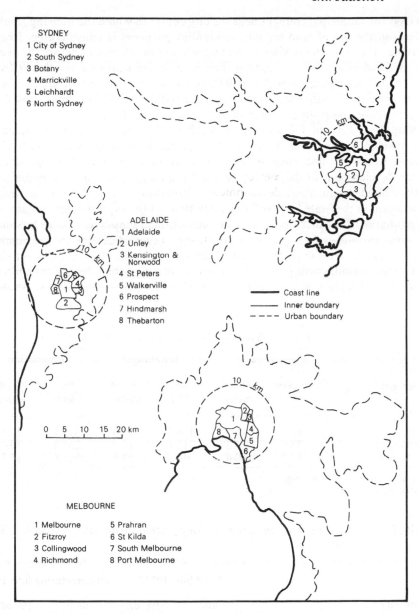

SYDNEY
1 City of Sydney
2 South Sydney
3 Botany
4 Marrickville
5 Leichhardt
6 North Sydney

ADELAIDE
1 Adelaide
2 Unley
3 Kensington & Norwood
4 St Peters
5 Walkerville
6 Prospect
7 Hindmarsh
8 Thebarton

Coast line
Inner boundary
Urban boundary

0 5 10 15 20 km

MELBOURNE

1 Melbourne   5 Prahran
2 Fitzroy   6 St Kilda
3 Collingwood   7 South Melbourne
4 Richmond   8 Port Melbourne

MAP 1.1.   Inner areas and urban boundaries of Sydney, Melbourne and Adelaide, 1971

(LGAs) for municipal councils near the city centre in which the housing stock is older and the use of land for non-residential purposes is considerable. Nearly all these areas, shown on Map 1.1 had significant development before the age of the car, and most of them reached their population peaks during the 1920s or earlier. Although inner suburbs in all three cities comprise very little of the total urban area, and house only about 10 per cent of the cities' residents (Table 1.1), they provide about 40 per cent of the jobs (Table 1.2).

Maps 1.2, 1.3 and 1.4, show how much of the inner areas are occupied by non-residential land uses. In all three cities, the inner areas are the hub of the statewide railway and road systems; they contain nearly all the high-density office development in the metropolis, and the major roads into them are lined with ribbon commercial development. Government in Australia is heavily centralised at the State level and the inner areas of the capital cities contain very large shares of the metropolitan areas' government employees, large hospitals, universities and other public institutions. Inner Adelaide has abundant parklands (the renowned park belt of the original plan) but no port activities and little manufacturing. Inner Sydney is distinguished by its magnificent harbour and high-density commercial development in North Sydney. Another

TABLE 1.1   *Sizes of inner Sydney, Melbourne and Adelaide, 1976.*

Inner city	Area		Dwellings[a]		Population	
	sq.km	% of metro	no. ('000)	% of metro.	no. ('000)	% of metro.
Sydney	81.0	5.7	136.1	12.8	319.9	10.6
Melbourne	83.6	6.3	112.6	12.7	259.6	10.0
Adelaide	57.7	10.4	45.3	14.6	114.8	12.7

[a]includes unoccupied dwellings
Source: Census, 1976

TABLE 1.2   *Employment in inner Sydney, Melbourne and Adelaide, 1971 and 1975.*

Inner city	Total jobs 1971[a]		Manufacturing jobs 1975[b]	
	no. ('000)	(% of metro.)	no. ('000)	(% of metro.)
Sydney	533.4	44.3	114.1	31.9
Melbourne	430.8	41.5	101.9	27.6
Adelaide	113.3	37.4	19.1	19.1

Sources: [a]Census, 1971
          [b]ABS (1977a).

TABLE 1.3   *Occupied housing types[a] in Sydney, Melbourne and Adelaide, 1971 (percentage of total)*

	Houses	Self-contained flats	Non-self-contained flats	Non-private	Total
Inner area					
Sydney	52	37	9	1	100
Melbourne	48	44	7	1	100
Adelaide	84	12	3	1	100
Total metro.					
Sydney	74	23	2	1	100
Melbourne	81	15	3	1	100
Adelaide	92	6	1	1	100

[a] For definitions of housing types, see the section of this chapter on data and terminology.
Source: Census 1971.

difference, not apparent on the maps, is that the inner areas in Adelaide and in Melbourne have wider roads than does Sydney.

The attraction of accessibility to jobs, and high land costs, are the main reasons why the inner areas have high proportions of flats (Table 1.3). Inner Melbourne has a higher proportion of flats than the inner areas of the other cities, as a result of redevelopment by the Victorian Housing Commission. Despite the advantages to inner areas of accessibility, Table 1.4 shows that rents are relatively low because the old housing is often small, obsolete, poorly maintained, or near incompatible land uses. Owner-occupancy rates are also relatively low. Compared to the two larger cities, inner Adelaide is more suburban in character; the advantages of accessibility are fewer, and there is less obsolescence of housing and intrusion of non-residential land use.

Table 1.5 shows that among the residents of all the inner suburbs, there are relatively fewer children, while there are more young adults, old people and migrants. Inner Melbourne and inner Sydney have been especially important reception areas for the post-war, non-British migrants, who comprise almost a third of the residents, not counting their Australian-born children. The higher proportion of children in inner Melbourne, is largely due to the many families with children resident in the large amount of public housing, and the numerous children of many southern European migrant families. Inner Adelaide has low occupancy rates (Table 1.4) and a high proportion of aged people. The high proportion of upper-status, white-collar workers in inner Adelaide reflects the relative scarcity of manufacturing industry and the higher-quality housing in the inner areas.

A general overview of the inner suburbs obscures the considerable diversity

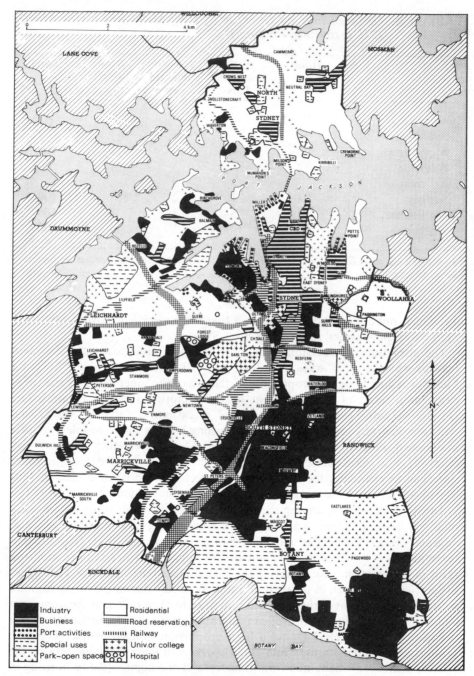

MAP 1.2.   Zoning of inner Sydney, 1971
Source: Local government planning schemes. (see note 6, Chapter 1)

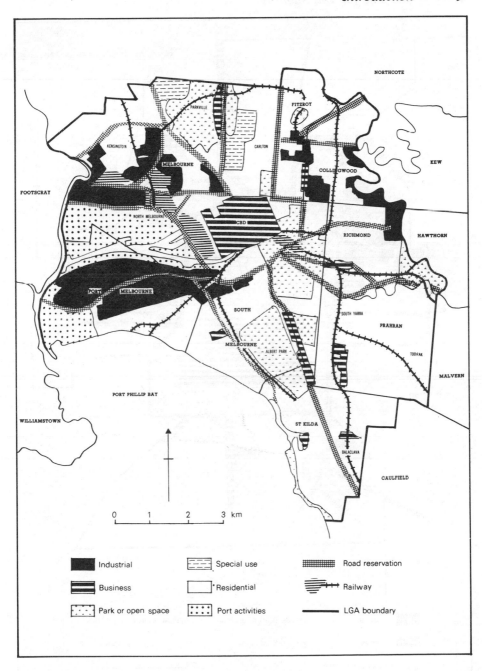

MAP 1.3.   Zoning of inner Melbourne, 1968
Source: Melbourne and Metropolitan Board of Works (1968).

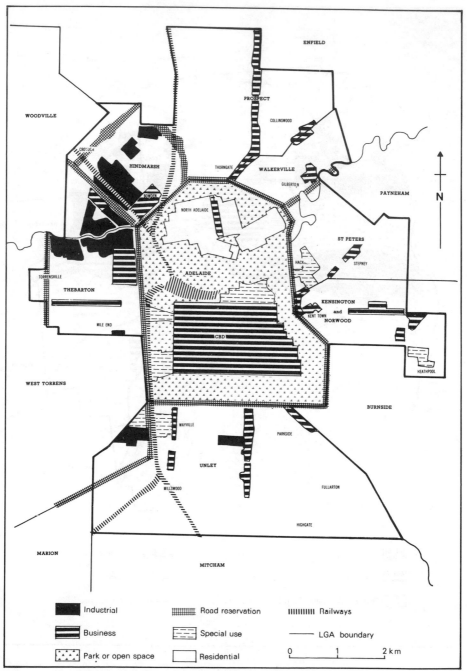

MAP 1.4.   Zoning of inner Adelaide, 1962
Source: South Australian Town Planning Committee (1962).

TABLE 1.4 *Selected housing characteristics in Sydney, Melbourne and Adelaide, 1971.*

Area	Houses			Self-contained flats		Govt. dwellings [c]
	Owner-occupied (%)	Rent [a] ($)	Occupancy rate [b]	Owner-occupied (%)	Rent [a] ($)	% of housing stock
Inner area						
Sydney	61	15.51	.63	21	18.64	3.1
Melbourne	62	16.71	.66	11	19.16	8.7
Adelaide	71	12.27	.55	12	15.18	1.3
Total metro.						
Sydney	79	18.90	.64	28	20.61	4.7
Melbourne	81	18.20	.66	17	19.48	3.6
Adelaide	75	12.88	.64	12	15.30	9.9

[a] Average weekly rent for unfurnished, privately tenanted dwellings
[b] Average number of occupants per room
[c] Proportion of occupied, self-contained houses and flats
Source: Census, 1971.

TABLE 1.5 *Selected population characteristics in Sydney, Melbourne and Adelaide, 1971.*

	Age (% of total)			Non-British born (% of total)	Labourforce (% of total)	
	Children (0-14)	Young adults (15-34)	Aged (65+)		Upper white-collar [a]	Blue-collar [b]
Inner area						
Sydney	19	36	10	31	14	38
Melbourne	23	35	10	32	18	39
Adelaide	20	31	16	20	20	32
Total metro.						
Sydney	26	32	9	16	18	34
Melbourne	28	32	8	19	18	35
Adelaide	28	30	9	13	19	35

[a] Per cent in professional, technical, administrative and related occupations
[b] Per cent craftsmen, process and production workers, and labourers
Source: Census, 1971.

within them. Inner Sydney is characterised by higher-status areas near and north of the harbour and lower-status areas south of it; inner Adelaide has higher-status northern and eastern areas and a lower-status centre and western area; inner Melbourne has a more complicated structure of better-quality dwellings and higher-status residents in elevated areas and poorer housing in the lowlands. North Adelaide, Toorak in inner Melbourne, and Potts Point in inner Sydney are renowned for having some of the most expensive housing anywhere in Australia. Within a few kilometres of these areas are poorly built houses badly blighted by traffic and industrial pollution. The development of flats has been concentrated in the high-amenity areas like North Sydney, the southeast of inner Melbourne, and the northeast of inner Adelaide.

This brief review shows that the inner areas of Sydney, Melbourne and Adelaide have a number of common features. Each inner area offers a large share of the metropolitan employment opportunities, serves as the focal point for government and business, and contains industries and warehousing. Some of the terraces and other older housing in the inner areas have been converted or redeveloped for flats or for a variety of non-residential purposes. The residents, like the housing and the uses made of the land, are diverse. Inner areas generally have more migrants, fewer children and more lower-status workers. Sydney and Melbourne are more extreme than Adelaide in these respects and are older, larger, denser and more congested.

Outline

This book explores the extent, causes and consequences of inner-suburban residential change since the second world war. Chapter 2 provides a background to later empirical analysis by reviewing a variety of theories and concepts that can be used to understand competition for and change of land use in inner areas. Chapters 3 and 4 describe the features of the inner-suburban areas and their residents, and show the advantages and disadvantages of inner-city living. The residential conditions and their effects are shown to differ considerably between households in different income and ethnic groups and at different stages in the family life-cycle. The analysis helps to understand the reasons for moves into and out of the inner areas, and identifies some of the social and economic costs imposed on the lower-income residents by urban change.

Chapters 5 to 9 analyse post-war changes in inner areas. Chapter 5 describes how the post-war housing and population changes in the inner areas have varied between the cities and from the overseas experience. Population losses are explained by the changes in the amount, composition and use of the housing stock. Chapter 6 provides a more detailed description and explanation of non-residential incursion, mainly in inner Sydney, up to 1971. It explains why some business and industries expanded in inner areas while others decentralised to the outer suburbs. It shows the amount of housing taken, and the jobs provided, by business, industry and a variety of public developments.

The characteristics of those displaced by these developments are also identified.

Chapters 7 and 8 explain the considerable rejuvenation of inner-area housing. Although, soon after the second world war, this housing was considered as slums requiring replacement, there has since been extensive private improvement of the housing, which, by almost all available measures, has exceeded the average extent of improvement throughout the metropolis. Private and public development of flats has provided additional inner-suburban housing. These developments and changes in the residential composition are explained.

The last two chapters analyse the intense competition for inner-suburban housing during the 1970s. Although the rate of non-residential incursion has slowed down, so has the building of flats, while demand for inner-suburban housing has remained high. People on low incomes are being forced to pay high rents to get housing in the inner suburbs. To preserve and improve inner-city living for the poor, this study argues for decentralisation of employment and public institutions, rehabilitation rather than redevelopment by the housing authorities, and selective neighbourhood improvements that do not displace low-income renters.

Terminology and Data

This study uses empirical data to answer questions of 'how much?' and 'to what degree?'. The terms 'inner city' and 'inner areas' are used interchangeably to refer to the areas shown on Map 1.1; the 'inner suburbs' refers to the residential parts of the 'inner areas'; 'urban areas' or 'metropolitan areas' — shown for 1971 on Map 1.1 — refers to the areas designated as such in each census (except for analyses of changes over time, which use the census figures for the slightly larger Statistical Divisions that vary less in size between censuses). 'The suburbs' or 'areas elsewhere in the metropolis,' refers to the metropolitan area outside the inner-city as shown on Map 1.1. When different definitions of the 'inner areas' are used because of problems of data availability, the difference is noted.

The use of jargon is minimised but is unavoidable in some cases. Chapter 2 explains technical terms in the literature, such as 'filtering' (p. 25), the zonal model and ecological succession (p. 18), a transitional zone (p. 18), 'multi-nodal' (p. 20), and 'higher' land uses (p. 21). Occupancy rates means the number of people per room, infill is new development on vacant land within developed areas, and gentrification is the movement of higher status residents into housing formerly occupied by lower-status people. Incursion, encroachment, and succession are used interchangeably to refer to the replacement of existing land uses with new land uses. Other special terms associated with particular data sources are listed below.

Most data from the Census and other major sources are available for local government areas (LGAs). These boundaries are shown for inner Sydney on Map 1.1 and Map 1.5, and for inner Adelaide and inner Melbourne on Map 1.1.

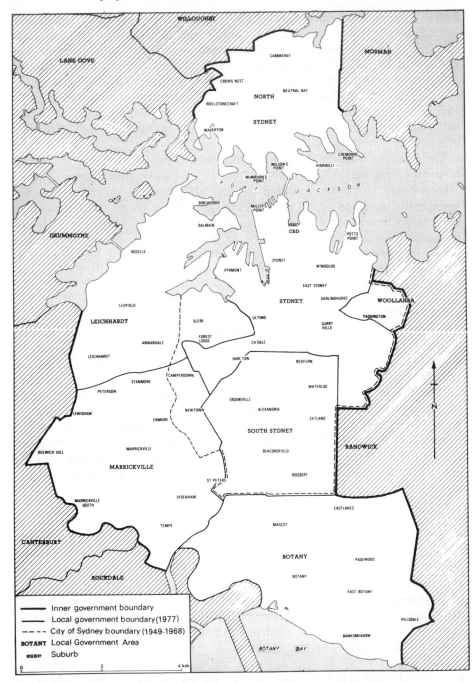

MAP 1.5.   Suburbs and Local Government Areas in inner Sydney, 1977

Because of changes over time to the City of Sydney boundaries, the 'old City of Sydney' refers to the enlarged areas from 1949 to 1968 shown on Map 1.5.[4] The names of suburbs, which are defined by postal code boundaries, are shown for inner Sydney on Map 1.2 and Map 1.5, and for inner Melbourne on Map 1.3 and for inner Adelaide on Map 1.4. For Sydney Census data was also obtained for the 600 very small Collectors Districts (CDs) which, in 1971, each contained an average of about 200 households. Because the boundaries of CDs varied between censuses, the 1971 CDs were amalgamated into 374 areas for which the figures from each post-war census could be aggregated into the same geographical areas. Changes of the dwelling counts in these small areas are used to estimate construction, demolitions and conversions in inner Sydney. For inner Melbourne and inner Adelaide, no analysis was conducted by CDs; detailed results for small areas are produced only for inner Sydney.

The primary data sources were the Censuses for 1947, 1954, 1961, 1966, 1971 and 1976. The Census is conducted on a 'defacto' basis and includes people temporarily in the area on the night of the Census. Unfortunately, only preliminary LGA figures from the 1976 Census were available in time for use in this study. Unless otherwise specified, the study uses the published census data on LGAs, or unpublished data on CDs. The latter were available on magnetic computer tape for the 1971 Census and in unpublished tables for earlier Censuses provided by the Australian Bureau of Statistics in Canberra. Information for CDs was very scarce for the earlier Censuses: in 1947 and 1954, the only housing data was a count of total occupied dwellings; data on unoccupied dwellings and on type of occupied housing have only been added since 1961; data on tenure, rent, and other variables was available only in 1971. Even for the LGAs, for which more information is generally available, no data on the occupations of the labourforce was available until 1966.

The housing data are limited further because the Censuses enumerate *'households'* — defined as people who live and eat together — not physical housing structures. A building counts as one dwelling if the residents live and eat together, or as two or more dwellings if occupied by separate households. This means that an old mansion subdivided into twenty rooms counts as a single dwelling if the residents have common meals but counts as twenty dwellings if they do not. The number of dwellings can therefore vary considerably if there are enumeration inconsistencies or small changes in the use of a dwelling that involve no structural change.

The definitions of *types of dwelling,* employed in the 1971 Census, and differences from definitions in earlier years, are as follows:
Private dwellings
Private houses: Detached houses, semi-detached house, house/shops, terrace houses, or villa units that contain only one household and thus return only one Census schedule. (Villa units, which form a significant proportion of the inner-suburban houses only in Adelaide, were apparently counted as self-contained flats in 1961.)

Self-contained flats: Part of a house or other building that can be closed off completely and has its own toilet and cooking facilities.

Non-self-contained flats: Rooms, shared houses, shared flats, or other dwellings that are not self-contained. (In 1961 and earlier Censuses, shared houses, shared flats and tenements or apartments were separated.)

Non-private dwellings: Boarding houses, hotels, institutions, caretaker quarters and related kinds of dwellings.

Some of these distinctions can be difficult to make, especially in the inner areas where the buildings are diverse and are used in a wide variety of ways.

The Censuses provide almost no data on the kinds of people living in different kinds of inner-suburban housing. This problem was partly overcome in this study by using the 1971 Sydney Area Transportation Study's (SATS) data on a sample of 2 per cent of Sydney's households. Unpublished SATS data on computer tapes were analysed to cross-tabulate different types of families by their income, housing, travel and other characteristics.[5] Data on life cycle was available only for household *heads,* and thus excludes boarders and all but the first head in shared accommodation. Following are the definitions used for *life-cycle groups:*

Pre-family: Households having no children and heads under forty years of age. They include single people living alone, groups and childless couples.

Family: Households of any age having children living in them. *Single-parent families* are those with only one spouse, while *large families* are those having four or more children.

Post-family: Households having no children and heads aged forty years or over. The *aged* are heads aged over sixty-four.

The SATS data on *income* is for gross total annual incomes. *'High income'* is defined as $8000 or more (21 per cent of Sydney households) and *'low income'* is under $5000 for families with children and under $4000 for others. The *'low income'* category is very large, containing 42 per cent of Sydney's households, because SATS had no income categories under $4000. Some of this data is provided for the outer southwest region of Sydney, which is defined as the LGAs of Penrith, Blacktown, Holroyd, Fairfield, Liverpool, Bankstown, Campbelltown and Sutherland.

Unpublished tables from the 1973 Income Survey, conducted for the Poverty Inquiry (Henderson, 1975), were made available by the Australian Bureau of Statistics. This 2 per cent sample of Sydney's households provided information on poverty rates, certain characteristics of families, and housing tenure. The data is based on *'income units'*, which are somewhat different from families. The aged, family members who could work (except for spouses and students), boarders, lodgers, and other individuals sharing accommodation each count as separate income units. *'Poverty'* is defined as the equivalent of a 1973 income of $63 weekly for a family of a father, mother and two children (the actual level is more or less depending on family size) (Henderson, 1975:24). Only 10 per cent of Sydney's *'income units'* are poor by this definition. *'Low income',* when used for data from the 1973 Income Survey, is defined as less than 150 per cent of the poverty line.

The 1973 Income Survey identified family characteristics in terms of *'Disability'* groups designed largely to fit with social security pension schemes: aged singles; aged couples; single parents; childless, single females; large, intact families (four or more children); the sick or unemployed; recent (post-1961) non-British migrants; Aboriginals; and multi-disability groups (those fitting into more than one of the earlier categories). North Sydney was excluded from the inner city in all of the Poverty Inquiry data because restrictions in the sampling procedures and file construction meant that it could not be separated from Mosman.

Land uses for inner Sydney, shown on Map 1.2, were estimated from maps of the planning schemes for the areas.[6] The accuracy of these estimates is limited by recent modifications to the schemes and by the use of land for purposes not prescribed by the plans. This study also makes extensive use of the data reported in the Australian National University's Urban Research Unit (URU) case studies of properties and households in Redfern in inner Sydney (Neutze, 1972; Vandermark & Harrison, 1972) and of North Melbourne (Johnson, 1972; URU, 1973). Although most of the data were gathered for purposes different from those of this study, they can be used to draw a reasonably consistent picture of the inner suburbs.

CHAPTER 2

Perspectives on Inner-suburban Change

This chapter provides a conceptual overview of the changes in the use of land, of redevelopment and of the supply of low-cost housing in the inner suburbs. Rather than view the inner city from any one disciplinary perspective, some key ideas of a variety of spatial, economic, social and political theories are assessed and, to some extent, integrated. The source of most of these is America, where the literature on city structure and housing markets is strongest; however, the discussion covers only those topics relevant to Australia. The chapter considers the descriptive models of spatial structure, the market forces that influence competition for inner-city land and the problems of an unconstrained market, which governmental actions attempt to overcome.

Spatial Patterns
Many of the roots for an understanding of urban development are deep within the descriptive work of the 'Chicago School' of urban ecology (Park, Burgess & McKenzie, 1925).[1] Confounded by the problems of social change during rapid urbanisation, researchers of this school looked carefully at Chicago and postulated that a spatial model of concentric rings could organise a description of the distribution of land uses, and especially of social groups and social problems. Proceeding outwards from the city centre, the zones are described as, first, the central business district (CBD); second a transitional area of mixed land uses and poor housing; third, an older area of 'workingmen's' homes; fourth, an outer zone of better residences, and finally, of ex-urbanites. The proportion of land used for residential purposes, the degree of social status, and the proportion of families with children, were seen to be lowest in the innermost ring and increased in each subsequent ring away from the city centre.

The definition of the inner city employed in this study generally aligns with the first two zones and the inner part of the third zone. The first zone, the CBD, contains retailing and cultural facilities, headquarters of business and government, and a wholesaling area around the downtown areas. Burgess' description of the transitional zone, the next zone outward from the CBD, includes most of the features commonly thought to be distinctive of the inner city:

... areas of residential deterioration caused by the encroaching of business and industry fron Zone 1 (the CBD) ... a Zone in Transition, with a factory district for its inner belt and an outer ring of retrogressing neighbourhoods, of first immigrant or rooming house districts, of homeless-men areas, of resorts of gambling, bootlegging, sexual vice, and of breeding places of crime ... As families and individuals prosper, they escape from this area into Zone 111 (older working men's homes) beyond, leaving behind as marooned a residuum of the defeated, leaderless and helpless (1929:115-16).

The third zone, the one of workingmen's homes, is '... largely constituted by neighborhoods of second immigrant settlement. Its residents are those who desire to live near but not too close to their work...' (Burgess, 1929:117).

These definitions show that Burgess also used his zonal model for describing inner-suburban change. He postulated that growth pressures start from the city centre and ripple outwards, causing each zone to expand and to overflow into the next one. Dominant non-residential land uses — offices, retailing, warehouses and light manufacturing — expand outwards from the first zone to displace older, deteriorating housing in the next zone, the transitional area. Much of this housing had previously been subdivided into small cheap units to defray owners' costs until speculative profits could be made by conversion to land uses that could afford higher land prices. This loss of housing, along with growth of the inner population due to immigration and natural increase, push the low-status residents outwards, invading and eventually succeeding old, but hitherto respectable, working-class communities. At the same time, the original residents of the invaded areas also move outwards to newer housing, leaving the area to the lower-status newcomers moving in.

Burgess' description of urban structure and change were not supported by any casual model. His descriptive concepts of invasion and succession have nonetheless been mistaken as 'sub-social' explanations that imply inevitability and a lack of human control or responsibility: '"Natural areas" are ... territorial units whose distinctive characteristics — physical, social, economic, and cultural — are the result of unplanned operation of ecological and social processes' (Burgess, 1964:458). However, as Suttles (1972:8) and others have taken pains to point out, Burgess probably was simply trying '... to emphasize the way in which urban residential groups are not the planned or artificial artifact of anyone but develop out of many independent personal decisions based on moral, political, ecological, and economic considerations.' If Burgess is interpreted in this way, then more specific explanatory theories, discussed later in this chapter, elaborate rather than contradict much of the original zonal formulation.

It is unfortunate that the urban ecology movement was side-tracked into seemingly endless empirical tests of Burgess' model. A mass of Australian and American studies confirm that inner-city areas in both countries are generally characterised by concentration of ethnic groups, low social status and high transiency of residents, and few children or middle-aged adults (Johnston, 1971). However, a variety of other studies, foreshadowed by Davie (1938), note that many of the land-use activities mentioned by Burgess as being characteristic of the inner city are often also found outside the inner areas. Non-residential activitiy is not always centralised: commerce is often located along many transport corridors and in subcentres; industry is traditionally near rail and water transport, which are often away from the city centre. Low-cost housing is usually near industry or railways. On the other hand, inner areas often contain high-cost flats (hardly an indication of uniformly low socio-economic status), office building frequently goes upwards instead of encroaching outwards, and wholesaling and industry have often moved out of inner areas (Hoyt, 1939).

The criticism of the zonal model led to alternative models which considered more specifically the reasons behind development patterns. For example, Hoyt's (1939) residential model of sectors of social status and rental costs explained the outward movement of higher-income groups in terms of both the 'push' from older, lower-quality, inner-area housing and the 'pull' of newer housing, better natural environments, and decentralised employment. Similarly, Harris and Ullman (1945) devised their multi-nodal model, which consisted of many subcentres that did not revolve solely around a dominant CBD. They emphasised the reasons why non-residential activities often cluster together (often outside the CBD); these activities are often interdependent, need common transport facilities, or are forced away from residential areas by governmental regulations.

Hoover and Vernon (1962) explained inner-suburban residential change as much by the age as by the location of the housing. After early stages of rapid construction of single-family housing, areas remain stable for some years. The next stage is the construction of flats on infill sites and redeveloped houses. As the neighbourhood becomes older, housing becomes run-down and over-crowded, then populations drop as households shrink, and finally the buildings deteriorate to the point when only public action can bring about renewal. The inner areas are the oldest parts of the metropolis and often have proceded through all of these stages.

Despite the later elaborations, the models and vocabulary of the urban ecologists, and more recently the social-area analyses and factor analyses (which describe and classify certain parts of the city), remain more valuable for description than for explanation. They seldom consider the social and cultural forces (Firey, 1947) and conflicts between public and private organisations, or 'actors', (Form, 1954) that actually determine land use. Even the 'accessibility' explanations are couched in generalities that are not linked to the interests and motivations of individual households and firms. Moreover, the ecological approach, like laissez-faire economies, can be misused to justify any existing urban structure as somehow natural and therefore good. It implies that government interference is inefficient, and it ignores conflicting interests, unequal distributions of power, and the influence of government.

A Market Analysis

The explanation of spatial patterns requires the use of other concepts besides simple spatial models. A market model provides a versatile framework for understanding competition for possible land uses. To understand the economic pressures behind inner-suburban change, the first step is to identify the attractions of inner areas relative to those of other areas. There is a limit to how much the attractions can be understood generally: different activities may compete for the same location for different reasons. To make the necessary specification, descriptions of land uses can be detailed further to specify various activities, within both non-residential and residential categories, each activity having very different requirements and abilities to pay for land. Because location is essentially about the spatial arrangement of activities with respect to each other, it is almost a truism to say that the interdependency between land uses is the key point. According to market criteria, the 'best' use of land is that for which the user is willing to pay most.

Accessibility is the fundamental reason for crowding human activities into cities, and the inner areas are theoretically the most accessible part of the entire city — providing access both to the rest of the entire metropolitan area and among the activities already densely congregated near the city centre. The market constraint on these centralisation pressures is that competition drives up prices and rents and these high costs limit the activities that can afford central locations. Hence the distributions of land values and the intensity of land use closely follow the accesssibility profile of a city. Successful bidders in the inner city can economise on expensive land and gain the greatest advantage from the accessibility.

The degree and nature of competition for central locations varies between cities and over time. In larger, more congested cities, the inner areas offer especially great metropolitan-wide access relative to any other single point. Established radial transport routes can maintain the relative accessibility of the original centre, even if uneven metropolitan growth has moved the geographical centre of the city. On the other hand, high rates of car-ownership and a freeway grid can reduce the accessibility advantages of inner areas because they lessen dependence on radial public transport. If, for whatever reason, development is already largely centralised, some heavily interdependent activities will seek location near each other in the heart of 'the action', even if this centre has poor accessibility to the rest of the metropolis. In larger cities, multiple subcentres, as suggested by the multi-nodal model, offer better access to residents, yet can still be large enough to reach peak economies of scale and agglomeration. The result of these pressures is that, as cities grow larger, the more land-intensive, specialised and interdependent activities usually expand in inner areas while other activities disperse.

In understanding the competition for inner locations, it is useful to work with a hierarchy of urban land-use activities, starting at the top with the most intense such as high-rise offices, followed roughly in order by specialised retailing, high-density residences, manufacturing, and ending with low-density single-family housing. Although there are exceptions for particular activities or locations, those at the top of this pyramid generally have the need for accessibility, the ability to use space intensively and therefore economically and the purchasing power which result in their securing more central locations. Spatial developments in inner areas thus depend on the relative growth, needs and resources of the various activities competing for land, as well as on the changing accessibility of locations as cities grow and transport facilities change.

Non-Residential Development

The activity most dominant in the inner city — intensive office development — takes advantage of nearly all the special features of the most central locations.[2] Businessmen, financiers, lawyers and government officials locate near each other because of their need for requent face-to-face interaction. Central locations also give them the best single access-point to their branch offices, customers and workers throughout the metropolis. Large organisations can afford high land prices and the construction costs of high-rise buildings, because the space required per office worker is small and can be efficiently used in upper storeys. The rapid post-war growth of the tertiary sector of the economy has increased the demand for space used for offices, particularly in the major cities. Although these accessibility advantages support Burgess's model of centralised office development, high-rise construction techniques mean that the new offices need not encroach into residential areas.

Most retailing and service activities neither need nor can afford central locations. Their optimum sizes and service areas are small enough for them to be accessibly distributed throughout the metropolitan area, rather than concentrated at the centre. An exception is that group of specialised business activities serving city-wide clienteles, especially those relying on agglomeration effects such as comparison shopping and entertainment areas. Another exception is those services like medical specialists which rely on centralised facilities such as hospitals. To the extent that inner-city workers shop and stay near work during lunch or after work, other retailing and services can remain relatively accessible although distant from the commuters' homes. But inaccessibility and congestion of the inner city, combined with the high land costs, encourages most retailing and services to disperse nearer to the homes of their customers and workers. Expansion of retailing outwards from the urban core, as suggested by Burgess, is therefore hardly an obvious consequence of city growth.

Manufacturing and wholesaling are frequently concentrated in inner areas, even though they seldom need centrality. Manufacturing locates near the heavy transport facilities — ports, railways, and freeways — that provide them access to raw materials and eventual markets. Largely for historical reasons, these transport facilities are often adjacent to the city centre, and old manufacturing areas originally on the outskirts of town have since become part of the inner area as the metropolis grew. Inner locations have also usually provided inner-city industry with good access to a semi-skilled labour pool, members of which cannot afford to travel far, an especially important fact when few workers owned cars. In the post-war period, new technologies led to the development of very large, single-floor factories. It becomes increasingly uneconomic for these land-extensive activities to be located on highly valued inner-city land and it is difficult to find big parcels of land or to amalgamate small ones suitable for their requirements. The need for trucks to carry materials and products, and cars to carry workers, further encourages decentralisation (Moses & Williamson, 1967).

Despite these incentives for decentralisation, many manufacturing and wholesaling firms remain or expand in inner areas for good reasons. Some industries, such as printing and clothing manufacturing, need little land and rely heavily on access to other firms or to labour. Although some of these kinds of industry are declining in importance, they are often replaced by other activities having similar needs. For example, warehousing, although to some degree following retailing and some manufacturing outwards, has an incentive to remain in locations that are near central ports and that offer metropolitan-wide accessibility. Equally important, firms that already have substantial fixed investments in inner areas may choose to expand their sites rather than move their entire plants. But, if there is no imperative for manufacturing to rush out of inner areas, nor is there necessarily an inexorable tide of centralised industrial expansion. Burgess excluded heavy manufacturing from his model, apparently because he realised that its particular site requirements are not based primarily on centrality.

As cities grow, non-residential activities also increase, although the rate of growth varies between particular kinds of land uses. Accessibility attractions can induce new activities that can make more profitable use of land to displace existing uses in the inner areas. In some cases, an existing structure can be converted from one use to another — for example, from manufacturing to warehousing. Similarly, professional offices or small commercial or service offices can use, and often prefer, existing residential structures. In these cases, the only expense is for the new user to pay more than the old one for the land and the building.

However, land-use succession in inner areas is hardly an inevitable process heedless of obstacles. To accommodate different, more intense uses, many land-use changes require rebuilding, or at least some structural changes to buildings. Because the demand for change in use almost always emerges while existing buildings are still useful, redevelopment incurs losses resulting from demolishing an otherwise adequate structure. Added to this are the costs of demolitions, transactions for any property amalgamation, and new construction. Thus, inner-city development is constrained severely by the economic considerations of modifying existing buildings which, although appropriate in the past, no longer fully exploit present and future accessibility advantages. The economies of high-rise construction, which partly overcome these problems, are limited by the expense of lifts and structural supports. As a result of these many costs, inner areas must offer large savings of travel costs if new activities are to displace existing inner uses rather than 'leap-frog' out to larger, vacant sites in outer areas.

Residential Development[1]

Non-residential and residential development are closely interrelated.[3] Although much non-residential development is of the existing non-residential areas, nearby residential areas often offer nearly as much accessibility, usually at lower land costs. The value of this land for non-residential uses is increased by accessibility and its residential value is decreased by the effects of traffic and pollution. These neighbourhood effects exacerbate the problem of old housing which is often small, obsolete and deteriorated. The result of these pressures can be the non-residential encroachment outwards from the city centre that was postulated by Burgess.

But non-residential incursion into non-residential areas can be resisted. Given a strong enough demand for accessible and low-cost housing, poor housing in undesirable environments can be subdivided into small units which yield high total rents for properties even though individual rents are low. The most threatened areas near the expansion of the core usually have especially dense housing on small lots, which yield high returns in residential use and would involve expensive property amalgamation before redevelopment. Non-residential encroachment is not inevitable; it depends on the relative strength of demand by the competing users.

A key notion in the spatial models of urban change is that the quality of housing inevitably declines with age. Intense residential subdivisions and occupancy by lower-income groups are viewed merely as temporary stages before eventual non-residential incursion or abandonment. However, inner-area housing should deteriorate only if expenditure on repairs or improvements cannot be recovered from increased rents or sale value. Buildings seldom have fixed physical lives. They are poorly maintained only if existing or potential tenants could not pay the rent increases necessary to cover repairs. Alternatively, if the quality of the inner-area buildings or locations is very poor relative to other available housing, tenants may not be willing to pay enough rent for owners to recoup the costs of improvements. Further limits are the high costs of maintaining and upgrading old buildings, and the classic 'slum dilemma' in which it is uneconomical for any individual owner to invest unless all the neighbouring owners do likewise. Finally, even if demand for well-maintained inner-area dwellings is strong, owners may choose not to continue investment in these dwellings because they anticipate profitable sales to those planning redevelopment for higher land uses.

On the other hand, reinvestment in old, inner-area housing can go beyond maintenance to improve the existing standards. If existing or potential occupants are willing and able to pay the costs, old housing can be modernised sufficiently to compete with newer housing (Grigsby, 1963): rooms and facilities can be added, deterioration can be repaired, rented dwellings can be returned to owner-occupancy, and subdivided houses can be changed back to single occupancy. The result can be the process known as 'filtering up': improvement of existing housing; this upgrading can be measured in terms of the occupation of an area by higher-income groups (Ratcliff, 1949), increases of values relative to other housing in the metropolis (Fisher & Winnick, 1951), or the absolute improvement of housing standards among low-income people (Grigsby, 1963). Any decline in these respects can be termed 'filtering down', as is postulated for inner-area housing by the zonal model. Being the opposite of slum formation, these processes are most likely to occur in the better inner-city housing in residential areas, away from the competition and noxious effects of non-residential uses. Compared to the newer housing of the outer suburbs, most inner-area housing is smaller and outdated, but can offer greater accessibility, a certain charm, and lower costs (although renovation costs partly cancel out price advantages). Compared to new flats in the inner city, old houses offer at least as much room, more 'character', ground-level living, private open space and, often, lower costs. Thus, old housing in inner areas can be adapted to very different levels of housing, depending on the kind of residential demand.

Flats are the only kind of new residential construction likely to be built in inner areas. Like office buildings, they can build upwards instead of outwards, thus buying accessibility and good environments without paying excessive land costs. But, except for the high-rise development for the rich, flats can rarely compete either with non-residential uses or with existing dense residences for the most accessible sites close to the city centre. Instead, flats are usually built a little farther out, in areas having bigger, cheaper sites and more opportunities for infill (i.e., filling the gaps between existing buildings). Sites near public transport, or natural amenities such as parks and beaches, are especially favoured, again, because, with flats, the costs of the advantages of such locations are relatively small per dwelling unit. If demand for new flats is strong and demand for cheap houses is weak, acquisition costs may be low enough for flats to replace old houses. For the residents of the remaining houses nearby, the development of flats means reduced privacy and views, more traffic and less kerbside parking, increased demands on local services, and perhaps transient or other less desirable neighbours.

The demand for inner-city housing is also affected by the alternatives available elsewhere. It is increased if new housing on the fringe is very expensive or inaccessible. Similarly, inner-area housing is more attractive in large cities in which jobs and other attractions are highly centralised and transport is poor. In addition to these considerations, development of flats in the inner area is influenced by the availability of sites elsewhere having attractions that substitute for centrality, like location near transport facilities or the coastline or other amenities.

The characteristics of householders entering the housing market — their income, life-cycle stage, ethnicity and life-style — affect the residential demand for inner locations. Inner areas attract poorer people because they cannot afford the transport required in outer areas, but can afford the rent for a minimal amount of old housing on its usually small site in the inner suburbs (Alonso, 1964:: Evans, 1973). If incomes are rising faster than are housing and transport costs, people can afford more of these goods and services and can therefore move to the outer areas which have the big sites necessary for large new homes. Rising incomes would encourage the abandonment or redevelopment of the worst, and improvement of the best, inner-area housing. On the other hand, a fall in income, or an influx of poor migrants, will strengthen demand for cheap, small housing in the inner suburbs.

If differences in the life-cycle stage of households are taken into account, the effects of income changes on them become more complicated. Rising incomes encourages the suburbanisation of families with children, who are best provided for by single-family housing. However, rising incomes also enable young adults to leave their boarding houses or parents' homes to reside in small, inner-city flats. Besides income changes, the relative demand for small, inner-suburban housing will grow with increases in numbers of childless households, particularly those in which all members work, for these people usually make less use of private outdoor space and make the most of the accessibility to jobs, entertainment and other city-centre attractions. Thus, demand for residence in the inner city can be heightened by such sweeping social changes as rising participation of women in the labourforce, postponement of child-bearing, and shifts toward more diversified, cosmopolitan life-styles.

Market Imperfections and Governmental Regulations

Government is heavily involved in urban development because of the inefficiencies and inequities of the private market.[4] Governmental controls are about the only way to constrain private parties from making developments harmful to others who have no voice in the decisions. Furthermore, the fragmented private market is seldom able to organise the provision of roads, services and other infrastructure necessary to support private development. As discussed in the next section, government also competes in the private market when locating its own facilities, including public housing. Finally, the quality of government services, and the costs of providing them, can differ between areas and hence influence locational decisions. These governmental influences are so persuasive that they affect nearly all aspects of land use.

Governmental regulations deal with interrelationship of neighbouring properties, which is most critical in the inner city because of the intensity, proximity, diversity and frequent change of land uses. Favourable interdependencies, such as economies of agglomeration and accessibility between land-use activities, increase efficiency and can provide windfall benefits to adjacent owners. Once some activities seeking these advantages can be located in the area, owners of neighbouring properties used for other purposes are encouraged to make profitable sales. Thus, the market mechanism extends pressures to realise positive interdependencies.

The private market, however, cannot equitably take into account the negative effects of development on nearby property investments and residential amenities. For example, single-family housing can come under pressure for change of use to flats or non-residential land uses. Because corporate property investors can outbid individual house-owners, the latter are encouraged to make profitable sales. If nearby owners were also willing and able to sell out for similar developments, then all would experience capital gains and leave the area; the problem is that all owners do not always want to sell, especially owner-occupants who often do not want to move. Furthermore, if all the properties were sold for the development of flats, few residents would have views and congestion would be too great. Partly for these reasons, there is seldom enough demand for all the houses in a given area to be replaced by higher land uses. Thus, the majority of owner-occupants remaining in an area where there has been non-residential development, or development of flats, must either endure a degraded environment or else sell or rent at a loss to someone who will accept it.

Given a demand for higher land uses, governmental controls are the only way to limit the sporadic dispersal of generally harmful land uses throught inner areas. The production and enforcement of realistic land-use plans can establish firm expectations which protect investment and amenities and encourage complementary developments. Although governmental controls can drive up the price of land for some uses by decreasing supply, they also limit the premature decline of residential values or of the housing stock that is caused by non-residential intrusion. These protective actions are opposed by the mobilised minority of a few owners seeking capital gains and potential developers and purchasers hindered by restrictions. Given an expectation of a land-use change, the political pressures against controls are heightened by speculative purchasers anticipating profitable changes of land use.

Another way to limit conflicting development is to place stringent requirements on those higher land uses that are permitted. For example, blocks of flats may be allowed only if they are built at low densities, with large individual units and ample outdoor and parking space (Patterson *et al.,* 1976). Such controls discourage development by raising unit costs, and any development that does occur is likely to produce fewer problems and attract more desirable residents. A more difficult method of pursuing this same end is 'performance zoning', which sets limits on the traffic, noise and other external effects of development, but does not specify the kind of development allowed.

Negative neighbourhood effects can also occur between existing land uses. Especially within the older, inner-suburban area, the maintenance and appearance of a dwelling can considerably affect the value of neighbouring dwellings. In the extreme case, nobody would repair or improve properties if the poor condition of neighbouring properties would limit the value increase to below the cost of improvements. Health, safety and housing standards can limit these problems with older dwellings, by requiring that owners make improvements; as do the minimum size of sites serve a similar purpose with new constructions. However, if the cost of improvements is beyond the rent that could be obtained for the improved structure, the owners are forced either to seek a more profitable use for their property, to operate at a loss, or even to abandon the property.

The external effects of developments are more complicated for many tenants, whose interests often conflict with those of landlords and other property owners. A possible advantage that tenants have over owners is that tenants can more easily move away from unpleasant developments, or else rents may be lowered. But both these possibilities are likely only if alternative rental accommodation is available at an acceptable price. More importantly, the private market provides no compensation for dislocated tenants when owners make profitable sales to new owner-occupants or for non-residential land uses.

Governmental regulations provide only partial answers for problems of low-income renters. Although enforcement of housing codes can improve or destroy the worst of the substandard housing, it decreases the supply of cheap housing and raises rents. Tenancy legislation, which ensures some security of tenure for low-rent occupants, can also reduce the supply of low-cost housing in the long run. Regulations are usually insufficient unless accompanied by additional steps either to raise incomes of the poor, or to increase the direct supply of low-cost housing or decrease demand by other potential users of low-rent accommodation.

Another group adversely affected by centralisation of development are the employees who commute there from outer suburbs. Theoretically, their interests are taken into account by employers, who should pay higher labour costs if firms are located far from workers' homes; however, employers can usually get sufficient labour no matter where they locate in the metropolis. If jobs for a worker are already heavily centralised, he or she may have no options. Paradoxically, some firms locate in inner areas even though sufficient workers reside in particular outer areas, simply because existing public transport systems focus on the core areas.

Governmental regulations in areas outside the inner city also influence demand for inner land. Middle and outer areas are often able to keep values high for their owner-occupied, single-family housing by severely restricting development of flats, non-residential uses and the subdivision of existing dwellings for low-cost rental accommodation. In fact, these areas were initially developed partly so that the middle classes could escape the mixed land uses and lower-status people in inner areas. This restriction of supply elsewhere, combined with the lesser power of inner-suburban residents to resist intrusion, can make the inner city the dumping ground for unpleasant land-use activities which provide mostly for landlords, proprietors and employees living in outer areas. Thus, residents of the inner city are exposed to a poor environment and to displacement pressures that may be caused by the market but cannot be regulated by governmental policies.

Competition can also arise between local governments if developments provide very high or low taxes relative to the costs of providing them with government services. If higher land uses are very profitable for local government, development would probably be favoured by ratepayers — except by those closest to the development. Alternatively, high taxes in an area can force out certain activities, especially when residential areas are zoned for higher uses and taxes are based on their value in their potential use.

Governmental Services and Facilities

The advantage to employers of the accessibility of the inner area results partly from publicly subsidised, radial road, rail and bus services. Because it can thus draw upon workers and customers from throughout the metropolis, non-residential development is encouraged into central areas. Low-cost radial transport should decrease residential demand in inner areas because it allows inner-area workers to live in more distant yet still accessible areas. However, building freeways also reduces supply by destroying low-cost inner-area housing, which especially increases competition at the lower end of the market. In the long run, therefore, improved transport to the core may not diminish congestion, travel times and demand for housing in inner areas unless land-use controls also constrain the centralised growth of jobs.

Government itself demands inner-city land for public facilities there. State capitals and regional centres contain particularly strong concentrations of offices, for the same accessibility reasons that attract private firms. Similarly, specialised hospitals, museums, universities and other activities serving the entire metropolitan area seek central locations. Moreover, government can bypass some of the market constraints against redevelopment by using resumption powers (i.e., which enable compulsory purchase); this lowers land costs and eases acquisition procedures. Government institutions do not experience the pressures of the market that encourages private enterprise to follow residents outward from the city centre; public institutions tend to expand large central facilities instead of establishing regional operations. Centralised location of government jobs can have a multiplier effect by increasing inner-city demand from firms that work with government authorities, and from government workers who want to live near their work. Government authorities appear to have no more scruples about the wider effects of their locational decisions, and perhaps fewer constraints, than do private enterprises. Those government departments that regulate land use are seldom able to constrain the locational decisions of other government agencies that are larger and more powerful.

Public provision of neighbourhood services, like private retailing, tends to develop concurrently with housing. Thus, the oldest areas of poorest housing tend to have the poorest schools, parks, conditions of local streets and other neighbourhood facilities. This can be an additional discouragement to private residential investment. If private redevelopment nevertheless does take place and increases residential populations, the adequacy of services drops even further unless their capacity is increased. On the other hand, the improvement of neighbourhood services, especially if combined with protective land-use controls, can encourage the 'filtering up' of houses in inner areas that offer some housing and natural amenities. Thus, poor local public services often parallel the poor living conditions that low-income people can afford, or else improved local services facilitate the upgrading of housing so that the poor are forced out.

The previous discussion showed that, unless the poor pay high rents relative to income, or crowd into the worst housing, low-cost housing is readily displaced. If comparable housing for the displaced becomes available through 'filtering down' of the housing elsewhere, the cost to the poor is only that of moving. If alternative housing is insufficient, government housing authorities can compensate by directly providing some housing for lower-income earners, thereby decreasing demand in the private sector and hence moderating private rents. If the government were to do this by purchasing and rehabilitating existing houses, the stock could be improved and kept available for renting to the poor. Alternatively, public redevelopment to higher residential densities increases the supply of inner-suburban housing, but it also incurs the high financial and social costs of displacement. Compared to building government housing in outer areas, providing public housing in inner areas — whether by redevelopment or by purchase and rehabilitation of existing dwellings — is more expensive but provides for better accessibility for the residents.

The application of governmental regulations and the provision of public services involves conflicting interests between inner-city and other residents and between different interest groups within the inner city. Low-income areas have a disproportionate share of the inner city's unpleasant yet essential activities, partly because the residents lack the political and economic power to keep them out. When there is conflict between property owners in an area about land-use changes, unpleasant development is not likely unless its proponents have exceptional political power, or unless the other owners can expect similar profits from development. This is more likely in inner areas than in others, because of the stronger market pressures for redevelopment and the smaller proportions of owner-occupants. Owners and developers wield more influence than tenants because they are better informed and they individually have more stake in the outcome. Inner-city tenants and outer-suburban commuters are especially disadvantaged by their lack of individual incentives to oppose development until it already is underway.

The organisation of governmental responsibilities is equally important. A small, powerful local government area containing little more than the CBD will tend to be dominated by property owners and others seeking permission for intense redevelopment. Neighbouring local government areas, in which housing demand and transport problems are increased considerably by centralised growth, have no say over these effects. A metropolitan or state government has the power to take account of relationships between local councils and to arbitrate conflict between them. However, state government tends to be less accessible to the less powerful and poorly organised, and it can more easily override local objections in the pursuit of metropolitan-wide concerns like increasing employment. State government also develops large service bureaucracies that can themselves demand inner-city locations for their facilities, which locals cannot resist. Interest groups that are not satisfied by either the private market or governmental processes frequently call on outside support, most notable the trade unions or the courts.

Summary

The number and kind of people living in the inner suburbs depends on the competition for various residential and non-residential uses, which in turn relates to the relative attractions of inner versus outer areas. Redevelopment for flats and non-residential activities, and investment in existing housing, depends on many market factors: the accessibility of the central area; the concentration of businesses and jobs in central areas; the effects of technological changes and of structural change in the economy on the requirements of firms for space and locations; the quality and density of existing inner-area housing; the accessibility, costs and amenities of alternative housing; and the life-cycle stages and incomes of people seeking homes. The situation is further complicated by the interdependencies between these factors and between various land uses. Finally, government is heavily involved in urban change, by regulating land uses, by providing roads and public transport, by providing local and metropolitan-wide services, and by directly competing for locations for its own activities.

Considering the complexity apparent even in this brief discussion, it is no surprise that urban ecologists could not develop spatial models that consistently fit the development patterns of cities. Even though the basic development pressures in Western cities are similar, the relative strength of these various pressures, and hence the spatial distributions of activities, vary widely between countries and between individual cities within countries. The partial descriptive success of the concentric zone model, notwithstanding the many exceptions, results from the basic fact that inner areas are the oldest and most accessible parts of nearly all Western cities. Among the few generalisations that can be made is that there usually is more central redevelopment in older, bigger and more centralised cities.

CHAPTER 3

The Structure of the Inner City

This chapter describes and briefly explains the features of inner Sydney in the early 1970s. It provides an introduction to the area and a basis for considering whether or not inner Sydney's features are consistent with the spatial models and other concepts discussed in Chapter 2. The analysis is factual and Australian; although most of it is from Sydney, where the features of inner-suburban areas are most sharply defined, most of the analyses apply equally to inner Melbourne and inner Adelaide. By dealing with one city, it is easier to consider both the diversity within the inner areas and the differences between inner and other parts of the city. The chapter discusses non-residential development and its consequences for job availability and residential amenity, the housing patterns that evolved during successive waves of earlier development; and the kinds of people who live in the inner city. Later chapters explain the importance of inner-city living to the residents (Chapter 4) and post-war land-use and housing developments (Chapters 5 to 9).

Non-residential Land Use

Consistent with the overseas spatial models, the most striking feature of inner Sydney is the pattern of non-residential land use, shown on Map 1.2. Industrial, office and commercial activities cover over a fifth of the inner-suburban land, compared to less than a twentieth of the rest of Sydney (SATS, 1974, vol.1:4-6). The inner areas also have disproportionately large shares of the metropolitan roads, railways, and various specialised non-residential land uses. The most dominant point is the CBD, hemmed in by the harbour on two sides and the Botanical Gardens and Hyde Park on another. Originally Australia's first settlement, the area now contains over 230 000 workers — almost a fifth of Sydney's jobs, in only 445 hectares of some of the most dense office development of any city. More than a third of the workers are government employees (Harrison, 1977:19). The smaller centre in North Sydney, also containing intense office development, is more of an extension of the CBD than an alternative to it. Around the eastern fringe of the CBD, especially in Kings Cross, are additional offices and the greatest concentration anywhere in the metropolis of live entertainment, movie theatres, restaurants, and specialised retail stores. (Inner Melbourne contains three-quarters of the metropolitan area's 'walk-in' cinemas, half of the restaurants, two-thirds of the hotels, and virtually all of the professional live theatre and music [MMBW, 1977:63-4].) Shops and services are found within the CBD, along the major arterial roads leading from the CBD, and in numerous small nodes within the residential areas.

Compared to offices and commercial land uses, manufacturing and wholesaling activities are far less intensive, covering much more land but providing many fewer jobs. Most warehousing is located on less expensive land to the west and south of the CBD, near to the port and manufacturing. Extensive parts of the flat southern areas, many of which were originally swampy, is zoned for and contains Sydney's heaviest and most bothersome industry. For example, the LGA of Botany contains paper mills and chemical plants and South Sydney contains a tallow refinery, brickworks, iron and steel yards, and even an incinerator to burn garbage produced in the more affluent eastern suburbs. The dispersed, less intense manufacturing in Leichhardt and Marrickville consists of 'light', labour-intensive activities such as clothing manufacture, food processing, and electronic assembly firms. Until the post-war period, these areas contained the vast majority of Sydney's manufacturing jobs and working-class accommodation.

The inner areas also contain a disproportionate share of the public facilities that serve the entire metropolis: Sydney University and various technical colleges, major hospitals, museums, the central mail exchange; there is even a naval yard within a kilometre of the CBD. Just west of the CBD is Australia's largest and Sydney's only port, the main point of entry for New South Wales' imports and of exit for the State's exports of wool, wheat, coal and other rural products. Because of the port and non-residential development, the state's extensive rail system is centred on the inner city; there is a large central railyard in the southern industrial area, a massive central station adjacent to the CBD, and a number of lines linking the CBD, port and industrial areas to each other, to sources of labour and to other firms beyond the inner area. Except for the Warringah Expressway, which runs to the north across the Harbour Bridge, and the short Cahill Expressway across the northern edge of the CBD, road transport moves along arterial roads or through the grid of small streets.

A measure of the intensity of non-residential land use in the inner area is the number of jobs concentrated there. The inner city contains 44 per cent of Sydney's total jobs (Table 3.1). Within the inner city there are almost two-thirds of the metropolis' clerical jobs, which demonstrates the importance of central locations for offices. As the transport and communication centre of the state, the inner areas contain almost half of the city's jobs in these industries. Sales jobs, which have suburbanised along with residents, are considerably less concentrated in inner areas, reflecting their tendency to follow markets out to the expanding residential areas. Some manufacturing is also less centralised than other activities, partly because it needs such extensive amounts of land. Within each major industrial group, the intensity of jobs per hectare is greatest near the city centre (Neutze, 1977:95).

TABLE 3.1   *Jobs and resident workers, in inner Sydney, by occupation, 1971*

Occupational group	Jobs		Resident workers		Jobs per resident worker
	no. ('000)	% of metro.	no. ('000)	% of metro.	
Professional, Technical,	61.2	45.5	19.4	14.0	3.2
Administrative, Managerial	40.7	45.0	8.8	9.5	4.6
Clerical	151.6	62.3	31.9	12.8	4.8
Sales	35.4	36.7	11.2	11.3	3.2
Transport and Communication	32.1	48.2	10.5	15.5	3.1
Craftsmen, Process workers and Labourers	153.4	37.1	71.2	16.8	2.2
Service, Sport and Recreation	34.7	40.0	19.1	21.0	1.8
Other	3.8	14.1	2.2	7.3	1.7
Not stated	20.3	44.3	16.3	28.1	-
Total	533.4	44.3	190.5	15.2	2.8

Source: Based on an analysis of unpublished 'Journey to Work' computer tapes, Census, 1971.

Residential Effects of Non-residential Land Uses

The concentration of non-residential land uses has both advantages and disadvantages for inner-suburban residents. One of the greatest benefits is the availability of a vast number and variety of jobs[1]; jobs outnumber workers by almost three to one. Because white-collar jobs are most centralised, and the resident workforce in inner areas has a smaller proportion of white-collar workers than the rest of the metropolis, the surplus of jobs over resident workers is especially high for these occupations. Even for blue-collar workers, more of whom live in inner areas, there are two jobs to every resident worker. As a result of the accessibility of so many jobs, more than 70 per cent of the workers living in in the inner city also work there. The concentration of activities also provides inner-suburban residents with nearby private and public services, including good public transport. Chapter 4 shows how this accessibility influences the travel behaviour of inner-area residents.

On the other hand, inner-area residents are exposed to heavy traffic and other problems generated by non-residential uses in the vicinity. If each of the 374 amalgamated CDS (see page 15) approximate neighbourhoods, then 45 per cent of inner-city neighbourhoods contain or adjoin land that is zoned for businesses (mostly retailing), 39 per cent for industry, 31 per cent for major roads, 23 per cent for railways and 6 per cent for ports.[2] Only a fifth of the inner-suburban neighbourhoods do not support, or are not next to, some kind of non-residential land use; these favoured areas are concentrated mostly in eastern North Sydney and in areas of Potts Point, Paddington, Darlington and Eastlakes. On the other hand, some other inner-area neighbourhoods, mainly in the CBD and industrial areas, are next to a number of unpleasant kinds of activities. Although the most populated CDs have the least amount of non-residential intrusion, the amenity of most inner-suburban residents is affected by these problems.

The most serious environmental problem is motor-vehicle traffic. Of the third of a million daily commuters into inner-area jobs, about 175 000 drive; many others drive within, through and into the area for shopping and other purposes. Moreover, the industrial areas, the CBD and the port areas carry large volumes of the heavy commercial vehicles that are especially bothersome in residential areas (SATS, 1974, vol.1: figs 6.36 and 6.37). Most commuter and commercial vehicles travel through narrow streets having house-fronts no more than three to six metres from the carriageway.

The effects of this traffic are severe. Noise in the inner suburbs, mostly from traffic, is the worst of any area in Sydney. Most of the three localities of Ultimo, Chippendale and Redfern, just south of the CBD, are estimated to have noise levels that exceed the limits considered acceptable for American and British residential areas (seventy decibels for 10 per cent or more of the time) (SATS, 1974, vol.3: x-15, and fig. 10.13). Measurements of noise levels along truck routes near the port container facilities in Balmain also exceed these levels (Fricke, 1975). The SATS study estimated that nearly all the inner-city areas have noise levels considered 'objectionable or intense' (fifty decibels at least half the time). Residents of the inner suburbs also comprise a large proportion of the 67 000 people who live in areas where aircraft noise is bad enough to generate substantial numbers of complaints (Ryder & Joy, 1976:65). None of these noise levels poses any direct health problems, but a vast majority of residents in the worst-affected areas describe them as 'distressing' or 'upsetting' (Balmain Residents' Case, 1975:App. 6B).

Heavy traffic causes other problems too. The inner LGAs have rates of pedestrian injuries that are twice to seven times those of the rest of Sydney, although many of the injured probably do not live in inner areas (Vinson & Homel, 1976:App. B). Residents of Redfern report that traffic noises and dangers are their most serious neighbourhood problem (Troy, 1971:40). (Similar reports have been made by residents in North Melbourne [Troy, 1972:39-41] and the City of Adelaide [Anglim *et al.*, 1975:App.III].) Another traffic difficulty, especially for the more affluent households that own cars, is that much of the street parking near their homes is taken by commuters and shoppers. These many problems have been found to reduce residential property values along heavily trafficked streets, for example by about $1000 per house in Balmain, Sydney (Gardner, 1975).

Heavy industry and port activities directly generate less extensive or frequent noises than traffic. But sporadic noise from these sources can be even more sharp and annoying. Noise from railways generally is less troublesome than noise from road transport or industry.

Road traffic and manufacturing, together with prevailing wind currents and geographical features, causes the inner-city area south of the harbour to have Sydney's worst air pollution, by almost any available measure (Ryder, 1976; SATS, 1974, vol.II: figs. 10.1, 10.3, 10.5 and 10.7). As with noise, the problems are greatest along major streets but also affect nearly all inner suburbs. Although the available data are poor, some inner areas have had concentrations of certain pollutants that exceed World Health Organisation standards and could cause health problems (South Sydney Community Aid Environment Committee, 1974:11-20).

Housing

More inner-suburban land is used for residential purposes than for business or industry. Chapter 1 showed that, consistent with the spatial models, the housing in the inner area is relatively old, dense, small, low-cost and often rented. Despite the considerable losses and changes during the post-war period, the inner city in 1971 still provided three-quarters of Sydney's terrace housing, over half of the non-self-contained flats, more than a third of the non-private dwellings (mostly boarding houses), and nearly a fifth of the rented houses. The inner area's boarding houses and non-self-contained flats were the cheapest accommodation in the metropolis. This section briefly describes the characteristics, spatial patterns and historical development of inner-area housing.[3]

To summarise the inner-city housing patterns, a mathematical technique known as cluster analysis was used to divide the 374 inner CDs into groups, according to housing similarities within groups and differences between groups.[4] These similarities were defined in terms of the following ten housing variables from the unpublished computer tapes for the 1971 Census.[5]

Housing type: Percentage detached or semi-detached houses (1), terrace houses (2), non-self-contained flats (3), non-private dwellings (4).

Housing tenure: Percentage owner-occupied houses, (5), owner-occupied flats (6).

Housing costs: Average rents of houses (7), average rents of flats (8).

Housing size: Average rooms per house (9), average rooms per flat (10).

A division of the CDs into four basic groups seemed to offer the simplest picture without obscuring critical differences between areas. These 'housing areas' were given names that best described them; and a brief summary of their characteristics (from Tables 3.2 and 3.3) follows.

'Non-private' dwellings: a small group of areas of cheap housing characterised by the boarding houses, hotels, institutions and non-self-contained flats that housed more than 80 per cent of the 6800 people in these areas.

'Terraces': a fairly large grouping, housing about 100 000 people, mostly in rented terrace houses, many of which have been subdivided into small flats.

'Detached houses': the largest group, containing almost half of inner Sydney's population, mostly in owner-occupied, semi-detached and detached houses of moderate value.

TABLE 3.2   *Housing types in inner Sydney by 'housing area', 1971*

'Housing area'[a] in Sydney	Housing types (occupied) (percentages)						Total occupied dwellings ('000)
	Det- ached house	Semi- det. house	Ter- race	Flats (s.c.)	Flats (non- s.c.)	Non- pri- vate	
Inner area							
Non-private	10	8	19	41	6	16	.8
Terraces	5	6	30	36	19	4	38.4
Detached houses	43	21	11	19	4	2	57.0
Flats	16	5	3	67	8	1	34.2
Total	25	12	14	37	10	2	130.5
Metro area	66	5	3	22	3	1	849.4

[a] 'Housing areas' were defined by a cluster analysis of census data (see text p. 36).
Source: Based on analysis of unpublished 'CD' computer tapes, Census, 1971.

TABLE 3.3   *Selected characteristics of houses and flats in inner Sydney, by 'housing area', 1971.*

'Housing area'[a] in Sydney	Houses				Flats (self-contained only)			
	Rent weekly ($)	Rented (%)	Publicly owned (%)	Rooms per house[b]	Rent weekly ($)	Rented (%)	Publicly owned (%)	Rooms per flat[b]
Inner area								
Non-private	12.81	76	0	4.6	23.59	75	0	3.5
Terraces	17.49	54	1	4.9	17.86	93	18	2.9
Detached houses	15.89	28	1	4.9	19.61	87	4	3.1
Flats	24.40	27	1	5.8	23.64	65	5	3.5
Total	17.81	31	1	5.0	20.35	73	10	3.3
Metro area	17.87	19	4	5.4	21.55	71	7	3.6

[a] 'Housing areas' were defined by a cluster analysis of unpublished 1971 Census data (see text p. 36).
[b] Actual differences between the dwelling sizes is considerably greater than is indicated here, because the older dwellings have far smaller rooms.
Source: Based on analysis of unpublished 'CD' computer tapes, Census, 1971.

'Flats': areas of expensive, newer flats and higher-quality houses, which accommodate some 85 000 residents.

Map 3.1 shows the consistency between the location of these housing patterns and the concentric zone model. The 'Non-private' areas are mostly in the CBD, some of the nearby arc of 'Terrace' areas resemble the zone of transition, and the other 'Terrace' areas and the 'Detached houses' areas a bit

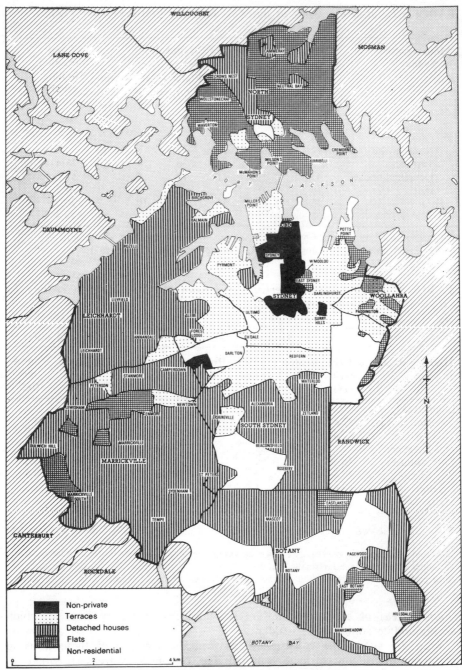

MAP 3.1. 'Housing area' distribution in inner Sydney, 1971
(See text p. 36 for method of identifying 'housing areas'.)

farther out are similar to the zone of workingmen's homes. The distribution of the 'Flats' areas, while not following the zones, are consistent with Hoyt's sectoral model, for they mostly spread northwards and eastwards toward higher-status areas offering the natural attraction of both harbour views and hillside locations.

The general similarity between Sydney and the Chicago-based, zonal model reflects similarities between the two cities. Both started in the early 1800s as ports serving vast rural hinterlands. Their first periods of growth were in the mid to late 1800s, when transport was mostly by foot, followed by another spurt of growth early in the twentieth century, during the period of trams and railways.

Inner Sydney's 'Non-private' housing areas contain vestiges of housing in the otherwise solely non-residential CBD. The majority of the residents are there because it is close to work. Many live in accommodation provided by the university or a hospital, some are in hotels on business trips, and a few live in expensive flats. The remainder of the accommodation is of very poor quality — old hotels and boarding houses as well as the oldest, smallest and cheapest of the inner-area terraces. Nearly all the terraces are rented and many are let as single rooms.

The 'Terrace' areas, mostly located within four kilometres of the CBD, contain a mix of housing, especially the terraces that are so characteristic of inner suburbs in Australia. Because of the major transport barrier imposed by the harbour only a few of the areas in North Sydney were classified as 'Terrace' areas. With Sydney's earliest housing demolished long ago, the terraces are the oldest of the remaining major types of housing, being developed as early as the 1830s but mostly between 1860 and 1890. They evolved during the 'walking city', when people had to live near their work places. At one extreme, they are minute, single-floored, stone hovels with frontages of two and a half metres, in the back alleys of Woolloomooloo (Sydney's first 'outer' suburb away from the city centre). At the other extreme, in Paddington, are the magnificent three-storey, Victorian terraces built fifty years later, complete with elaborate cornices and wrought-iron grating, with frontages of five to six metres.

The better 'Terrace' areas are those designed in the later part of the nineteenth century for middle-class occupants, mostly in environmentally favoured areas near commercial rather than industrial centres.[6] Many of the very best of them are on hillsides (supposed to be a health advantage in the early days) or have harbour views. Paddington, Potts Point, Darlinghurst and Glebe Point were the most fashionable of these areas. On the other hand, the small suburb known as 'The Rocks', located just north of the CBD, has a notorious history as Sydney's first and foremost slum, 'breeding' tuberculosis and other epidemics and harbouring criminals. The worst housing, generally, was built before the enforcement of building codes in the 1870s. Somewhere between the extremes lies the small, single-storey and double-storey terraces to the south and west of the CBD, built originally by companies for their factory workers. Even when new, many of these dwellings were interspersed among non-residential land-use activities. Thus, the basic quality of the terrace houses and their nearby land uses were established about a century ago when the dwellings were first built.

The 1971 Census describes only a third of the dwellings in these 'Terrace' areas as terrace houses, because many have been subdivided into flats, are let as single rooms, or are used as boarding houses. In the 'Terraces' area there are also a few blocks of flats built from the 1920s onwards, especially in Kings Cross, and both older and newer detached houses (some older mansions and newer infill). Over half of the houses in these areas are rented, at rents just under the average for inner-city houses. However, within the better half of the 'Terrace' areas, where there are a relatively large number of rooms per dwelling and few of them are subdivided, more than two-thirds are owner-occupied and the rest are let for rents that are about 10 per cent above those of all inner-suburban houses. In the 'worse-off' Terrace areas, houses have a number of obsolete facilities, most conspicuously the outdoor toilets. A significant number of these old houses have been replaced by government flats let at low rents. Public housing comprises more than half of the dwellings in a number of the CDs in Redfern, Surry Hills, and Waterloo.

The 'Detached houses', located in the next arc away from the city centre, are largely the product of the public-transport era of Sydney's development. The construction of the tramways and suburban railways before the turn of the century brought Sydney's first major wave of suburbanisation. Consistent with the zonal model of urban change, the improved transport enabled the middle classes to leave their rented terraces and move to become owner-occupants of newer houses farther out. In the first outward thrust lasting up to the first world war, a few more terraces were built, but most of the development was of semi-detached houses built to better standards on larger sites of about eight metre frontages. Later development consisted mostly of detached houses, often 'Californian' bungalows, on sites up to sixteen metres wide, mostly in the southern and southwestern parts of the inner city. Considerable numbers of the detached houses in Botany were built after the second world war on formerly swampy sites.

The areas of 'Detached houses' include a few terraces in their innermost areas and a scattering of flats. More than two-thirds of the houses are owner-occupied. Many of the detached houses were built in the heavy industrial areas, which had been on the edge of the metropolis until the twentieth century. Because the few rented homes are of poor quality and are mostly in these areas, house rents in the 'Detached houses' areas are much lower than in the 'Terrace' areas. House values are also depressed by the proportion built of timber or fibro-cement: over half in the 'Detached houses' areas in Balmain, Botany and Mascot. Flat rents are relatively higher in the 'Detached houses' areas because few are converted houses and nearly all were built since 1960.

The last grouping is the 'Flat' areas, in which three-quarters of the dwellings are flats. Nearly all the flats were newly constructed and very few were converted from houses. They are relatively large and are often owner-occupied or let at high rents. The few remaining houses are predominantly large, detached units, which are mostly owner-occupied but exact high rents if rented. They are generally far from heavy industry and are often in elevated positions or have harbour views.

The evolution of 'Flat' areas differs considerably from one to the other, depending on their location. In North Sydney, flat redevelopment and infill has occurred steadily since the 1920s, first on the foreshores served by ferries and later on the more distant ridges which became accessible to the CBD when the Harbour Bridge was opened in 1932. In Potts Point, many flats were built on sites which were formerly large gardens of old mansions. Both North Sydney and Potts Point have always been high-amenity areas which attracted higher-status residents. The 'Flat' areas in the south and the southwest are a post-war phenomenon, explained by the availability of suitable sites and the ready access by rail to the CBD. The relatively high rents in these latter areas result more from their newness than from any residential amenity.

The Residents

The distinctive inner-suburban living conditions are matched by a distinctive population structure. The most basic feature is the small number of families with children. Table 3.4 shows that considerably fewer than a third of the inner-area families include children, compared to over half in the rest of Sydney. Among the families with children, the inner suburbs have relatively more single parents and fewer large families. Young single people or couples make up nearly a third of the inner-area households but only 15 per cent of all metropolitan households. Older families without children, of whom the inner areas also have a higher proportion, occupy well over 40 per cent of the housing. Inner Sydney clearly has the relatively small proportion of families with children that characterises inner-suburban populations in most Western cities.

TABLE 3.4   *Stage of family life-cycle of household heads in Sydney, by sub-region. 1971.*

Area	Pre-family (%)	Family (%)				Post-family (%)			Total	
		Single-parent	Large	Other	Total	Aged	Other	Total	%	No. of cases
Inner	29	3	2	24	29	18	25	43	100	1 158
Middle	13	4	6	40	50	16	21	37	100	8 853
Outer southwest	12	4	7	48	59	12	18	29	100	2 503
Total	15	4	5	39	48	16	21	37	100	13 614

For definitions of terms, see section on Terminology and Data in Chapter 1 (p. 16).
Source: SATS.

Sydney's inner suburbs, relative to the rest of the metropolis, generally are less distinctive with respect to socio-economic status. They have a slight under-representation of higher-status, white-collar workers but considerable over-representation of lower-status, blue-collar workers (Table 3.7; see also Map 4.1). Table 3.5 shows that the inner suburbs have relatively few high-income families and more low-income families. However, contrary to any model suggesting that only the rich can gain fringe locations, the outer western suburbs have even more low-income households, mostly families with children and incomes just below the middle category.[7] But the 1973 Income Survey showed that the inner areas (excluding North Sydney) still have a proportion of impoverished people (13 per cent) that is twice the proportion of them in the outer areas and half as much again as that for all of the Sydney metropolitan area. The inner-suburban concentrations of people on low incomes reflect inequalities of income and socio-economic status in Sydney like those found in American cities, although the differences between sub-areas are much smaller.

TABLE 3.5   *Family income of household heads in Sydney, by sub-region, 1971.*

Area	Income (%)			Total	
	High	**Middle**	**Low**	**%**	**No.**
Inner	14	38	48	100	2 258
Middle	22	42	36	100	8 853
Outer					
southwest	16	28	56	100	2 503
Total	21	37	42	100	13 614

For definitions of terms, see section on Terminology and Data in Chapter 1 (p. 16).
Source: SATS

Table 3.6 shows the systematic influence of both income and life-cycle stage in determining which groups live in the inner suburbs. In addition to the independent effects of both income and life cycle, the inner-city residents in each life-cycle group have consistently lower incomes. The incident of low-income earners in the inner city does not, it seems, result only from a high proportion of residents in those stages of the life cycle (especially the aged) most likely to have low incomes. These relationships are best summarised by the extreme values: the inner suburbs contain only 7 per cent of Sydney's high-income families with children, and fully 39 per cent of the low-income single people and childless couples.

With regard to the impoverished, the inner suburbs also have a larger share of the people whose life-cycle characteristics or other 'disabilities' predispose

TABLE 3.6　*Proportions of Sydney's income groups and family types living in the inner city, 1971.*

Income group	Pre-family (%)	Family (%)	Post-family (%)			Total (%)
			Aged	Other	Total	
High	26	7	12	16	16	12
Middle	29	10	17	19	19	16
Low	39	12	19	24	21	19
Total	31	10	18	20	19	17

For definitions of terms, see section on Terminology and Data in Chapter 1 (p. 16).
Source: SATS

them to poverty: 53 per cent in the inner city, compared to 40 per cent elsewhere in Sydney. Within the inner city, only 12 per cent of those below the poverty line do not fit into one or more of these groups designated by the 1973 Income Survey (see p. 16 for terminology). The main reason is that recently arrived non-British migrants and families with multiple disabilities comprise 19 per cent of the 'income units' (see p. 17 for the definition) compared to only 5 per cent in other parts of Sydney. Large families are also slightly over-represented, despite the substantial under-representation of families with fewer children.[8] Though recent migrants and multi-problem families explain much of the higher poverty rates in inner areas, by far the largest group among the inner-suburban poor is still the aged (36 per cent).[9]

Inner Sydney serves as a reception area for recently arrived, culturally different migrants from overseas. Over a third of inner Sydney's residents are foreign-born, compared to a quarter throughout Sydney (Table 3.7). Inner Sydney has especially large shares of those who are most recently arrived and who are from non-English-speaking countries: only 12 per cent of Sydney's British migrants but nearly a third of the Southern European migrants, including more than half of the Greeks, a third of the Yugoslavs, and a fifth of the Italians.[10] There are also relatively greater concentrations of the less numerous, more recently arrived groups: Turks, Lebanese, Egyptians and South Americans. Because these figures exclude the Australia-born children of migrants, the number of persons with a non-Australian heritage resident in inner Sydney is probably considerably higher than the figure of 38 per cent the Census data gives for the non-British-born (see Table 5.3).

Table 3.7 shows that particular demographic groups are distributed within the inner city only partly consistently with the zonal model. The 'Non-private' housing areas — effectively the CBD — have a high proportion of higher-status workers because of the many visiting businessmen and resident nurses; the poorest residents are not in the labourforce. The 'Terrace' areas, which should contain the 'zone of transition' according to the Burgess model, do have relatively few children and many migrants. But the next housing area outwards, the 'Detached Houses' areas (analagous to the zone of workingmens' homes), have even fewer high-status workers and more southern European migrants. Finally, the 'Flat' areas, which were not in the zonal model, have high proportions of high-status workers, young adults, and the higher-status British migrants. Despite some similarities with the zonal model, the inner Sydney 'housing areas' do not show uniformly lower status nearer the CBD.

TABLE 3.7   *Socio-economic characteristics of 'housing areas' in Sydney, 1971.*

'Housing area in Sydney [a]	Occupational status [b] (%)			Population								
				Age group (%)				Non-Australian-born				Total ('000)
	High	Mid.	Low	0-17	1-34	35-64	65+	British	Sthn. Europe [c]	Other	Total	
Inner area												
Non-private	58	12	30	8	40	41	11	14	2	14	30	9
Terraces	37	19	44	20	34	35	11	10	11	15	36	99
Detached houses	29	23	48	27	31	33	9	6	20	10	36	181
Flats	58	17	25	18	37	34	11	16	6	15	37	84
Total	39	20	41	23	33	34	10	10	14	12	36	374
Metro area	42	28	30	37	20	34	9	10	6	9	25	2724

[a] 'Housing areas' were defined by a cluster analysis of unpublished 1971 Census data (see text p. 36).
[b] Percentage of employed persons. High status: professional, managerial, and clerical; low status: operatives and process workers, drivers, service workers and labourers.
[c] Southern European: from Greece, Italy, Malta, Yugoslavia.
Source: Based on analysis of unpublished 'CD' computer tapes, Census, 1971.

Summary

This chapter has shown that inner Sydney has an internal structure that, on first inspection, appears typical of large Western cities. There is a dominant CBD and a nearby belt of manufacturing and warehousing which supply many jobs and produce many problems in the living environment. Although Australian cities have considerable spread of residential land, employment remains highly centralised, probably more so than in most North American cities. The housing patterns in inner Sydney are generally consistent with the concentric zone model: 'Non-private' housing areas in the CBD, surrounded by 'Terrace Houses', and then by 'Detached Houses'. The innermost areas have often been subdivided for more intense use as flats or rooms and are mostly rented and relatively inexpensive. But the housing stock in most areas is diverse and there is no indication of any housing having reached the end of its physical life, or of slum formation, disinvestment in the housing, or abandonment of any housing. Newer flats, though concentrated mainly in a northern sector, are also spread through much of the inner city — further evidence of the attractiveness of the inner suburbs for residential investment.

The most distinctive feature of the inner-area population is the proportion of families without children, especially young, single people. The inner areas are also functioning as reception areas for recently arrived migrants from southern Europe and from elsewhere. But inner-Sydney residents are not the down-trodden and defeated masses described by Burgess. Unlike the North American ghettos, the proportion of households having low incomes is only slightly higher in inner Sydney. Although poverty rates are relatively high, only one out of every eight of the inner residents is poor. If the existence of impoverished, unemployed, and racially different people explain much of the disinvestment and decay in American cities, it is easy to understand why Australia has had no comparable experience.

CHAPTER **4**

Inner-suburban Life-styles

This chapter considers the influence of inner-suburban living on the everyday lives of the residents. Their needs and resources are related to the housing and amenities available, the neighbourhood environment and the accessibility of inner areas. Because the requirements of residents vary considerably during the life cycle, this analysis deals separately with each of the life-cycle groups defined in Chapter 1. The importance of economic resources is shown by comparing living conditions between high-income and low-income earners within each life-cycle group in the inner suburbs. To test whether inner areas exacerbate or compensate for the difficulties of the disadvantaged, residential environments of low-income people are compared between inner and other areas. The accessibility advantages and moving patterns of the different groups are also shown. These findings relate closely to later chapters which consider the demand for inner-city living.

Pre-family Households

The many inner-suburban residents in the childless, pre-family stage of the life cycle are well suited for inner-suburban living. More of the high-income households (people with considerable choice) are at the pre-family stage, than are low-income households. More than three-quarters of the pre-family households that are on high incomes are married couples on two incomes. These people have high incomes even though few have reached the top salaries in what are almost always white-collar jobs. On the other hand, almost none of the pre-family households on low incomes are married; most are single females in clerical jobs. Their average age of twenty-three years is about five years younger than their higher-income counterparts. Thus, of the two extreme income groups within the pre-family group, those with higher incomes are a bit further through their life cycle. The lower-income group also includes more tertiary students (10 per cent), and more young migrants who are often unemployed or have unskilled jobs.

The life-styles of pre-family groups at all income levels are generally oriented towards careers and consumerism and are facilitated by inner-city living. Unencumbered by babysitting problems or many household duties, pre-family groups can take full advantage of the many nearby cultural and entertainment facilities. A small dwelling with no yard and ready access to jobs is convenient to those with little taste for domestic duties. The small size of the family enables them to economise on high cost, inner-suburban housing space.

Of those on high incomes, the vast majority live in expensive new flats which are spacious for their typically two-person households. Most are tenants because, despite high incomes, few of them have yet the wealth or the urge to buy homes. Few share dwellings because most are married and the others can afford to live alone. Analysis of unpublished CD data shows that the proportion of flats in inner areas correlates strongly with higher-status workers (.65) and women in the labourfource (.45). Other correlations suggest that these groups live in expensive flats which, relative to other flats, have a high proportion owner-occupied.

Of the low-income, pre-family households, more than half share housing and nearly as many live in non-private housing as in flats (see Table 4.1). Those in non-private accommodation include students in colleges, nurses living in at hospitals, and recent migrants and others in hostels and boarding houses. Many of the flats that house lower-income, single people are probably non-self-contained units subdivided from existing houses. Unpublished figures from the 1973 Income Survey suggest that, in the inner city, about a quarter of women not classified as aged and a quarter of the recent migrants (both of whom were mostly in the pre-family stage of life cycle) were boarders. The 1973 survey for the Australian Population and Immigration Council found that, of the migrants resident in Australia for less than a year, 20 per cent lived in hostels and 11 per cent were boarders (APIC, 1976:94).

The low-income individuals at the pre-family stage can thus usually avoid paying high housing costs relative to income by either sharing accommodation or by living in smaller, poorer-quality units.

Families of all life-cycle stages are distributed throughout the inner areas; however, as was shown in Table 3.7, those in the pre-family group tend to be concentrated in the 'Non-private' and 'Flats' housing areas. Map 4.1 shows that the high-status workers, who are mostly in the pre-family group, are also in some of the most attractive 'Terrace' areas: Paddington, Glebe Point, Balmain, and around Sydney University. The minority of young, higher-status people who live in old houses concentrate where there are special locational advantages and higher-quality dwellings. Correlations indicate that the high-status workers are able to avoid the industrial areas and that other young adults — mostly lower-status workers and recent migrants — concentrate in rooming house areas to the east of the CBD.

These findings reflect the function of the inner city as a staging ground for young, upwardly mobile individuals. Young migrants from overseas and rural areas come for the jobs, while those from the suburbs leave their parents' houses to live near jobs and inner-city attractions and to establish their status as independent adults. Most of the young men have low incomes only temporarily at the beginning of their careers, while the women are typically typists for a brief period between childhood and child-bearing. As these groups grown older

TABLE 4.1   *Housing types of inner suburban residents in Sydney, by income and family type, 1971.*

Group	Detached house (%)	Semi-detached house a (%)	Flats b (%)	Non-private c (%)	Total
High income	30	18	50	2	100
Low income	28	28	33	12	100
Pre-family	7	9	45	38	100
Family	32	33	34	1	100
Single parent	29	27	42	2	100
Large family	42	50	8	0	100
Post-family	32	29	29	9	100
Non-aged	31	26	28	15	100
Aged	33	32	30	5	100
Total	30	25	40	6	100

For definitions of terms, see section on Terminology and Data in Chapter 1 (p. 16).
a Unfortunately, SATS combined semi-detached and terrace houses.
b Includes both self-contained and non-self-contained flats.
c Rooming houses, hostels, colleges, hotels, boarding houses; and nurses quarters.
Source: SATS.

and marry, often each other, several changes occur. In the first instance, their combined incomes raise them out of the lower-income group, and most begin to save for their shift to the child-bearing stage of the life cycle. The transition usually involves a number of closely interrelated events: the wife leaves her job and bears children, the husband is promoted out of the low-income level, and they leave the inner-city flat to buy a house in another part of the city where land costs are lower and the environment is better.

Families with Children

Inner-city living is more problematic for the families with children that do not move to the suburbs. They cannot easily economise on housing space and children are very vulnerable to cramped housing, lack of backyards and ground-floor entrances, traffic dangers, inadequate public facilities and social problems. For these reasons, the inner suburbs have relatively few families with children, especially those with high incomes. On the other hand, low-income families with children, particularly single parents and large families, are heavily over-represented in the inner suburbs. Relatively low house rents and prices are a major attraction, for they free money for other essential expenditures. Moreover, the houses are near jobs, which keeps down travel costs and increases opportunities for wives to work — a key factor in raising incomes from poverty levels. In the inner area, half of the middle-income and higher-

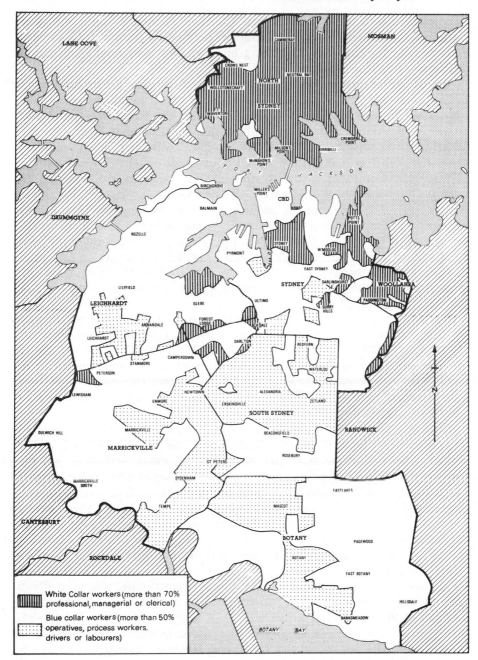

MAP 4.1. Distribution of selected occupational groups of inner Sydney residents, 1971
Source: Based on analysis of unpublished 'CD' computer tapes, Census, 1971.

income families with children depend for their economic status on wives working. Inner areas also have enough population turnover to provide opportunities for culturally different groups to form communities that ease their entry into Australian society.

Almost half of the inner-suburban families with children are probably non-British migrants.[1] The majority of migrants are young to middle-aged adults who either brought children with them or bore them relatively soon after arrival in Australia. More than half of the Greek, Italian and Yugoslav households throughout Australia are couples with dependent children, compared with less than a third for all households of inner Sydney (APIC, 1976:105-12). Compared to the Australian-born, migrants are less likely to leave the inner areas once children are born or approach school age (Burnley & Walker, 1977:7-9). Most of the children in South Sydney have non-British parents — commonly Greek (20 per cent), Yugoslav (9 per cent), Lebanese (7 per cent) and Turk (4 per cent) — even though only about a third of the total population is non-British-born (Piatkowska, 1974:4, 10). Southern European children are similarly concentrated within most of the City of Sydney, especially in the Italian sections of Leichhardt municipality, and in the Greek parts of Marrickville (see Map 8.4).

Southern Europeans comprise an even larger proportion of the poor families with children. The proportion's of families with children that are impoverished are 32 per cent Italian, 25 per cent Greek, and 20 per cent Yugoslav, compared to 5 per cent Australian-born (APIC, 1976; Henderson, 1975). A study of large families (four or more children) in the City of Sydney (pre-1968 boundaries) found that half were headed by non-British migrants, and about 5 per cent were Aboriginals (Halladay, 1971:120).

Three-quarters of the heads of low-income families with children in inner areas are blue-collar workers, compared to only a fifth of the pre-family heads. Unlike white-collar workers, the blue-collar workers seldom enjoy the increasing incomes with promotion that enable families of white-collar workers to leave the inner suburbs when child-bearing begins. Southern European migrants, who sometimes can speak little English, have even higher rates of blue-collar jobs. Nearly three-quarters of the post-1962 migrants throughout the mainland capital cities, including the many white-collar British workers, are skilled (30 per cent), semi-skilled (32 per cent) or unskilled (1 per cent) workers (APIC, 1976:26).

Southern European families in the mainland capital cities also have a high proportion of mothers at work; two-thirds of each the Yugoslavs and Greeks, and half of the Italians (APIC, 1976:105-12). If the wives were not employed, the poverty rates of these families would rise to over half of each the Greeks and Italians and to 44 per cent of the Yugoslavs. The main problem, of course, is child care. Of those married migrant women who do not work, more than half would do so if child-care problems could be overcome (APIC, 1976:105-12). In a number of primary schools near the CBD, about a quarter of the children enrolled, most of whom are migrant, are 'latch-key' children, who have nobody to mind them after school (City of Sydney, 1974*a*:46-50). By living near jobs, working parents are at least able to minimise the time these children spend alone. This problem also applies to Australia-born single parents (40 per cent work), spouses of large families (36 per cent work), and other wives with children (33 per cent work).

Table 4.1 showed that very few of the low-income families with children live in non-private housing, two-thirds live in houses, and only 4 per cent share housing costs by living with unrelated people. A third of these inner-area families live in flats, compared to only 14 per cent elsewhere in Sydney. These are probably mainly the smaller families with younger children, and many are single parents, living in cheap flats near the CBD or in Housing Commission flats in South Sydney. Almost a tenth of the large families live in flats, which must be very crowded. Living in flats presents major problems for child-rearing and nearly all these parents would prefer to live in houses (Stevenson & O'Neil, 1967; Sutton & Richmond, 1975).

The lower-income families with children are forced to make other compromises. Terrace houses usually have only a few bedrooms and can be crowded when families are occupying them. Some, especially tenants, put up with poor housing standards. For example, a small survey of some of the worst private housing areas in South Sydney found that most dwellings had one or more of the following problems: outside bathrooms and toilets, inadequate water heating, excessive dampness, and vermin (Piatkowska, 1974:§ G). A survey of occupants of rented dwellings in the inner-Melbourne LGAs of Collingwood and Fitzroy found that two-fifths reported poor heating; a third, poor plumbing; and a fifth, extensive dampness (Fitzroy Ecumenical Centre, 1975:91). A third had spent their own money on maintenance and repairs because landlords refused to do so. Owner-occupants, who have more incentive and resources to spend on their dwellings, probably live in a considerably better standard of dwelling.

If housing costs are taken into account, poverty rates increase slightly within the inner suburbs compared to elsewhere in Sydney (1973 Income Survey). The explanation is that there is a higher proportion of renters in inner areas rather than that housing costs are higher than in other areas. However, because inner-city house rents are relatively low, the poverty rates, if calculated after housing costs, would be even higher if they rented elsewhere in Sydney. Although data on tenure by life cycle are unavailable for the inner areas, it is likely that the Australian-born families with children tend to rent while trying to save, sometimes unsuccessfully, to purchase housing elsewhere in Sydney. Renting presents a number of problems, especially the possibility of eviction and the near-certainty of ever-increasing rents. Nonetheless, the rent levels — however high they may be — do not require the saving of a deposit of a house. Renting old, inner-city houses is one of the few housing options available for many low-income families with children.

Southern Europeans often expend an extraordinarily high proportion of their incomes on the purchase of a house. In Redfern, more than two-thirds of the Greek-born householders were owners or buyers of their homes, compared with only a fifth of the Australian-born and British-born residents (Neutze, 1972:15). Of all the post-1961 overseas migrants in Australia the proportions of home buyers or owners were 75 per cent Greek, 69 per cent Italian, and 62 per cent Yugoslav (1973 Income Survey). Only in the inner-city areas were prices low enough for many of them to gain the security of home ownership. However, the short-term costs of buying are high: if housing costs are taken into account, poverty rates double for recent, non-British migrants but drop by more than a third for other households.

Families having four or more children face special difficulties. Of the large families in the City of Sydney (1968 boundaries), more than half lived in terrace houses and, although more than 90 per cent wanted to own their homes, only 44 per cent did so (Halladay, 1971). Overcrowding was severe: the average number of people per room was 1.4, compared to less than .7 for the average inner Sydney household. Because the Housing Commission has no large units in the inner city, less than 2 per cent lived in government-subsidised housing. In addition to their housing shortage a third of these large families said they had been short of food during the past year and a fifth had either gone hungry or asked for food from outside sources. Not surprisingly, 75 per cent wanted to move, but few could afford to do so.

Although families with children are found throughout inner Sydney, they are concentrated in the 'Detached houses' areas and, to a lesser extent, the 'Terrace' areas (Table 3.7). The few who live in 'Flat' areas are mostly in the newer but lower-quality flats in areas like Hillsdale. Although children are endangered by heavy traffic from nearby factories, they are nonetheless more likely than other inner-city residents to live in the industrial areas (correlation .32), which have more houses relative to flats than other areas. Heavy traffic often restricts children from using the little open space that is available. For example, in Redfern more than half the families reported that their children could not safely cross a major road to get to a nearby park (South Sydney Community Aid Environment Committee, 1974:1). Many of the families with children are able to rent or purchase homes only by living in the most environmentally degraded areas, which have old, inadequate schools and poor neighbourhood facilities.

Location is especially important for the non-British migrants, who have congregated sufficiently to establish ethnic enclaves of shops, churches and pubs. (The location of non-British migrants in Sydney in 1971 is shown in Map 8.4.) This geographical concentration provides cultural and social opportunities, which are critical for the many non-English-speaking members, especially wives. It also facilitates the formation of self-help groups and small businesses which provide a foothold on the ladder of social and economic advancement. Italians, Greeks, Yugoslavs and almost every other of Sydney's migrant communities have certain localities where some of their cultural traditions can be maintained. Fortunately, the ethnic groupings are not so great as to form ghettos. None of the inner city CDs has a majority of population born in Southern Europe, let alone in any single one of its countries.

Inner-suburban families are aware of the problems of their areas. In a survey of Redfern residents (Troy, 1971:40-41), the respondents (almost two-thirds the households had children) rated their environment slightly more poorly than did the residents of other Sydney study areas. The inner suburban residents were also much more likely to think that 'families here live far too close together'. Nonetheless, three-quarters of them thought the area was 'a good place to live' and only 6 per cent more than the residents in other areas felt they would be happier in another suburb. Although the findings partly reflect low expectations, they still indicate that the area provides for those on low incomes.

In summary, the people that remain in the inner city after children are born differ substantially from the pre-family groups. Among the low-income group, most are migrants or blue-collar workers (or both) and many avoid poverty only because their wives work. More than two-thirds live in houses, affordable because of their low quality and poor environments. Despite problems of poor housing and neighbourhoods, inner locations offer these families cheaper housing and easy access to work, which frees them to spend more of their incomes on other necessities such as food and clothing.

Post-Family Households

These households comprise over 40 per cent of all inner-suburban households and over half of those with low incomes. Within this group, aged people make up 40 per cent of the total and 60 per cent of the low-income households. A majority of them are probably working-class couples or widowed people remaining in homes after children have left; others are the more transient, life-long poor who have never established secure families or jobs; and a very few are higher-income couples who have either returned to or remained in the inner city because it suits their life-styles.

Compared with the rest of Sydney, those in the inner-city who are at the post-family stage are far worse off. Higher proportions have low incomes (more than half compared with a third in the rest of Sydney) and there is greater poverty among aged single people (almost half compared with a quarter).[2] In the inner city about a quarter of those in the post-family group are married or have spouses still living, compared with almost half in the rest of the metropolis. In the inner suburbs very few of the household heads who are aged and on low incomes, and only half of the other post-family household heads on low incomes, are employed full time. Though only a minority need accessibility to work, the inner city offers low-cost housing, access to shopping and health and welfare agencies and, most importantly, continuity of familiar housing, neighbourhoods and friends.

Table 4.1 shows that almost two-thirds of the low-income, post-family groups live in houses, even though their needs and resources are small. Many of them are continuing to live in the houses that they first occupied during their middle years when they had both families and jobs. Excluding those living rent-free (mostly boarders and lodgers in relative's homes), over 40 per cent of single, aged people, and nearly two-thirds of aged couples in the inner city owned their dwellings; none of the aged owners in the sample had a mortgage debt (1973 Income Survey). The aged are relatively well served by public housing and about 5 to 10 per cent of them in the inner city rent from the government. These ways of economising on housing explain why the poverty rates of aged throughout Australia reduce sharply from 24 per cent to 8 per cent once housing costs are taken into account (Henderson, 1975:240).

The greatest economic difficulties arise for those who rent privately: half of the aged single people and a third of the aged couples in the inner suburbs — about twice the proportions of those living elsewhere in the metropolis. For these people, poverty rates probably remain high even after housing costs are taken into account. Although some are protected from high rents and eviction by rent-control legislation, most of these renters are unprotected tenants living in flats, mostly not self-contained, or boarding houses. Those people who are not yet aged are more likely than the elderly to live in boarding houses because their poverty is often life-long, not just during old age. Older tenants face special difficulties in asserting their rights to landlords, in moving from intolerable conditions, or in overcoming fixed personal habits to share accommodation and housing costs. They frequently pay extraordinarily high proportions of income on rent.

The aged are more evenly dispersed throughout inner Sydney than any other life-cycle group. The owners in the more outlying 'Detached houses' areas are generally balanced by aged people renting single rooms in 'Terrace' and 'Non-private' areas. Among the cheap flats and private hotels of Kings Cross, the proportion of older people is over 30 per cent, compared to the metropolitan average of under 10 per cent. Two-thirds of aged people living in the inner city throughout Australian capital cities report no dislikes about the areas in which they live (EHCD, 1976a, vol. 1:55). Moreover, the old people living outside the inner suburbs were found to be slightly more likely to have neighbourhood dislikes, mainly because more felt 'too far' from various facilities.[3] The most frequently reported of the few dislikes in the inner suburbs was a 'catch-all' category of poor environmental conditions, crime, and distance from the country — mentioned by 16 per cent of the respondents.[4]

Another measure of housing and neighbourhood satisfaction, albeit an imperfect one, is the desire to move. Only 14 per cent of old people in both the inner and other parts of the capital cities 'wanted to move' (EHCD, 1976a, vol. 1:45). Of the inner-suburban aged who did want to move, a third wanted to move within their own neighbourhoods and another third to move to another inner suburb. Less than 2 per cent of all the aged in the inner suburbs wanted to move to other parts of the capital cities. Moreover, throughout Australia, those old people who wanted to move — especially the vulnerable single aged — wanted to be near public transport and shops, which are most accessible in inner areas. The American situation of the old people trapped in deteriorating, racially changing, inner-area neighbourhoods, would appear to be inapplicable to Australia.

Social Problems

In the traditional models of urban structure, high rates of personality and social disorders are considered characteristic of inner-suburban residents. Moreover, it is sometimes suggested that the inner-area environment is largely responsible for them; for example, poor housing has long been viewed as a principle cause of disease and social problems. More plausible, at least in today's context, are the theories that the inner areas exacerbate personal difficulties because of a breakdown of community order caused by high transiency rates and concentrations of the disadvantaged. If there is any norm, it is a culture of poverty, in which 'deviancy' becomes the rule rather than the exception. The test of these 'environmental determinism' models would be to find out if these particular individuals would have more or fewer problems if they were dispersed throughout the metropolis.

Contrary to the arguments of social pathology and social dysfunction, this study takes the simpler view that, at least in Australia, the problems of the inner areas result overwhelmingly from general social problems that are not areal in origin. The disadvantaged are somewhat more likely to come from inner areas because that is where most disadvantaged parents live, not because of the poor living conditions. Other disadvantaged people have moved to the inner city for the low housing costs or to escape the strictures of suburban life-styles. Indeed, if there is any agglomerative or interactive effect between 'deviants' in inner areas, it is probably a beneficial one; communities of common interest provide mutual self-help and companionship. The local economy makes some adjustments to the specialised needs, to the poverty and, in some cases, even to the limited employment capabilities of people who cannot or do not want to make it in the mainstream of Australian society. If the 'deviants' were to locate elsewhere, they would be more likely to divert meagre funds from food to pay more for housing, to suffer from either isolation or social stigma or, in some extreme cases, to be institutionalised.

The inner city, certainly, contains a disproportionate share of the most disadvantaged people in Sydney. Virtually all of the estimated 3000 homeless men live within a few kilometres of the CBD (Darcy & Jones, 1975). A quarter of Sydney's 5000 Aboriginals are in the inner suburbs, clustered mostly around Redfern and Chippendale. The City of Sydney — followed by South Sydney, Leichhardt, and Marrickville — consistently rank the lowest of all of areas in New South Wales in terms of health, social orderliness, family stability, and educational performance (Vinson & Homel, 1976). These results have been widely publicised, including a headline in the Sydney *Daily Telegraph* (7.12.76):

'Five suburbs choked by misery, despair'. Except for Liverpool, the 'misery' suburbs were all in the inner city.

A study in Melbourne (Little *et al.,* 1974:6) reported similar findings: 'Melbourne is dramatically dichotomised into an inner core area with high levels of social and related economic problems, and the remainder of the metropolitan area where the socio-economic pathology is not so evident'. The use of the term 'socio dysfunction' in the title of the report implies a 'culture of poverty' cause. The report also claims that poverty, and therefore various social problems, are on the rise because jobs for the poor are moving out of the inner areas (this thesis is reviewed critically in Chapter 9). The study did not consider that the inner city might attract and provide benefits for, individuals who are predisposed to have social difficulties or to lose jobs.

How severe *are* the social problems of the inner city? Table 4.2 shows the relative levels in the inner suburbs of a few problems having fairly typical spatial distributions. By these selected measures, the inner suburbs have roughly twice the state-wide rate of mental illness, needs for emergency assistance, juvenile delinquency and family breakdown. No studies are available to show the extent of under-estimation of problems in the high-status areas. The relative rates of social problems tell only part of the story. Even if problems are twice as prevalent in the inner suburbs, more than three-quarters of all such problems in Sydney are found among people not living in the inner suburbs. Moreover, only a small proportion of inner-area residents have such problems. On a yearly basis, one out of every three hundred inner-area adults is admitted to mental hospital, one out of every fifty households receives

TABLE 4.2   *Percentage of people in inner Sydney having selected social problems, 1971-74.*

Area	Mental hospital admissions [b]	Emergency cash assistance [c]	Juvenile court appearance [d]	Divorced separated [e]
Inner area [a]				
City of Sydney	.3	1.5	1.3	11
Other	.2	1.8	1.2	7
Total	.2	1.7	1.2	8
NSW average	.1	1.0	.5	4

[a] Because North Sydney and Botany have relatively fewer problems, they have been excluded from this definition of the inner city so as to not understate inner-urban problems.
[b] First admissions to mental hospitals (yearly average 1971-73) per 100 people aged over fifteen.
[c] Persons receiving emergency cash assistance (fiscal year 1973-74) per 100 people aged over fifteen.
[d] Juvenile 'Crimes Act' appearances (fiscal year 1973-75) per 100 people aged eight to seventeen years.
[e] Permanently separated or divorced people (1971) per 100 people over age fifteen.
Sources: Calculated from Vinson and Homel (1976, App. B) and the 1971 Census.

emergency cash assistance, and one out of every hundred juveniles made a court appearance. Moreover, multi-problem individuals or families probably account for many of these incidents, which suggests an intensity, as much as an extensiveness, of social problems. Although it is not possible to quantify the numbers of inner-city residents having various social problems, it is clear that they comprise only a small minority.

Unless people having social problems were highly concentrated within particular inner suburbs, it is unlikely that spatial sub-cultures of poverty could develop. Yet, even in the most disadvantaged suburb in inner Sydney — around the CBD — only 26 per cent of the households received pensions, compared with 9 per cent for the rest of the metropolitan area.[5] In no other inner postal-code area does the proportion of pensioners exceed 15 per cent. There is no evidence to suggest that the inner parts of Australian cities have concentrations of social problems in any way comparable to those of the American ghettos.

In the United States, the concentration of the poor in public housing has given rise to much of the strongest arguments against the harmful effects of segregating the disadvantaged. Some of the more vociferous opponents of high-rise development suggest that similar, if less intense, problems are emerging in Australia. It is true that there are a number of CDs, mostly in Waterloo, in which many more than half of the dwellings are government owned. However, unlike America, Australian public housing serves a wider range of needs: mainly of the lower-middle classes, rather than solely the most intensely disadvantaged level of society. Only 17 per cent of the occupants of Sydney's government housing are below the poverty line (1973 Income Survey). Government housing is characterised more by low-status workers, although all occupational levels are represented (Jones, 1972:29). Table 4.3 shows that, although government housing has more than its share of single parents and large families, still only a small minority of the residents fall into these categories. In sharp contrast to the American experience, Australian public housing has little concentration of ethnic and multi-problem families. The reason is the fairly generous income limit for first admission, the absence of any income reviews after admission, and the eviction of those who are unable to pay their rent or who regularly create disturbances.

One of the most important questions is whether the inner city produces or attracts people having social difficulties. The only data available to test this issue are in the information on family breakdown (see Table 4.2). Vinson and Homel (1976:App. B) present data which show that, although the inner areas have proportions of divorced and separated adults almost twice as high as those of other areas, in fact the rates of petitions for divorce among adults in inner Sydney do not exceed the New South Wales averages. Indeed, Bankstown, a middle suburb, had rates one-third higher than those in the inner suburbs. Part of the explanation is that the low-income people in inner areas are more likely to separate and not apply for divorce; but a more important reason is probably that people with personal problems to resolve frequently prefer to escape from

TABLE 4.3   *Disability groups in government housing in Sydney, 1973.*

'Income units'	Disability groups (percentages)						Total
	Aged	Single parent	Large family	Sick or un-employed	Migrant, Aboriginal, or Multi-disability	No Dis-ability	no. of Dwellings ('000)
Government housing	29	10	7	3	8	43	37.3
Private housing	17	3	2	3	7	68	898.3

For definitions of terms, see section on Terminology and Data in Chapter 1 (p. 17).
Source: 1973 Income Survey.

an all-too-familiar setting into the anonymity of inner areas, where there is cheap housing.

As well as cheap housing, the inner areas have proximity to a wide variety of social services. The inner city contains a massive surplus of hospital facilities relative to the needs of local residents. Although serving specialised metropolitan needs, these facilities also provide a 'safety net' of virtually any kind of medical service at minimal or no charge (Donald, 1977). Many private services — most notably the Smith Family, the Salvation Army, St Vincent de Paul, and the Sydney City Mission — are located in or near the CBD, even though they may serve far larger areas. These agencies report that their main categories of clients are multi-problem families, itinerant and alcholic men, pensioners, and single people (usually middle aged) having psycho-social problems; there are few migrants among their clientele (City of Sydney, 1974*a*:12). Other services, such as the Aboriginal Health Service, are located in inner areas to be near their target populations. For a wide variety of historical and practical reasons, the inner city has developed important resources for those dependent on public or private assistance.

In summary, the inner suburbs do contain a disproportionate share of people having social problems. However, such people still comprise a relatively small proportion of the inner-suburban population. Rather than causing the problems, it is likely that the inner areas attract people with emergent problems. The housing is cheap and, although often unpleasant, is not nearly so bad as to cause health or social problems. The anonymity, social services, and wide variety of cheap cafes and pubs are additional attractions. For those with limited economic and social capabilities, the inner suburbs, for who choose them, are one of the best places to live.

Travel Behaviour

Accessibility, together with low housing costs, are the most important attractions of the inner city for low-income residents. Studies in Sydney (Troy, 1971), Melbourne (Troy, 1971) and Adelaide (Anglim *et al.,* 1975), have shown that the most valued feature of inner-city living is location near jobs and shops. Residents gain either time or money, or sometimes both. Although limited by inner-city congestion and the use of slower modes of transport, the time saved in travel by living in inner locations can still be enough to provide more time for family activities, recreation and entertainment, or even to hold a second job. The costs are low because the distances travelled by inner-area are short, and cheaper public transport is readily available. If a first or second car is not needed, the savings could easily approach $1000 a year for each car. Put another way, the availability of public transport and nearby job and services can overcome some of the inconvenience or isolation for people who cannot afford cars, or for wives whose husbands commute in the family's only car.

In 1971 only half of the inner-suburban households owned cars, compared to three-quarters elsewhere in Sydney (Table 4.4). The difference is only partly due to the lower income of inner-area residents, because it also applies at each level of income. Among the low-income groups, a quarter in the inner city own cars compared with over half elsewhere in the metropolis; large differences between inner and other areas also occur between different life-cycle groups within the low-income population.[6] The exception here is that high-income families living in the inner city, who presumably keep cars for their convenience, own nearly as many cars as high-income families living elsewhere. The vast majority of the lower-income groups economise by not owning cars.

Among the low-income residents of the inner city, there are important differences between life-cycle stages in car ownership rates. Very few of either the pre-family or post-family households own cars. The young one have less need for cars, because they can walk easily, carry their groceries, and have time to wait at bus stops. Many of the older ones are unable to drive, particularly in the hectic inner-city traffic. On the other hand, half the low-income, inner-city families with children have cars. When cars can be kept full there are greater savings compared with public transport, and many of the heads of households have blue-collar jobs that are not on the main public transport routes into the

TABLE 4.4   *Percentage of households owning cars, by income, family type and sub-region of Sydney, 1971.*

Area	High income group	Pre-family	Single-parent	Family Large family	Total	Post-family Aged	Total	All families	All Incomes
Inner	83	14	27	17	51	12	16	25	47
Other	95	29	51	83	76	29	34	54	75
Total	94	23	47	71	73	26	30	49	69

For definitions of terms see section on Terminology and Data in Chapter 1 (p. 16).
Source: SATS.

CBD. Unlike the majority of families with children, few of the single parents or large families can afford cars, even though they probably need them more than other households. The high rates of car ownership among the large, low-income families outside the inner city, despite the considerable financial sacrifice they have to make, indicates the importance of the car for all but the most impoverished or those with easy access to amenities.

The SATS data, if used cautiously, indicate some of the travel advantages of inner-suburban living. In interpreting the results, it should be borne in mind that differences in travel habits result from differences between people as well as between environments.[7] Table 4.5 shows that nearly 60 per cent of inner-city workers use public transport or walk to work, compared to 40 per cent of workers living elsewhere in Sydney. The drop in car use associated with inner-city living is least among the high-income people, who presumably use cars for convenience and speed even when public transport is available. Low-income, inner-area workers use buses (28 per cent) and walk (24 per cent) nearly as much as they use cars (31 per cent) for journeys to work. The low-income workers without cars rely most heavily on buses (40 per cent) in inner areas and trains (42 per cent) elsewhere. Thus, the availability of nearby jobs and public transport makes possible, or compensates for, the low car-ownership of inner-suburban residents.

Despite the use of slower modes of travel, the average, one-way trip to work takes twenty-six minutes in inner areas and thirty-four minutes elsewhere in the metropolis (Table 4.6). These time differences result mainly from the sharp reduction of the proportion making trips of over forty minutes: from 31 per cent in other metropolitan areas to 17 per cent within the inner city. The time saved is greater for the low-income workers who do not own cars.

TABLE 4.5   *Mode of journeys to work in Sydney, by sub-region and income group 1971.*

Sub-region and income group	Mode of journey (% of sample)					Total no. of journeys
	Car	Bus	Train	Walk	Other	
Inner area						
High-income	44	21	12	16	7	610
Low-income	31	28	12	24	5	637
No car	7	40	17	30	6	379
All incomes	38	23	13	19	7	3 329
Other metro areas						
High income	60	11	20	5	4	4 059
Low income	54	11	23	7	5	1 937
No car	13	24	42	16	5	873
All incomes	60	11	20	6	4	18 146

For definitions of terms, see section on Terminology and Data in Chapter 1 (p. 16).
Source: SATS.

TABLE 4.6 *Duration of journeys to work of income groups in Sydney, by sub-region, 1971.*

Area/income	Duration (one-way)			
	Average (minutes)	Percentage less than 10 minutes	Percentage more than 40 minutes	Total no. of journeys
Inner area				
High income	26	21	17	606
Low income	27	23	16	637
No car	29	18	21	379
All incomes	26	21	17	3 329
Other metro areas				
High income	34	16	32	3 993
Low income	35	20	31	2 937
No car	41	15	41	873
All incomes	34	18	31	18 146

For definitions of terms, see section on Terminology and Data in Chapter 1 (p. 16).
Source: SATS

The advantages of inner locations for the journey to work are especially important for the many families that depend heavily on the wife's earnings to lift them out of the poverty and low-income categories. Over 80 per cent of the low-income, working wives in the inner area have children. These women had exceptionally short journeys to work (average twenty-two minutes), even though only a quarter used cars. If these women could not get jobs nearby, they would be forced to spend more time away from the children and domestic duties, to purchase cars and hence reduce severely their net earnings, or not to work and suffer from even greater economic hardships.

Shopping trips are generally less important than trips to work, except for aged people and for other households that have no workers. SATS coding procedures resulted in an underestimation of walking trips to the shops, which are probably the shortest trips, made mostly to corner shops or shopping centres along major streets. Despite this measurement problem, Table 4.7 still shows that low-income, inner-area residents use cars for shopping only half as often as those living elsewhere in the metropolis. High-income, inner-suburban residents use cars about one-eighth less often than those in other areas, preferring the convenience and speed of their cars for shopping even more than for the trip to work. Low-income groups rely especially heavily on buses, which are used by two-thirds of those without cars. Another inner-city advantage, not shown in the table, is the availability of taxis, which are used on 7 per cent of inner-area shopping trips and only 1 per cent in other areas. Taxis enable those without cars to gain the speed and convenience of car travel in the particular circumstances when it is most necessary. Unlike work trips, shopping trips take

TABLE 4.7   *Mode and duration of shopping trips in Sydney, by sub-region and income group, 1971.*

Area/income	Mode (%)			Time (minutes, one-way)		Total
	Car	Bus	Other[a]	Average	Less than 10 minutes (%)	no. of trips
Inner area						
High income	71	15	14	16	55	75
Low income	28	42	30	26	29	105
No car	3	63	34	33	18	62
Aged	19	50	31	33	10	42
All incomes	41	29	23	21	46	370
Other metro areas						
High income	83	8	9	12	64	1 009
Low income	55	26	19	19	52	1 457
No car	9	54	12	25	36	441
Aged	43	34	23	20	49	332
All incomes	68	18	14	17	56	5 351

For definitions of terms, see section on Terminology and Data in Chapter 1 (p. 16).
[a] Two-thirds of the 'Other' category are walking trips.
Source: SATS.

significantly more time in the inner areas, probably because of slower modes of travel, inner-city congestion and the greater decentralisation of retailing than of employment in outer areas.

The general thrust of these findings has wider implications. The data for personal business trips are similar to those for shopping. Recreational and medical trips have not been analysed (sample sizes were too small) but they are probably facilitated in inner areas by the concentrations of these facilities and by public transport. Furthermore, the accessibility advantages of inner areas extend beyond those of mode of travel and time spent: within any fixed travel distance or time, there is more choice in the inner areas. For example, the number of jobs available within five kilometres is over 200 000 in Marrickville (an inner industrial suburb), compared to only 40 000 in Hurstville (a middle suburb) and 15 000 in Blacktown (an outer suburb) (Black 1977:26). Workers thus have a wider range of job opportunities nearby. With regard to shopping and entertainment, the inner-suburban resident can usually have access to greater choice in price and quality within a relatively short distance from home. As a result of these advantages, it is not surprising that a number of community studies have found accessibility to be the most liked feature of inner-city living (for example, Troy, 1971). The savings of time and money spent in travelling are important compensations for inner-area residents' housing, which is often quite expensive for its size and quality.

Residential Mobility

This chapter has suggested that the inner areas serve as a transitory staging area for the young, upwardly mobile, white-collar workers, and provide longer-term accommodation for lower-status families throughout the life cycle. The SATS data on people moving house between 1966 and 1971 generally confirm these findings, by showing that residential mobility drops sharply as people progress through the life cycle. In the inner suburbs, the average number of years since the last move was 1.5 for those at the pre-family stage, 6.3 for families with children, and 17.1 for those at the post-family stage. Within each life-cycle group, there were few differences in the rates of moves of income groups. Mainly because of the large proportion at the pre-family stage in the inner area, the number of movers since 1966 comprised 42 per cent of inner-suburban households, compared to 34 per cent for the rest of Sydney.

Of the inner-city households that have moved since 1966, half moved out of the inner city (Table 4.8). Thus, a fifth of the inner-area families in 1966 left in the next five years. Those with higher incomes who move are more likely to leave the inner city, while moves by low-income households are more likely to be within the inner areas. The inner city is either more attractive for low-income groups, or else these groups have more difficulty finding appropriate housing elsewhere.

The proportion of movers who leave the inner city also varies among life-cycle groups. Movers with children, especially the higher-income groups (who presumably have more choice), and the large families (who presumably have more need), tend to leave the inner city. This strongly suggests that movement out of the inner city, probably to larger and more costly housing, will take place

TABLE 4.8 *Percentage of movers leaving inner Sydney (1966-71), by income group and family type.*

| Family type [b] | Movers out of inner area (%) [a] | | | |
	Low income	Middle income	High income	Total
Pre-family	38	45	53	45
Family	51	63	68	58
Single parent [c]	-	-	-	62
Large family [c]	-	-	-	42
Post-family	42	52	40	46
Aged	-	-	-	47
Total	46	54	57	51

The data of course excludes those who left the Sydney metropolitan area, and those whose address in either 1966 or 1971 was not coded.

[b] Family types and income categories are based on 1971 characteristics. For example, the 'family' category includes some heads who had their first children after 1966.

[c] Sample sizes are too small for disaggregation by income.

Source: SATS.

as incomes rise and families grow. On the other hand, families without children, whether the heads of the households are young or old, are inclined to move within the inner city. Pre-family groups with higher incomes are slightly more inclined to move out (perhaps in anticipation of families), while the low-income groups, again, are more likely to move within the inner city. Of the few post-family people that did move, both those with high and with low incomes are more likely than the middle-income families to move within the inner city. It may be that those on low incomes stay because rents are lower, while those on high incomes stay for the convenience of the many two-worker families in this group.

A limitation of the preceding discussion is that movers to the inner city are not taken into account. Table 4.9 shows that people tend to move into the inner city before having children and move out when children arrive or are anticipated.[8] Despite the exclusion from the data of the many pre-family household heads from outside Sydney, those moving in number 40 per cent more than those moving out for this group. The figures are reversed for heads of families with children, which have only 42 moving in for every hundred moving out. As expected, the relationship is stronger for the larger families that need large houses, and weaker for the single parents who usually have small families and low incomes. Old people move into the inner city about as often as they move out of it. Using unpublished Census data from 1966 and 1971, Burnley and Walker (1977:7-9) have confirmed some of these figures for the non-British-born: the strong net immigration into the inner suburbs of young, foreign migrants and their children, the equally significant exodus of Australian-born people of similar age, and the less notable net migration losses of both Australian-born and foreign-born people aged forty or older.

TABLE 4.9   *Families moving into inner Sydney per 100 families moving out (1966-71), by family type and income group.*

| Family type | Income group | | | |
	High	Middle	Low	Total
Pre-family	116	108	217	139
Family	52	27	50	42
Single-parent	-	-	-	89
Large family	-	-	-	22
Post-family	121	77	111	98
Aged	-	-	-	97
Total	86	62	92	78

See qualifications in Note 8 and notes to Table 4.8. For definitions of terms, see section on Terminology and data in Chapter 1 (p. 16).
Source: SATS.

Summary

This chapter has tried to show how the inner city facilitates or impedes the life-styles of the residents. The small flats and non-private accommodation are well suited as staging areas for the young, white-collar, pre-family groups. The families that remain once children are born, mostly headed by blue-collar workers, gain accessibility and cheap housing at the expense of poor neighbourhood conditions. The aged especially value the familiarity, low-cost housing and accessibility of inner city living. Although the inner suburbs have a high incidence of social problems, people in trouble still are only a small minority of the inner residents, and inner-city living probably compensates for rather than causes these problems. The majority of the families want to continue living in the inner city. If housing costs in inner areas rise, low-income households must either consume less housing or pay more for it by reducing expenditures on food, clothing, and other necessities. Alternatively, if they are forced outward, journeys to jobs or shops will probably be longer and may require either the purchase of a first or second car or the wife's departure from the labourforce.

CHAPTER 5

An Overview of Post-war Change

This chapter briefly describes the post-war housing and population changes of the inner suburbs in Sydney, Adelaide and Melbourne. Both absolute change and change relative to the rest of the metropolis are discussed. The study tests whether or not the Australian developments have been consistent with either overseas experience or its zonal theories of urban change. It also explains why the inner suburbs in the different cities did not change in the same ways. More detailed explanations, based mainly on data from Sydney, are taken up in later chapters.

The inner city has developed against a background of urban growth and suburbanisation, which were assumed by the spatial models, and which also have typified North American post-war development. Sydney, Melbourne and Adelaide almost doubled their populations from 1947 to 1971. The immediate post-war housing shortage was overcome by a sustained boom in the construction of detached houses: by 1971, single-family dwellings had comprised four-fifths of the net dwelling increases since 1947 in Sydney and Melbourne, and nine-tenths in Adelaide. Since the late 1950s, the construction of flats has accompanied housebuilding. Since 1947, the growth in numbers of dwellings outpaced population gains by more than 25 per cent in all three cities.

The quality of housing throughout the three metropolitan areas also improved. The new dwellings were generally bigger, made of better materials (more brick and tile) and were better equipped. Within the existing stock, the numbers of subdivided or shared dwellings fell, many dwellings were improved and occupancy rates (measured by people per room) declined markedly. Home ownership rose from an overall average of about 50 per cent to 70 per cent, partly because many rented houses became owner-occupied. Contrary to the assumptions of the spatial models, urban housing improved as a result of changes to the existing dwellings as well as the new construction. This chapter will examine how much the inner suburbs took part in these improvements.

Housing differed considerably between the cities. Immediate post-war housing conditions, and improvements since then, were best in nearly all respects in Adelaide and worst in Sydney, reflecting the greater competition for housing in bigger, more geographically constrained cities. It also shows how active participation of the South Australian government moderated housing competition throughout the housing market. The chapter will consider if these differences for the cities also applied to their inner suburbs.

Housing Stock

The spatial models predicted non-residential incursion and little residential development in the inner suburbs. Yet, from 1947 to 1976, the number of dwellings increased slightly in inner Adelaide and significantly in inner Sydney and inner Melbourne (Figure 5.1). In the immediate post-war years, there was little building and few losses of existing housing stock to non-residential incursion. During the late 1950s, there were net losses, in the inner suburbs, especially in Sydney and Melbourne. Only during this one period were the changes consistent with the models that predict incursion in inner areas and residential building on the fringe.

During the 1960s, the building of flats has more than compensated for incursion and has increased the number of inner-suburban dwellings significantly in the two bigger cities and slightly in Adelaide. In the early 1970s, the rate of both incursion and flat-building have slowed and total numbers of dwellings have remained about level. Consistent with the greater relative accessibility of inner areas in larger cities, inner Sydney and inner Melbourne have had more incursion in early years and more residential redevelopment in recent years.

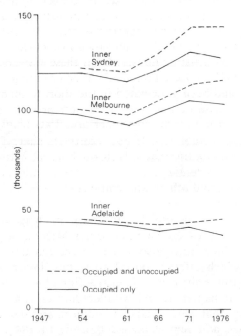

FIGURE 5.1.   Occupied and unoccupied dwellings in inner Sydney, Melbourne and Adelaide, 1947-76
(Adjustments were made in these and later figures for the boundary change to Walkerville in Adelaide and the City of Sydney.)
Source: Censuses.

Vacancy rates have increased considerably in the inner areas during the post-war years (Figure 5.1). These rates were very low in 1954, increased slightly in the late 1950s in Sydney and Melbourne, and then rose sharply in Sydney during the 1960s and in Melbourne and Adelaide in the 1970s. By 1976, the proportion of dwellings vacant was 11 per cent in inner Sydney and Melbourne and 7 per cent in inner Adealide. These were nearly twice the metropolitan averages.

At first sight these figures suggest that Australia may be following America in the abandonment of unprofitable and unattractive dwellings. However, analyses in later chapters show that the slight increase in rates in the 1950s only brought the rates up to more normal levels after the severe housing shortage of the 1940s. The large increases in the 1960s and 1970s resulted from the increases of turnover in population caused by increases of flats, more vacancies for renovations and prior to redevelopment, and more temporary absences and frequent turnover in occupation of all dwellings as residents became more mobile. The smaller amount of development of flats and non-residential incursion in inner Adelaide explains the smaller vacancy rates there.

The sharp rise in numbers of flats built, especially in inner Sydney and inner Melbourne, explains the general increases in numbers of dwellings (Figure 5.2). A third of the increase in the number of flats in metropolitan Melbourne and a quarter in Sydney and Adelaide occurred in the inner suburbs. Only a small proportion were consistent with the 'filtering down' posited by the zonal model, being subdivided from existing houses. Even these conversions were relatively expensive; they would not have been made if the next step of 'filtering down' — redevelopment — had been anticipated in the short to medium term. The vast majority of the increase of flats was from new private constuction. This is contrary to Burgess's notion of most inner-area flats being merely temporary uses before eventual demolition. It also contrasts sharply with Hoover and Vernon's (1962) presumptions that only through public action could inner areas be redeveloped for residential use. The findings conform most closely with those of Evans (1973) and others who emphasise accessibility as a determinant of population densities.

Variations in city structure largely explain why inner-suburban flat development differed between the cities. Inner Melbourne had larger gains of flats than inner Sydney. In Sydney much of the flat development was in the eastern suburbs, which offered coastal amenities, lower land costs, and still fairly good access to the city centre. Construction of new flats was also easier in inner Melbourne. It had more old wooden houses, many of which were on relatively large sites that were cheaper to acquire and demolish than Sydney's dense brick terrace and semi-detached houses. In 1947, the proportion of wooden structures was 28 per cent in inner Melbourne compared with 10 per cent in inner Sydney. Another explanation is that the Housing Commission constructed over a sixth of the flats in inner Melbourne but only a tenth in inner Sydney. In Adelaide, low land costs and good accessibility to jobs,

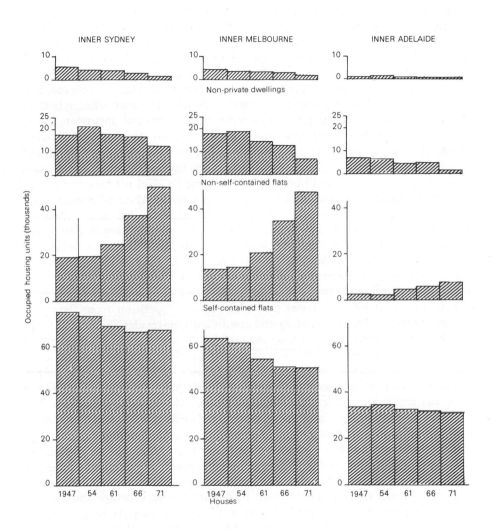

FIGURE 5.2.   Occupied dwellings, by type, in inner Sydney, Melbourne and Adelaide, 1947-71
Source: Censuses.

moderated demand for flats throughout the city. This explains why half of its inner-area flats (2620 units in 1971) were single-storey villa units.

Consistent with the zonal model, all of the inner areas had losses of houses despite the massive increases in the metropolis in general. Although inner-suburban houses were generally poorer in quality, the majority were still in demand and had many years more of potential use. They were displaced because of their location rather than their condition; attracted by the accessibility, developers could make more intensive use of the costly land. The net loss of houses was least in Adelaide partly because redevelopment pressures were not as intense; flats in any location were not in such strong demand, and industry expanded outside the inner areas. Although the inner areas of both of the larger cities experienced considerable non-residential incursion, inner Sydney had much smaller net losses, partly because the inner-Melbourne weatherboards had less potential for renovation, were cheaper to redevelop and were more likely to be condemned or redeveloped by the Housing Commission.

Another reason for the differences between the cities of net losses of houses was the variation in degree of infill of new houses compensating for losses. New houses, though concentrated on the urban fringe, were also built within the existing urban area. Being a smaller, more loosely developed city, inner Adelaide had more opportunity for infill. From 1947 to 1961, it had an increase of more than 3000 new houses — 60 per cent more than in the much bigger inner Melbourne and almost as many as in the much larger inner Sydney. The building of new houses in the inner areas declined later in the post-war years, due to the availability of fewer sites and more competition from flats.

Despite reduced house building and continued non-residential incursion, the number of occupied houses during the late 1960s remained about constant in inner Melbourne and actually increased in inner Sydney. The explanation is that many previously shared or subdivided houses were reconverted to single-family use. Here is another indication of the inadequacy for Australian cities of a model assuming irreversible 'filtering down' of inner-area housing. The numbers of the cheapest and poorest-quality dwellings — non-self-contained flats (mostly shared houses and single rooms) and non-private dwellings (mostly boarding houses) — declined far faster than houses in all inner areas; most in Adelaide and least in Sydney. In this respect, the quality of housing in the inner areas improved as much as in other parts of the metropolitan areas. Except for small gains during the early post-war housing shortage, the losses of this poorer-quality accommodation due to non-residential incursion and conversions exceeded by far the number of houses and flats that were converted to these uses. These losses of this type of accommodation were greatest during the 1960s, when their occupants began to live in flats.

Housing Characteristics

Other housing changes also indicate that inner residential areas were not declining. Most importantly, the proportion of houses that were owner-occupied jumped from a quarter to almost two-thirds in inner Sydney and Melbourne, and from a half to three-quarters in Adelaide (Table 5.1). These increases were far greater than those for the rest of the metropolis, partly because the proportion of owner-occupation in 1947 was so much lower in inner areas. Such a rise of home ownership is inconsistent with theories that hold that housing 'filters down' into rental occupancy as it ages. The proportion of owner-occupied flats also rose considerably, especially in Sydney, where high housing costs and poor accessibility of low-cost, fringe estates resulted in more owners living in home units instead of houses.

TABLE 5.1   *Changes in housing characteristics in inner Sydney, Melbourne and Adelaide, 1947-1971.*

Inner city	Houses			Flats (self-contained)		
	Owner-occupied	Persons per room [a]	Relative rent [b]	Owner-occupied	Persons per room [a]	Relative rent [b]
Sydney						
1947	27	.80	76	5	.70	100
1971	61	.63	80	21	.66	92
Melbourne						
1947	27	.77	83	5	.65	112
1971	61	.63	90	11	.72	104
Adelaide [c]						
1947	47	.73	90	18	.67	107
1971	79	.55	94	12	.60	99

a Excludes houses with two or more families in 1947. Thus, occupancy rates are underestimated in 1947.
b Average, unfurnished, private, inner-area rents as a percentage of those elsewhere in the metropolis.
c All figures exclude Walkerville because of the boundary changes.
Source: Censuses, 1947 and 1971.

One of the many indications of rising housing standards was that overall occupancy rates declined faster in the inner suburbs than in the rest of the metropolis. As with the home-ownership figures, the inner areas had more improvement, partly because they started from a lower position. The more stable occupancy rates in flats, both within and outside inner areas, resulted from newer flats having 'open plan' layouts of fewer but larger rooms. Occupancy rates of flats in inner Melbourne rose because of the large increases of publicly owned flats containing many children.

Unfortunately, the Census provides no data on the movement of inner-suburban housing values relative to the rest of the metropolitan stock. However, various case studies, discussed in later chapters, show faster appreciation in inner areas. Moreover, in all three cities, the Census shows that private house rents increased relatively faster in inner areas, even though many more of the rented houses elsewhere were newer and bigger (Table 5.1).[1] However, in all three cities, private house rents in inner areas were still lower in 1971 than those in the rest of the metropolitan area.

In the inner city, house rents, as a proportion of private flats rents, also rose from as little as 65 per cent to 75 per cent in Sydney and as much as 54 per cent to 84 per cent in Adelaide. This happened even though most of the flats in 1971 were new and most of the best 1947 rented houses were owner-occupied in 1971. The faster rise of house rents that still occurred reflects the growing shortage of single-family housing for rent and the increased demand for it. Relative to other areas, inner-area flat rents fell slightly in all three cities, probably because more of the inner flats were conversions. Flat rents nonetheless remained close to the level of metropolitan averages.

Population Losses

The large losses of population are usually considered one of the most important post-war developments in inner areas. From a million residents in 1947, the populations of the three inner-city areas dropped to just over 700 000 people in 1976 (Figure 5.3). The losses were 35 per cent in Melbourne, 30 per cent in Adelaide, and 28 per cent in Sydney; they occurred continuously and were recorded at every Census in the period 1947-76.

The increase of dwellings in the inner suburbs during the post-war years

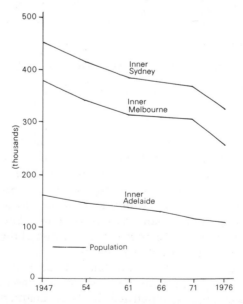

FIGURE 5.3.   Populations of inner Sydney, Melbourne and Adelaide, 1947-76
Source: Censuses.

suggests that the population losses did not result primarily from forced moves out of the inner areas caused by non-residential incursion. The population losses were associated more with the changes of the composition and use of the inner suburban housing stock discussed in the previous sections. The increasing availability of housing throughout the metropolitan areas made it possible for the inner area housing to be used less intensively. This suggests that the population losses resulted more from 'pull' factors attracting people out of inner areas than from 'push' factors forcing them out.

Figure 5.4 provides more detailed evidence for this interpretation. A quarter of the net population losses resulted from decreased occupancy rates in houses. These losses almost always reflects freely chosen moves; new suburban construction, especially up to the mid-1950s, made it possible for families over-crowded in inner areas to move out to better housing. During the late 1950s, these losses were smaller, especially in Melbourne and Adelaide, because intense crowding had already been relieved and because of the increase of the numbers of overseas migrants, who often shared housing and who remained in inner-areas during child-rearing. Further losses of occupancy rates during the 1960s resulted from post-war children leaving home, deaths of aging adults, and the replacement of larger migrant families moving out with younger childless couples moving in. Only the last of these later changes could have involved many forced moves out of inner areas.

The quarter of the population loss that was attributable to a loss of the number of occupied houses does suggest 'push' factors. Although some of these resulted from higher vacancy rates (a 'pull' factor made possible by the increasing availability of housing elsewhere in the metropolis), most resulted from there being more losses than additions of houses in inner areas. These losses were greatest during the 1950s, especially in Melbourne, when pressures for non-residential incursion were high.

Almost half of the losses between 1947 and 1971 were of people living in non-self-contained flats and non-private dwellings. The main explanation was the large losses of these types of dwellings but there was also a reduction of the number of people per dwelling in those that remained. Because these kinds of housing command higher rents than houses in single occupancy, these population losses for the most part indicate a reduction of demand for them rather than forced moves out of them caused by redevelopment (see Chapters 7 and 8). The losses were smallest during the early post-war housing shortages, and largest during the early 1960s when flats were replacing them in the market. If it were not for flat construction, the post-war population losses in the inner suburbs would have been 77 000 greater in Melbourne, 71 000 in Sydney and 12 000 in Adelaide.

Population Composition

Changes of the kind of people in the inner suburbs is an important concern for policy. If the more affluent have fled the inner areas, it would imply the

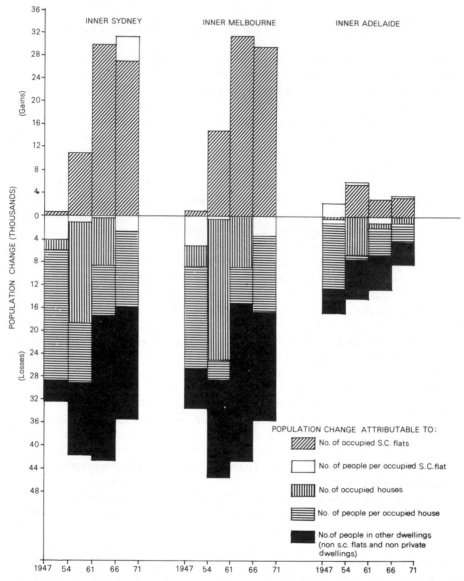

FIGURE 5.4. Population changes attributable to housing changes in inner Sydney, Melbourne and Adelaide, 1947-71

The estimates were calculated as follows. The population changes due to changes of the number of occupied houses (or flats) were defined as the change of the number of occupied houses (or flats) times the occupancy rate of houses (flats) at the end of the period. The population changes caused by changing occupancy rates were calculated by multiplying the number of occupied houses (flats) at the beginning of the period by the change in the number of persons per occupied house (flat). The change of the number of people living in 'other dwellings' (non-self-contained flats and non-private dwellings) was calculated by subtracting from the total population change, the change in the number of the people living in either houses or flats. This last measure of course does not separate losses due to losses of stock or to change in occupancy rates.

applicability of the 'slums and blight' model. Conversely, an increase of these people would tend to confirm the 'gentrification' hypothesis.

Over the entire post-war period, the inner suburbs' proportionate losses of manufacturing workers, most of whom are of low status, were considerably above the metropolitan average in Melbourne and slightly below the metropolitan averages in Sydney and Adelaide.[2] The proportions of higher-status workers in finance and property industries increased in the inner suburbs of the three cities by about the same amounts as in their respective metropolitan areas. The inner area thus kept pace with the rest of the metropolis in its rising proportions of white-collar workers. This suggests that, for the post-war period as a whole, neither the 'slums and blight' nor the 'gentrification' models applied; the housing improvements largely benefited relatively low-status people like those in the inner suburbs immediately after the war.

The occupational data available since 1966, however, is more consistent with the 'gentrification' model. The proportion of high-status workers in inner areas increased both absolutely and relative to the metropolitan averages. But the biggest change was the replacement of low-status with middle-status workers, especially in the inner suburbs of Sydney and Melbourne. These findings are directly contrary to the recent American experiences of middle-class flight to the suburbs and increasing polarisation between the very rich and the very poor in the inner suburbs.

The inner suburbs would have had even greater increases of social status had they not served their traditional role as a staging area for non-British migrants with lower-paid, blue-collar jobs. Non-British-born residents increased from only a few per cent of the inner area poplulation in 1947 to over

TABLE 5.2   *Changes in occupational status of labourforce in Sydney, Melbourne and Adelaide, 1966-71.*

City	High status [a]		Middle status		Low status [b]	
	Inner area	Metro.	Inner area	Metro.	Inner area	Metro.
Sydney						
1966	13.2	17.2	40.2	43.7	46.6	39.1
1966-71	+1.2	+1.0	+7.8	+4.4	−9.0	−5.6
Melbourne						
1966	15.8	17.4	40.5	41.2	43.7	41.4
1966-71	+1.9	+ .8	+8.3	+5.4	−10.2	−6.2
Adelaide						
1966	18.7	18.4	41.9	42.3	38.4	39.3
1966-71	+1.7	+ .3	+4.5	+3.7	−6.5	−4.2

[a] Professionals, Technical, Administrative and related jobs.
[b] Craftsmen, production workers, process workers, and labourers.
Source: Censuses 1966 and 1971.

30 per cent in 1971 in inner Sydney and inner Melbourne, and to 20 per cent in inner Adelaide. In all three cities, the inner-area proportions of the total population born in the British Isles remained constant at just under ten per cent despite immigration, because British-born migrants were more likely to live in middle or outer areas. The especially small representation of British-born migrants in inner Adelaide is explained by their privileged access on arrival to the public housing, very little of which is in the inner areas (see Table 1.4).

The more culturally diverse and more recently arrived groups of migrants are concentrated in the inner areas of all three cities. But in Melbourne, where the Italian immigration was earliest and largest, Italians were not concentrated only in the inner suburban area (Table 5.3). Since 1961 the proportion of Italians in the inner suburbs has dropped from 8 per cent to 5 per cent, despite continued city-wide increases. They moved outwards as part of their cultural and economic assimilation, and newly arrived compatriots joined them there. Italians, Maltese, and Poles in inner Sydney show a similar pattern of concentration and then dispersal.

TABLE 5.3   *Place of birth of residents of Sydney, Melbourne and Adelaide, 1971 (percent of total populations).*

City	Aust	Brit. Isles	Greece	Italy	Yugo.	*Other*
Sydney						
Inner	61.4	8.0	6.4	3.4	3.1	17.7
Metro.	75.1	9.1	1.7	2.3	1.4	10.4
Melbourne						
Inner	61.1	8.1	8.7	4.9	2.9	14.4
Metro.	72.5	9.0	3.0	4.3	1.7	9.5
Adelaide						
Inner	72.1	7.6	5.9	5.9	1.2	7.9
Metro.	71.9	14.9	1.5	3.5	.8	8.4

Source: Census, 1971.

Changes of the age and sex profile of the inner suburbs accompanied the other population changes (Figure 5.5). Bearing in mind the considerable shift from houses to flats, it is not surprising that the greatest losses were among adults in the prime ages for home purchases and child-bearing. There were smaller net losses of men because most of the newly arrived migrants were men. The losses of children were surprisingly small, considering the suburbanisation and the losses of houses, probably because of the child-bearing of overseas migrants and also because the war and depression had resulted in small numbers of children at the start of the period. The loss of middle-aged adults and children was largest in Adelaide, despite few losses of houses or gains of flats, because of more suburbanisation and less non-British immigration. For this same reason, the numbers of aged people, especially women, increased

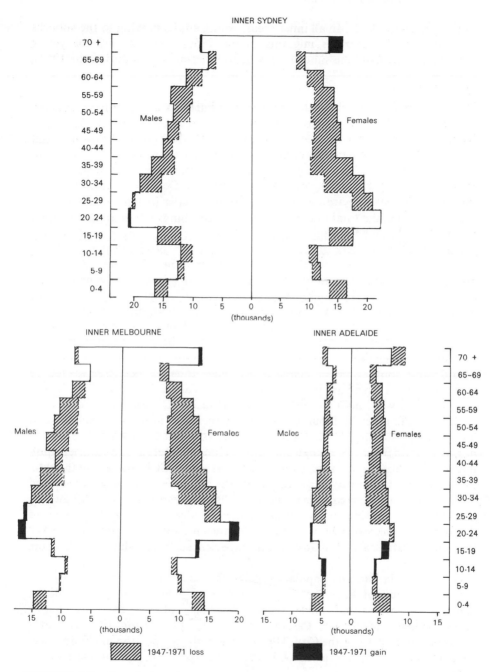

FIGURE 5.5.   Population changes, by age and sex, in inner Sydney, Melbourne and Adelaide, 1947-71
Source: Censuses, 1947 and 1971.

most in inner Adelaide. In all inner areas, young adults moving to the suburbs were replaced by overseas migrants in the 1950s and then by the young Australian-born from the suburbs moving to inner-area flats during the 1960s.

Spatial Patterns

The previous findings show that the inner suburbs as a whole have avoided problems of urban decay. However, the inner areas are relatively large and diverse. In Burgess' terms, they include the CBD, the zone of transition, and large areas of 'workingmen's homes'. This section examines changes within individual LGAs to test whether some inner areas improved while others declined (see Map 1.1 for the location of the LGAs). Developments in different parts of inner Sydney are considered in more details in later chapters.

In Melbourne, the total number of occupied dwellings fell in all inner LGAs except St Kilda and Prahran, which had the most flat development. Contrary to the traditional pattern of incursion radiating from the city centre, the losses were not concentrated in the City of Melbourne. In fact, they were proportionally largest in South Melbourne, partly because of incursion, but mainly because shared houses were converted to single occupancy. Many houses were also lost in Collingwood, due to non-residential incursion and redevelopment for flats, especially by the Victorian Housing Commission. In St Kilda and Prahran, house losses were very low despite considerable flat development, because of the absence of much non-residential incursion and considerable conversions of shared houses back to single occupancy. Outside these two LGAs which are in the attractive southeast sector, more than half of the new flats were built by the Victorian Housing Commission.

All LGAs in inner Melbourne experienced increases in home ownership and lessening of crowding. The reduction of occupancy rates was least in centres of non-British migration, Collingwood and Richmond. Relative to the metropolitan average, house rents rose in all inner LGAs except St Kilda, where they still exceeded metropolitan averages and where the biggest houses were redeveloped for flats. The large increases in rents in the City, and especially in Collingwood, resulted from the increasing attractiveness of some areas and widespread demolition of the worst housing by the Victorian Housing Commission. Even the innermost, least desirable areas experienced their share of housing improvement.

Only St Kilda had any population gains. The innermost area of the City of Melbourne did not have the greatest rate of population loss, as would be expected by the zonal model, mainly because of the extensive public redevelopment. Moreover, the increase in the proportion of high-status workers was greatest in the City. The increase in the proportion of children was generally greatest in the areas of immigration reception and public housing development.[3]

The unique feature of change in inner Adelaide — the exceptional change in all respects in the City itself — was due mostly to its very small area. Consistent with the changes expected in transitional zones, commercial intrusion in the City explains its large losses of people and houses, and increases in vacancy rates. The poor initial quality of the houses, and therefore the demolition of the worst of it, explains the dramatic improvement in average quality of accommodation in the City, as reflected in declining occupancy rates, rising relative rents and increasing social status. Unlike the other cities, there was an increase in the number of houses in half of the LGAs, especially in the higher-income areas to the north and south where there was still space for infill. Otherwise the changes in the LGAs were similar, except that only the three industrial LGAs and the City lost houses. Another difference was that the area having the most migrant settlement, Thebarton, had the smallest fall in occupancy rates and in the proportion of low-status workers, and the smallest increase in the proportion of high-status workers.

Summary

Over the post-war period, development in the inner suburbs of Australia's major cities generally contrasts sharply with either the predictions of the invasion/succession model or the American experience. Indeed, it is remarkable how the old zonal model, which had rougly fit Australian inner-area development during the first half of the century, had in many ways been turned inside out. By any of the established measures — subdivision of dwellings, overcrowding, conversion to rental occupancy, price and rent changes, new private residential investment, and socio-economic status of the residents — inner areas were 'filtering up' rather than 'down', both absolutely and relative to the rest of the metropolis. The population losses have been symptomatic of these improvements rather than of decline. Moreover, the innermost areas in the inner city shared in these improvements. Rising affluence and suburbanisation in Australia resulted in the improvement, not the deterioration of inner-city housing.

The traditional spatial models have applied in Australian in several respects. Especially in the larger and more centralised cities, the increasing relative accessibility resulted in a number of houses being redeveloped for non-residential uses. These changes are considered in the next chapter. The inner areas have also served as reception areas for large numbers of overseas migrants which, as shown in Chapter 7, was a major factor in the improvement of inner-city housing.

CHAPTER 6

Non-Residential Development, 1947-71

A major theme in the early chapters is the strong interrelationship between residential and non-residential land uses. This chapter describes and explains the economic and political forces behind the post-war inner-city development of offices, factories, public institutions, roads and other non-residential activities. The study tests whether Australian capital cities have had the centralised non-residential growth posited by the early zonal model, or the dispersal characteristic of post-war American cities. A major emphasis is the direct residential consequences of these developments, especially in displacing housing and increasing jobs.

The early post-war planners, heartened by Commonwealth reconstruction proposals, saw a tremendous opportunity to plan for the development expected after the standstill during the depression and the war. In this spirit of optimism, the Cumberland County Council (CCC) was established in 1945 to develop a plan for Sydney's future. Preservation of old, inner-suburban housing was regarded as only a temporary expedient until the war-time housing shortage was relieved and public redevelopment had commenced. The plans in Sydney (CCC, 1948) and Melbourne (MMBW, 1954) thus allowed for considerable incursion into the housing within the unpleasant environments of the established industrial and business areas. It was proposed that other inner residential areas be protected from incursion, in order to avoid the congestion and commuting associated with further job growth in central areas and residential development on the urban fringe. Post-war planners, especially in Sydney, tried to encourage a more decentralised metropolis, despite expectations of strong market pressure for continued centralisation of firms and government agencies.

Whether or not the planners succeeded depends on how decentralisation is defined and measured. Most non-residential development has been outside inner areas; this suburbanisation is contrary to the predictions of the old zonal model. However, it is equally valid to show that, contrary to the American experience, the already dominant inner areas gained a considerable share of the post-war, non-residential property boom. The change induced by this centralised development had important effects in the inner areas, notwithstanding the equally important structural changes elsewhere in the metropolis.

Non-residential development can be measured by building investment,

80

employment changes and land use. These measures often do not vary together; for example, high-rise building can substitute for spatial expansion, and building automated factories on larger sites can be an alternative to having more workers. The number of jobs — important for the demands employees place either on the transport system, or for those who want to live close to their workplaces on nearby housing — are fairly easily measured. But little information is available about spatial expansion, which is important for identifying residential incursion. For example, the numbers of dwellings demolished could be found out only by contacting the firms or organisations responsible for demolition — which was practicable only for such public activities as roads, universities, schools and hospitals. Even this task was so tedious that it could only be done for Sydney. There is no direct way to measure the greater housing losses caused by industrial and business incursion.

However, for the purposes of this study, an estimation of commercial and industrial incursion was made. All housing losses for any inter-censal period were attributed to whatever non-residential use was permitted in 1971 in the particular CD.[1] Each area experiencing residential losses was then considered individually and, after close examination of the data, discussions with local experts[2] and some field visits, was finally allocated to a non-residential use. Some of the losses in the areas zoned for non-residential uses were due to dwelling amalgamations and increased vacancy rates rather than to incursion, and this could tend to overestimate incursion. On the other hand, incursion was underestimated in areas where the number of dwellings increased due to subdivisions or new building. On balance, the estimates appear accurate enough to establish the general magnitude of incursion.

COMMERCIAL DEVELOPMENT
Investment and Land Values
Offices have been, by most measures, the most significant non-residential development during the post-war years. The office boom started earlier in Sydney (late 1950s) than in Melbourne (early 1960s) or Adelaide (late 1960s). In the late 1960s, each of the three inner areas captured over 90 per cent of metropolitan investment in office building (Vandermark, 1974:229-31). Moreover, the inner-city share actually rose in Sydney from 81 per cent in 1961 (the earliest available figure) to 93 per cent in 1975. Together with the rapid growth of office activities, this explains why offices and banks account for over half of the $1,000 million spent on non-residential development in inner Sydney from 1969 to 1975 (Table 6.1). Even within the inner-city areas, office development in all the cities was heavily concentrated in or next to the CBD, or in nearby areas like North Sydney, St Kilda Road in Melbourne, or south and east of the parkland in Adelaide. The accessibility and status of inner-city locations, together with the rent-paying capacity of office activities, explains the continuing dominance of the CBD for office building. Office development was accompanied by building for a number of complementary activities,

TABLE 6.1   *Non-residential building investment in inner Sydney, 1969-75 (in millions of dollars).*

Land-use activity	Sydney[c]	North Sydney	South Sydney	Leich-hardt	Marrick-ville	Botany	Inner-area total	Metro. total
Commerce								
Office & banks	362.6	139.7	7.3	2.6	2.5	6.2	520.9	675.1
Shops	27.0	3.6	4.1	3.5	1.8	.9	40.9	197.2
Hotels[a]	42.2	7.8	.4	3.5	.5	0	54.4	102.2
Entertainment & recreation	65.1	2.0	1.5	3.3	2.2	1.0	75.1	153.0
Industry								
Factories	20.9	2.9	28.6	5.7	13.6	20.8	92.6	486.2
Other business[b]	33.0	2.4	22.1	8.8	3.7	47.8	117.8	292.6
Community services								
Education	26.1	5.0	1.8	3.0	5.4	1.5	42.8	258.6
Health	16.6	1.9	.1	2.6	1.2	0	22.5	102.6
Other	13.9	2.6	1.8	2.1	1.5	2.5	24.3	173.0
Total	607.3	167.8	67.7	35.2	32.4	80.8	991.2	2440.5

[a] Includes motels, hostels, and boarding houses
[b] Includes wholesale stores and warehouses
[c] LGAs defined by current boundaries; Sydney as at post-1968 boundaries
Source: ABS (1972-1977a).

including half of Sydney's building of hotels and recreation and entertainment facilities since 1969.

Unlike the other commercial activities, inner-suburban retailing has declined by almost all measures. As a result of rising car-ownership and residential suburbanisation, the real value of sales has fallen in the CBDs of all three cities (Pak-Poy & Sherrard, 1966:12; Alexander, 1976:11) and there have been large net losses of retail establishments (mostly small shops), especially in residential areas (Neutze, 1972:86; URU, 1973:48). However, the inner city in 1975 was still gaining a fifth of Sydney's building investment in retailing, mainly due to modernisation and redevelopment of CBD stores. There has also been improvement of existing shops along major roads and the building of modern shopping centres, accessible by car, in inner areas like Crows Nest in Sydney, and Prospect and Unley in Adelaide. Inner-suburban retailing has avoided stagnation by shifting from small to large shops and by specialising.

The rising values of property also indicate the continuing demand of inner-city sites for commercial development. Sydney City Council studies have shown that from the mid 1950s to the mid 1960s, CBD land values rose much faster than the Consumer Price Index (Clutton, 1966:11; *Sydney Morning Herald,* 21.4.67). In 1970, land prices per square metre had reached $5000 in the CBD core and exceeded $600 throughout the rest of the CBD. The Melbourne CBD also had large rises (Sandercock, 1975:160) and by the late 1960s some sites were valued at over $1100 per square metre (VCOSS, 1975:55). Comparable figures at the time in nearby North Melbourne (less than a kilometre away) were $110 for intense retailing, $44 for small shops, $33 for industry, and $18 for houses (URU, 1973:31). When land used or zoned for residential purposes is wanted for redevelopment, it requires strong political action to retain it in its existing use.

Employment

Office and related development has brought a large number of additional workers into inner Sydney. In the late 1940s, the Cumberland County Council expected a 10 per cent increase, by the early 1970s, of the 80 000 office workers then in the CBD (CCC, 1948:107). It feared that this would cause considerable traffic and other problems. The actual increase was almost 80 per cent: to 128 000 in 1961 (NSWSPA, 1967:55) and to 142 000 in 1971 (Alexander, 1977:12).[2] In other office areas in the inner city, (the rest of the City of Sydney, North Sydney and South Sydney), there were another 70 000 office jobs in 1971 (Alexander, 1977:12). Table 6.2 shows that, between 1961 and 1971, the only industries to increase their employment significantly in the CBD were 'finance, community, and business services' (an increase of about a third) and 'public administration' (an increase of almost 40 per cent). Government employment growth in the inner areas has been almost entirely in the CBD, but private office employment has extended into the rest of the City and to North Sydney.

Despite the size of the office boom, total CBD employment grew by only 20 per cent from 1945 to 1961, and apparently declined slightly during the 1960s. This decline resulted from the large loss of jobs in other industries (retailing, wholesaling and manufacturing).

The number of retail-sales workers in the CBD fell precipitously from 40 000 in 1945 (CCC, 1948:107) to 27 000 in 1961 and to 20 000 in 1971 (Table 6.2). The slight increases elsewhere in the City, and only small total losses from the whole inner city, shows that some retailing decentralised only small distances. These losses of retail jobs, despite substantial investment in shop buildings, are explained by the improvement and redevelopment of existing buildings and the change in sales techniques from labour-intensive, small shops to larger self-serve shops and supermarkets.

Inner Melbourne had similar increases of office jobs, small losses of total jobs in the CBD, and precipitous losses of retail-sales jobs in the CBD (MMBW, 1977:34). The main difference was that inner Melbourne had a distribution and growth of office workers that was slightly less centralised in the CBD. Inner Adelaide experienced similar kinds of employment change (City of Adelaide, 1974:21). The inner areas of all three cities had large increases of office workers which, in the CBD, were balanced by about equal levels of losses of other kinds of employment.

Governmental Policy

The strong commercial development in the inner suburbs conflicts sharply both with the models of city-centre decline and with the CCCs goals of 'limited

84 New Life for Old Suburbs

SUBURBS

TABLE 6.2   *Employment, by industrial group, in inner*

Industrial group [a]		CBD	Remainder of City [c]
Commercial			
Finance, community —	1961	52.9	4.8
business services	1971	69.6	9.5
Retailing	1961	26.6	11.6
	1971	19.7	13.1
Public administration	1961	19.7	3.4
	1971	27.3	3.9
Communication	1961	9.8	1.8
	1971	9.0	5.3
Industrial			
Manufacturing	[1945]		[138.1]
	1961	33.8	88.5
	1971	18.4	66.6
Wholesaling	1961	27.9	13.3
	1971	20.4	16.9
Transport & storage	1961	18.5	12.3
	1971	19.6	13.6
Elect., gas & water	1961	13.2	1.3
	1971	9.2	2.3
Community services			
Health	1961	3.5	7.9
	1971	4.2	9.0
Education	1961	2.8	5.5
	1971	1.7	7.0
Building &	1961	-	-
construction [b]	1971	9.8	7.5
Total	[1945]	[200.1]	[139.3]
	1961	244.0	177.6
	1971	228.3	178.3

[a] The 'no location stated' responses were, for each industrial g
of work.
[b] In 1961 most building workers were not allocated to a p
[c] LGAs are as defined by pre-1968 boundaries.
Sources: CCC (1948:44-6), and unpublished tables from the

Sydney local government areas, 1961-71 (thousands of jobs).

North Sydney	Leich- hardt	Marrick- ville	Botany	Inner- area total	Metro. total
3.5	.5	1.0	.5	63.2	82.7
9.2	1.2	1.4	.9	91.8	141.8
2.4	2.0	3.0	1.1	46.7	104.5
3.0	2.6	2.9	2.5	43.8	146.3
.8	.4	.3	.3	24.9	29.4
1.7	.3	.4	.4	34.0	42.2
.9	.2	1.2	.1	14.0	20.3
.9	.2	.3	.1	15.8	25.3
[3.6]	[15.1]	[24.2]	[7.8]	[188.8]	[250.0]
4.4	13.1	17.3	13.8	170.9	337.3
4.4	9.6	15.2	14.2	128.4	343.2
1.5	2.0	1.9	1.6	48.2	63.7
3.6	2.1	2.9	3.2	49.1	90.6
.6	1.4	1.2	7.3	41.3	62.7
1.2	1.9	1.6	8.7	46.6	68.8
.5	.6	.2	.2	16.0	22.2
.4	.5	-	.1	12.5	22.1
1.0	1.1	.9	.1	14.5	34.2
1.2	1.6	1.3	.1	17.4	54.1
1.0	.5	.6	.1	10.5	28.1
1.0	.4	.7	.2	11.0	42.8
-	-	-	-	-	-
2.3	1.7	1.7	1.5	24.5	85.7
[9.5]	[26.3]	[27.3]	[14.1]	[416.5]	[630.0]
20.5	24.9	31.7	29.3	526.0	952.9
35.5	24.5	31.7	33.7	532.0	1205.2

allocated to areas in proportion to the number having given that area as a place

work.

and 1971 *Journey to Work* Censuses. After Neutze (1977:104).

centralisation and satellite development' and a 'planned central city of determined size' (CCC, 1948:60-61). Although the Council accepted that 'centralisation has greater advantages for industrial, commercial and administrative interests', it argued strongly that 'solutions involving decentralisation offer the greater social benefits', particularly by reducing the journey to work. The Council was backed by a state Labor government espousing a 'social reformist approach to city planning' (Sandercock, 1975:177). Yet even this level of political support was not enough to resist the intense market pressure behind city-centre office development.

Most importantly, in the Planning Scheme of 1951, the CCC could not take on the responsibility for planning the city centre. Except for Paddington and Potts Point, which were declared 'living areas', the plan left the control of the CBD and nearby suburbs to the City Council. The CCC claimed that more information was needed before a plan could be established for these areas, and that the issues were of a 'detailed' and 'local' nature (ignoring the regional effects of the city centre). More plausibly, it probably anticipated that any attempt to limit city-centre growth would be unsuccessful and would also hinder the Council's more feasible pursuits, like trying to preserve the green belt on the fringe.

The City Council's enlarged boundaries from 1948 to 1969 incorporated a number of working-class suburbs that provided a solid Labor majority. While firmly opposed to displacing the voters who put them into office, the councillors were willing to accept redevelopment to more intense use of existing non-residential areas, presumably because they believed that allowing intensive CBD redevelopment may have discouraged redevelopment and conversions to commercial use in nearby residential areas. Other reasons for their acceptance of redevelopment were that the councillors were relatively ignorant of the traffic consequences, hoped for increased rates to fund local welfare services, and feared charges that they were limiting economic growth by diverting it to Melbourne. The Council's draft planning scheme of 1952, which considerably limited approval for non-residential redevelopment of residential areas, faced a number of technical and political obstacles that prevented approval by the state government. By the mid 1960s, over 1300 objections had been lodged to the revised plan adopted by the Council in 1958 (*Sydney Morning Herald,* 22.3.66). The Pitt Street Property Owner's Defence League savagely attacked it for 'causing great capital loss' and for its 'immorality' (quoted in Harrison, 1972:72). A later director of the business-oriented Civic Reform Society remembered that: 'The Scheme ... was essentially a document devised to preserve worn-out residential areas housing thousands of traditional Labor voters. It thus penalised the city's industrial and commercial growth...' (Spooner, *Sydney Morning Herald,* 21.8.67).

The Labor City Council delayed and often refused approvals for development and building applications that would destroy housing. Although the draft planning scheme was of some help, refusals were frequently overruled in appeals, if the developers could afford the necessary time and expense. City-centre development was limited most by the state Minister for Local Government, who, on the advice of the Height of Buildings Committee, generally refused development approval for buildings having floor-space ratios of more than 12:1 (a floor-space ratio is the floor area of the building divided by the site area). This was more than twice the highest density allowable for London's post-war building.

In 1967 the recently elected Liberal state government replaced the Labor councillors with 'independent' commissioners. With their favourable view on development and strengthening of demand, applications for development in the CBD worth over $300 million were approved in less than two years, at an average floor space ratio of 10:1 (Sandercock, 1975:197). After the state made boundary changes which drastically reduced the Labor vote, the 1969 Council elections were won by the Civic Reform Association, a group heavily supported by commercial interests.

Nonetheless, a planning scheme for the enlarged City of Sydney was finally adopted in 1969. The plan has probably protected some threatened residential areas from commercial redevelopment (East Sydney, Darlinghurst and Kings Cross). However, the Council continued to approve commercial development in these and other areas designated for residential and industrial uses. The plan also allowed floor-space ratios of over 12:1, which did little to restrict the amount of central growth; densities well above the limits of the plan still were approved. If the CBD could have been developed to its approved 1971 potential, there would have been space for 750 000 workers — triple the actual level.

Nor did other governmental agencies in Sydney restrict office development. Property interests in North Sydney, without opposition from nearby residents, obtained approval for massive office developments. The Council itself proposed a $47-million civic centre which included two seventeen-storey office blocks. Commonwealth, state, and local government all contributed to the growth of CBD jobs, despite the planners' calls for decentralisation. Moreover, both the Labor and Liberal state government developed proposals for massive office redevelopment of the old residential areas in The Rocks and in Woolloomooloo, on either side of the CBD. The Rocks area proposal involved a $500-million government loan, mostly to provide space for government workers, while the Woolloomooloo proposal involved planning incentives for private development. These two schemes proposed accommodation for an additional 90 000 workers, nearly all office workers. The failure of these schemes, partly as a result of growing opposition to office development during the 1970s, is discussed in Chapter 9.

The lesser amount of office development in inner Melbourne and inner Adelaide reflect a smaller market demand rather than more governmental control. In Melbourne, the 1954 plan (MMBW, 1954) called for considerable CBD growth and neither the state government nor the City Council have been controlled by Labor since the mid 1950s. City-centre property organisations represented by the City Development Association, and later by the Chamber of Commerce, advocated city centre growth and redevelopment as a way to increase property values (VCOSS, 1975:55-70). The 1964 City plan (City of Melbourne, 1964) was designed to encourage CBD growth and the series of Metropolitan Board of Works plans (e.g. MMBW, 1968), though sometimes espousing decentralisation, never proposed constraints on the city centre.

In Adelaide the City Council tried to increase its rate base by encouraging central development (Sandercock, 1975:140-43). The Metropolitan Plan of 1962 designated the entire City of Adelaide (except for North Adelaide) for CBD development (South Australian Town Planning Committee, 1962). To hasten land-use transition, the Council refused approvals for residential rehabilitation in the mid 1960s, and acquired and demolished dilapidated buildings, the sites of which were used as parking lots before offices were built. The Council even produced a proposal for a large retail centre in affluent North Adelaide, which the politically powerful residents managed to stop. Until the 1970s, the only constraints on the private commercial market were sporadic bans against office building by a plumbers' union.

Commercial Incursion

Commercial development generated environmentally degrading traffic (discussed in Chapter 3), attracted to inner housing more white-collar workers wanting to live near their work (considered in Chapter 8), and replaced dwellings through either redevelopment or conversion for commercial use. Between 1947 and 1971, the estimate of 6800 inner-Sydney dwellings lost in this way amounted to almost half of the total number of dwellings taken for all kinds of non-residential development. Because some of the incursion in industrial areas was probably for commercial purposes, the actual share is probably considerably larger.

During the early 1950s, the residential losses in inner Sydney were limited because the pace of development was slow, there was opposition to housing losses until the war-time shortage was relieved, and perhaps some protection

TABLE 6.3   *Estimated dwellings lost to business and industrial Incursion in inner Sydney, 1947-71*

Type of	Number of dwellings lost (net)			
incursion	1947-54	1954-61	1961-71	Total
Business	1 775	2 834	2 148	6 757
Annual average	253	405	215	280
Industry	1 329	2 062	1 778	5 169
Annual average	190	295	178	215

See text (page 81) for methods of estimating.

was afforded tenants by rent control (see Chapter 7). After accelerating in the late 1950s, residential losses reduced again during the 1960s, despite the massive office development, because most of the redevelopment was in non-residential areas. Another factor here is that the building of flats during the 1960s obscured intrusion in some areas.

Map 6.1 shows that few of these losses were within the CBD, where there was little housing left by the end of the war. Even the much larger 'County Centre' area — the CBD and nearby areas zoned for high-density commercial development — accounted for only a quarter of the total losses due to business. The losses within this area were concentrated on the CBDs eastern edge, in Woolloomooloo, and along Oxford and William Streets in East Sydney. Even though the 'Loo' was never extensively redeveloped, hundreds of dwellings were demolished in anticipation of change. Except in the 'Loo' during the 1960s, most of the losses in these innermost areas occurred during the 1950s, after which time there were few dwellings left to be redeveloped.

There were more losses (a third of the total) to the east of the central area, in Kings Cross and Darlinghurst. Many of the businesses that in the late 1950s were either displaced by the CBD development or were newly established near the city centre, were located in this very small area, which had many, intensely subdivided, residential buildings. A number of buildings here, and in the Rocks area on the other side of the CBD, were converted from residential to commercial uses without any redevelopment. North Sydney, which has absorbed more of the CBD overflow during the 1960s, experienced about a fifth of the losses caused by commercial incursion. Along the ribbon development in Leichhardt and Marrickville, the use of some houses changed without redevelopment, some combined house/shops were converted to solely commercial uses, and a few dwellings were demolished for small expansions or car parks.

Table 6.4 shows the changes of different types of dwellings in areas experiencing commercial intrusion during the 1960s. Surprisingly, these areas generally had net increases in numbers of self-contained flats, especially where the business expansion was modest and residential environments were good. Few flats were lost to incursion because most were built during or after the war and few were located in areas of subsequent commercial encroachment. However, consistent with the zone of transition, there were large losses of buildings subdivided into single rooms (non-self-contained flats) or used as boarding houses (non-private dwellings). In the CBD and nearby areas to the east, these usually were large terrace houses, occasionally old mansions, and frequently old hotels. In areas farther from the CBD, there were more losses of shared houses or shopkeepers' residences attached to shops.

It appears that housing for about 24 000 people was lost as a result of business incursion.[3] Because most of these losses were in areas of very poor housing, most of the displaced must have had low incomes. Table 6.5 shows that many of the occupants in these areas, and those apparently displaced, were

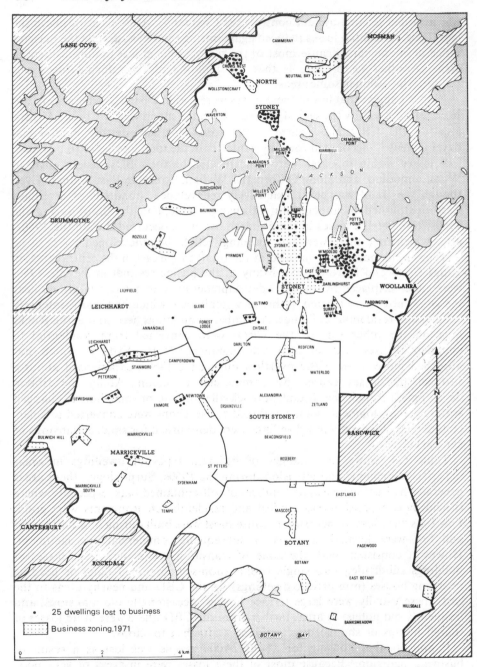

MAP 6.1.   Incursion of commercial land uses in inner Sydney, 1947-71
(see text p. 81 for method of identifying incursion.)
Source: Based on analysis of unpublished 'CD' Census data, 1947-71.

TABLE 6.4   *Changes of dwellings, by type, in areas of commercial and industrial incursion, inner Sydney, 1961-1971.*[a]

Area	Commercial intrusion					Industrial intrusion				
	Houses	(s.c.) Flats	(n.s.c.) Flats	Non-private	Total	Houses	(s.c.) Flats	(n.s.c.) Flats	Non-private	Total
City of Sydney [b]										
'County Centre'[c]	-152	+41	-154	-113	-378	-	-	-	-	-
Other	-358	+100	-359	-104	-721	-724	+152	-291	-185	-1048
North Sydney										
'Milsons Point'	-472	-128	-402	-33	-779	-	-	-	-	-
Other	-63	+45	-40	-21	-79	-	-	-	-	-
Leichhardt	-103	+203	-238	-27	-165	-63	+56	-160	-13	-180
Marrickville	-15	+18	-23	-6	-26	-265	+96	-130	-18	-417
Botany	-	-	-	-	-	-189	+105	-43	-6	-133
Total	-1163	+535	-1216	-304	-2148	-1341	+409	-624	-222	-1778

[a] See text (page 81) for the method of identifying areas of incursion.
[b] The enlarged boundaries existing from 1948 to 1969.
[c] The 'County Centre' includes the CBD, East Sydney, and Woolloomooloo.
Source: Based on analysis of unpublished 'CD' Census data, 1947-71.

TABLE 6.5   *Changes of population and labour force in areas of commercial and industrial incursion, inner Sydney, 1961-71.*

Area	Population (%)				Resident labour force (%)			
	Aged 15 yrs		Aged 65+ yrs		Manufacturing [a]		Finance & Property	
	1961	1971	1961	1971	1961	1971	1961	1971
Commercial Incursion	26	16	20	12	31	20	4	9
Industrial incursion	30	22	14	10	45	36	2	4
Inner *Total*	19	19	12	10	37	29	3	8
Metro. *Total*	26	26	9	9	35	28	5	9

[a] A definitional change caused most of the reductions from 1961 to 1971.
Source: Based on analysis of unpublished CD data of Censuses 1961 and 1971.

the most vulnerable people: children and the aged. The small numbers of manufacturing workers declined even further. On the other hand, the proportions that were young adults, or working in finance or property rose, particularly in North Sydney, as a result of flat development.

No comparable figures on commercial intrusion are available for inner Melbourne or inner Adelaide. Although it had less commercial development than inner Sydney, inner Melbourne may have had nearly as much incursion. The CBD spread more than in Sydney and there was a very large loss of houses in the City (see Figure 5.3). Development in East Melbourne, South Carlton and North Melbourne involved especially large losses, similar to those in East Sydney and Kings Cross (VCOSS, 1975:36-7). In North Melbourne alone, between 1950 to 1969, 560 dwellings were lost to non-residential incursion, especially commercial development (Johnson, 1972:96). Adelaide had even less but equally spread office development, which probably caused most of the loss of 4000 dwellings in the City from 1947 to 1971. There is little doubt that those displaced were, as in inner Sydney, among the poorest and most vulnerable people in the metropolis.

INDUSTRIAL DEVELOPMENT
Investment, Expansion and Land Prices
Unlike offices, most industrial uses have been decentralising. In all three cities, the building of factories in the inner areas during the mid and late 1960s has been small relative to the building of offices, and has declined in real terms and as a proportion of the metropolitan total (Vandermark, 1974:227-31). For example, inner Sydney's share of the metropolitan total of factory building fell from a third in the mid 1950s down to a fifth in 1971. Inner Adelaide had an especially small amount of manufacturing development. Except for some new development in Botany, most of inner Sydney's investment in industrial building has been in the improvement of old buildings and in limited expansion within the established industrial areas by firms dependent on the port for access to materials and markets. Most factories increasingly preferred cheaper, outer-suburban sites, where they could use space-extensive technologies, be easily serviced by trucks, and be near suburban workers. The investment in inner-suburban buildings for wholesaling, storage and transport terminals, has been larger, on the other hand, especially in recent years, growing faster and comprising a larger metropolitan share than the investment in manufacturing. These activities continue to be attracted by the metropolitan-wide accessibility and the nearness to the centralised port, railyard and airport.

There was a 40 per cent increase in land used for industrial purposes in inner Sydney from 1956 to 1972 (Table 6.6). However, this amounted to only 12 per cent of the metropolitan increase during this period and the inner-area share thus fell from 40 to 25 per cent. The increases were greatest during the 1950s but lessened in later years 'due to the shortage of suitable land in the older inner suburbs' (AIUS, 1975:15). Of the increases in land used for industry, 40 per cent was for large, space-extensive developments in the lowlands of Botany. Among the LGAs, only North Sydney had net losses, mostly due to the encroachment of commercial development. Similar incursions in Surry Hills and other City areas were more than offset by increases elsewhere. This increase in use of industrial land was caused largely by non-factory industrial uses, which displaced some factories and by 1972 covered a third of the industrial land (AIUS, 1975:17). The investment figures and land uses permitted (discussed in the next section) suggests that inner Melbourne had comparable increases of inner-suburban industrial land.

TABLE 6.6 *Expansion of land used for industry in inner Sydney LGAs, 1956-72.* [a] *(in hectares)*

Area	To 1956	1956-61	1961-67	1967-72	Total
City of Sydney	109.9	7.0	1.6	.4	114.9
South Sydney	373.4	23.7	20.2	12.6	429.9
North Sydney	15.4	3.2	2.8	-6.9	14.5
Leichhardt	61.2	5.3	2.0	20.7	89.2
Marrickville	95.6	49.6	17.0	13.8	176.0
Botany	128.4	48.6	55.9	28.3	261.2
Inner *total*	783.9	134.4	99.5	89.6	1 085.7
Metro. *total*	1 810.3	762.9	879.3	784.0	4 236.5

[a] Land use was measured from aerial photographs.
Source: AIUS (1975:78)

Up to the early 1960s, the value of factory and wholesaling sites in Redfern and in North Melbourne rose considerably faster than the Consumer Price Index (CPI) or the values of nearby house sites (Neutze, 1972:107; Johnson, 1972:202). In fact, house-site values in the City of Sydney stagnated partly because land-use restrictions prevented profitable conversions from residential to industrial uses. Problems of congestion, the availability of only small land parcels, and the conversion to other uses of the most attractive industrial properties are other reasons. Yet in the early 1970s, prices of industrial land in inner areas were still well above those in middle or outer areas in both Melbourne and Sydney (PLI, 1976:142-3; AIUS, 1975:61).

In a review of Sydney's industrial development of the 1950s, Logan (1963:158) noted that the inner areas still had the highest industrial land prices in Sydney. He concluded that:

> Sydney's CBD is the main product market and raw material source for many industries. The centralisation of shipping, road and rail services makes contact with the centre inevitable for firms serving other than peculiarly local markets. The continuing concentration of wholesaling, commercial and professional services in or near the CBD has forced manufacturers to bypass local commercial centres in their search for these services .... the growth of suburban industry, although dispersed, has not led to any diminution of the 'dominance' of the city centre (Logan, 1963:160).

Employment

Despite the extent of building and the use of more land, inner Sydney's industrial employment fell considerably, especially during the 1960s (Table 6.2). The loss of 60 000 manufacturing workers by 1971, a third of the 1945 total, resulted mainly from shifts to more capital-intensive, space-extensive technologies. Many factory jobs in the CBD were also displaced by office development during the 1960s. Elsewhere, some factories were replaced by transport terminals and wholesale stores. Only Botany had increases, mostly during the 1950s. On the other hand, transport, storage, and wholesaling jobs increased slightly in all LGAs except the City. Inner Melbourne experienced similar losses of blue-collar jobs during the 1960s (MMBW, 1977:26). These losses of jobs reflect the modernisation of industrial activity and the high cost of land.

Policy

Industrial decentralisation was considered desirable in the early post-war plans. However, consolidation within existing inner industrial areas, was advocated to remove the worst of the slum housing. In Sydney the Cumberland County plan allowed large-scale, inner-city expansion only in the undeveloped lowlands of Botany. There were also plans for the replacement of scattered industry with residential uses in some inner residential areas. This would have offset the population losses caused by consolidation in the main industrial areas. However, this latter part of the plan failed because the Commonwealth refused the funds for the acquisition of factories in residential areas. Intrusive industries could only be declared 'non-conforming' uses, which limited their expansion but seldom resulted in changes to residential uses. Net housing losses to industry were therefore far more than had been expected. The planners' predictions of large losses of manufacturing employment nonetheless proved to be very accurate, because they had underestimated how much modernisation would lower job densities.

The 1954 Melbourne plan allowed for 1093 hectares of inner-suburban industrial land, 405 hectares more than in 1947 (MMBW, 1954:134). Nearly all of the increase was on swamplands near the River Yarra, or in residential areas where there was already a lot of industry. The inner city was to have less than 10 per cent of the metropolitan increase expected until the 1970s. From 1961 to 1973, the area in inner Sydney zoned for industry remained about constant at about 600 hectares while, throughout the metropolitan area, it increased 50 per cent, to over 4000 hectares (AIUS, 1975:75). Considering that the inner areas had most of the existing industry in both cities in the early 1950s, these plans were ambitious for the time. Although Adelaide had no comparable land-use plans, the state government's initiatives in decentralisation had similar effects.

The planners were more successful in controlling industrial development than commercial development for a number of reasons. First, planning controls and market pressures worked in the same direction. Second, it was easier to control the expansion of industrial uses. The land was not worth so much more for industrial use than for housing, and the adverse consequences of industrial expansion (house demolitions and environmental degradation) were obvious to all and opposed by most residents. Labor councillors almost always controlled the industrial wards and strongly resisted the displacement of their constituents.

Disagreement about industrial zoning, between the State Planning Authority (NSWSPA) and the Sydney City Council, was one reason for the long delay in implementing the City planning scheme. In the early 1960s, both organisations wanted to restrict inner-suburban industrial expansion and to increase the residential population by about 10 per cent. But the NSWSPA wanted to follow the Cumberland County Council's policy of allowing industrial encroachment in ten housing areas already surrounded by industry (a loss of 10 000 people) and the replacement of 147 small, non-conforming industrial nodes with residential uses (a gain of 25 000 people) (*Sydney Morning Herald,* 25.11.64). This would improve housing quality as well as increase residential populations. The problem was that land-use controls, the only available policy tool, were insufficient to ensure the replacement of non-conforming industry with dwellings. Residential properties would be replaced in industrial areas but zoning alone was no guarantee that industries in residential areas would be removed.

On the other hand, the City Council sought to limit non-residential encroachment on an ad hoc basis whenever possible. But it could only delay, not stop, encroachment in the zoned industrial areas of the CCC plan. Nor could the City Council prevent the NSWSPA from rezoning for industrial uses an area of Pyrmont that contained 4000 residents. In the mid 1960s, City Council proposals to zone millions of dollars-worth of industrial land for park space foundered under NSWSPA opposition and demands by the industrialists for immediate acquisition by the City Council at industrial-use value (*Sydney Morning Herald,* 12.5.67). The City Council also tried during the 1960s to rezone from industrial to residential uses, several hundred homes in Beaconsfield (Quinn, 1974:32-3). Despite the support of most residents, firm objections were received from twenty-seven affected industrialists, some of whom had already purchased sites for their future expansion plans. The state Minister for Local Government disallowed the rezoning on the grounds that the area had no future for residential use.

Inner Adelaide had few limitations on industrial incursion until the 1962 Metropolitan Plan was adopted (South Australian Town Planning Committee, 1962). However, governmental incentives for decentralised development proved to be very effective. The industrial construction programme of the Housing Trust has supplied outer-area land and built factories for particular clients, who either leased the buildings or bought them at cost from the Housing Trust. Other state agencies have also encouraged industrial decentralisation. A survey of manufacturing firms in the northern sector (all outside the inner city) found that governmental assistance was the most important factor in their locational decision (Hume, 1975).

Industrial Incursion

In addition to considerable environmental degradation, industrial development in inner Sydney took about 5200 dwellings between 1947 and 1971 (Table 6.3). Even though industrial expansion used far more land, it caused about 30 per cent fewer residential losses than commercial redevelopment, which was in areas of very dense housing. As with commercial development, the losses were relatively small until the mid 1950s. They nearly doubled during the late 1950s, when the inner-area market for industrial properties was strongest, and then fell in the 1960s back to the early post-war rates.

Map 6.2 shows the location of the dwellings lost in inner Sydney to industrial incursion. The most striking feature is that a fifth of them were in the small, dense Surry Hills area, which absorbed some office development and much of the CBD overspill of warehousing and small firms in the fields of clothing, printing and business service. The indirect cause for much of this incursion was the office development in the CBD that had either displaced these activities or attracted them to near-city locations. Unlike the other areas of industrial incursion, Surry Hills was something of a transitional zone, as indicated by its large loss of terrace houses used as boarding houses or let as single rooms.

Most of the industrial incursion scattered farther south, where larger firms were expanding into areas of small terraces and cottages that were often in shared occupancy. The losses around the harbour, especially in Pyrmont, resulted from the expansion of firms, like Colonial Sugar Refineries, which were dependent on the port. There were few losses in Botany, except those due to expansions by old factories in Mascot or new transport facilities near the airport because there the newer, heavy-industrial firms had room to expand.

The housing that was taken for industrial development was generally of poor quality. Unlike some of the elegant but dilapidated terraces taken for city-centre commercial development, industry mostly took poorly constructed workingmen's terraces or cottages. Moreover, most of the losses were of dwellings run-down in anticipation of conversion, in areas already dominated by unpleasant land uses. The vast majority were houses, many shared by several families (non-self-contained flats), and there were few boarding houses or flats because of the unattractiveness of the locations (Table 6.4). Even among the houses, most were probably rented and many were purchased by industrial companies many years before the eventual change of use. As with commercial incursion, acquisitions were seldom impeded by 'irrational' owner-occupants refusing profitable sales.

The high proportion of houses explains why nearly as much population loss resulted in the industrial areas — about 19 000 — as in the commercial areas — 24 000 — where more dwellings were lost. Both uses displaced many old people and children but the industrial encroachment took the homes of more blue-collar workers (Table 6.5). Because some flats were subsequently built in these areas, there were small proportional gains of higher-status, white-collar workers.

The close parallels between inner Sydney and inner Melbourne — with respect to industrial land use, employment and investment — suggest that the population losses in inner Melbourne from industrial encroachment may have been almost as large as in Sydney. Although inner Adelaide had far less

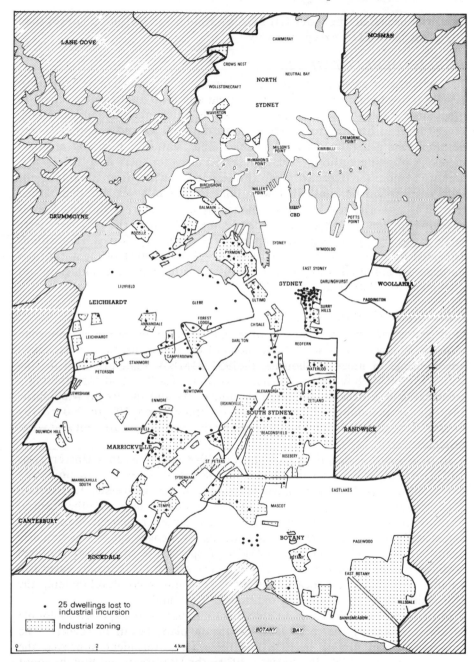

MAP 6.2.   Incursion of industrial land uses in inner Sydney, 1947-71
(See text p. 81 for method of identifying incursion.)
Source: Based on analysis of unpublished 'CD' Census data, 1947-71.

industrial incursion, the industrial LGA of Hindmarsh lost more houses than any other inner LGA except the City.

PUBLIC DEVELOPMENT

The activities of government were also a major factor in urban development; besides trying to control private development and locating their own offices in inner areas, public bodies were also responsible for changes in land use, taking inner-suburban housing for roads, schools, universities and hospitals. These developments generally occurred under similar statutory planning arrangements. A planning authority usually reserved areas for them as a 'special use' area well before the expected need. This restricted owners from making major improvements on buildings that were only to be purchased and demolished later. The authority had virtually a monopoly on the market and faced fewer development controls than private development. Most of the purchases were made privately by agreement, although the threat of forced acquisitions remained for those who were not happy to sell. A number of the authorities purchased years in advance of their needs, and either left the dwellings vacant or rented them (often to their staff).

Educational Facilities

Only Sydney had much expansion of tertiary institutions into inner-suburban housing. In inner Adelaide, virtually none of the major institutions has taken any housing. In inner Melbourne, the1954 MMBW Plan provided for the University of Melbourne's expansion into South Carlton and for building a technical college nearby. Although the university and the Royal Melbourne Institute of Technology have occupied or redeveloped 100 to 200 nearby houses, large-scale incursion was stopped by the increasingly affluent and vocal residents.

In New South Wales, the CCC report of 1948 viewed Sydney University as an '... overcrowded island in the slums'.[4] Decentralisation of new university development was dismissed, presumably because the University had certain scale economies (such as for libraries) and needed to be near other central institutions and to have city-wide accessibility. Another alternative to spatial expansion — more intensive use of the existing low-density site — was similarly dismissed. The CCC therefore provided a special-use area of thirty-three hectares on the main campus and thirty hectares for expansion eastward. Unable to displace the nearby hospital or commercial development, the University was to move into an old, mixed-use 'slum'.

In the late 1950s, when student enrolment numbers were expected to double to about 17 000 by the mid-1960s, expansion plans began in earnest. The University began buying in 1958 and the state government approved the expansion plans in 1960. By the early 1970s, the University had bought about 650 dwellings, displacing almost 2500 residents in the Darlington area (Map 6.3). Most of the dwellings were terraces, many occupied by either old,

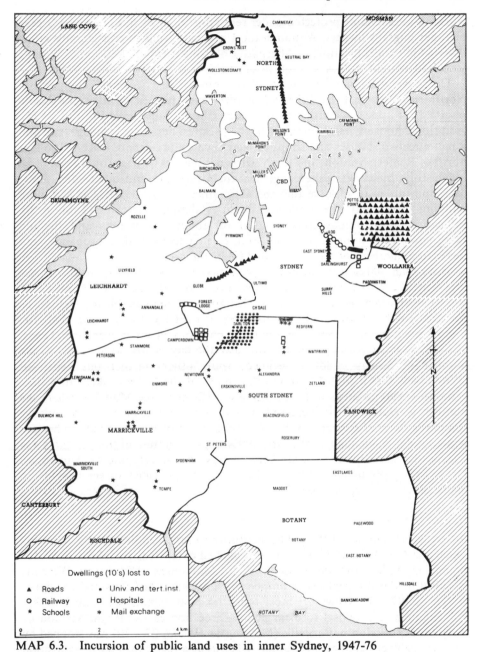

MAP 6.3.   Incursion of public land uses in inner Sydney, 1947-76
(See text p. 81 for methods of identifying incursion.)
Source: Data on roads and railways by the NSWDMR, on schools by the NSW
Education Department, on the University by James Colman Pty Ltd (1976), on the
hospitals from their superintendents or property officers, and on the mail exchange by
Neutze (1972:7).

working-class tenants protected under rent control, or by newly arrived Greeks or other migrant owners. Although the University went to considerable effort to assist in their relocation, no alternative housing was built and some migrants who had bought homes at high prices sold at a loss (McInnes, 1966).

The move of Sydney Teachers College from Sydney University campus into North Newtown had, by 1972, taken fifty-seven houses on a site originally reserved for a local school (Jackson Teece Chesterman Willis Pty Ltd, 1975). Additional housing has been taken by the Moore Theological College (two and a half streets of houses and shops in Newtown), a pre-school teachers' college north of Redfern Station, and the Newtown Teachers College (on the site of an old historic building). Taken together, the University and other educational developments were so large that the City, since the late 1960s, has had more building investment in educational facilities than in factories (Table 6.10). Educational institutions took a total of about 750 houses and the old Darlington community centre, as well as increasing traffic problems, and increasing numbers of students and staff in the area.

More than 400 additional houses were taken for school expansions in the inner areas, mostly during the 1960s, even though the number of inner-suburban children declined. Comparable figures are unavailable for Melbourne but the South Australian Education Department has taken more than 100 houses since the mid 1960s for similar expansions in inner Adelaide (Lewis, 1978:7). In inner Sydney, old schools near the city centre were closed as the number of nearby children declined, while others farther out expanded (Whiteman, 1966). Map 6.3 shows that most of the houses taken for school expansion were in areas of heavy migrant settlement (see Map 8.4) where the number of children had increased. Expansions were also made to improve standards of inner-suburban schools: a school site of less than half an hectare was considered adequate in the early 1900s but a minimum of four hectares was set for the same number of students in post-war developments. Unlike the University development, the school expansions provided direct benefits to many nearby low-income families.

Health Facilities

Hospitals are another of the public institutions of metropolitan importance for which the MMBW and CCC plans established extensive special-use areas for expansion within the inner suburbs. In Melbourne, the Royal Womens Hospital in Carlton replaced a number of houses by staff flats and car parks (VCOSS, 1975:37). However, most other hospital expansions were blocked. For example, a proposal to clear eighty-three houses for Royal Melbourne Hospital's expansion in Parkville (Melbourne *Herald*, 27.7.70) was stopped by the state cabinet (Melbourne *Herald*, 4.11.70) as a result of intense opposition from residents.

As proposed in the 1948 CCC Plan, the Royal Prince Alfred Hospital near Sydney University replaced an estimated eighty-seven dwellings between 1954 and 1961, for similar purposes. Sydney Hospital, the other general hospital, never did relocate, as was proposed in the Plan, to the Victoria Barracks site (considered historical buildings today) and the twenty-four hectares of 'depressed housing' near it. Nor have the plans for the Hospital's decentralisation to Parramatta been carried out. St Vincent's Hospital, Royal Alexandria Hospital for Children, Royal North Shore Hospital and other inner-city hospitals have been allowed to expand into nearby housing, despite a shortage of hospitals in outer areas (Donald, 1977). These various developments of health facilities have involved $16 million of building investment since 1969 in the City of Sydney (Table 6.1), an increase of over 3000 medical personnel during the 1960s (Table 6.2), and the probable loss of about 200-300 dwellings (Map 6.3).

Road Development

The large post-war growth of jobs and port activities in the inner areas, together with residential decentralisation and rising use of cars and trucks, greatly increased the demand for roads to the city centre. The post-war plans in Sydney and Melbourne anticipated this demand. The Melbourne Plan provided for a major ring-road around the CBD and a dozen 'major arterials' leading out to the suburbs. The Cumberland County Plan made reservations for 140 kilometres of freeways that have been incorporated in the detailed planning schemes as shown on Map 1.2.

Proponents for freeways suggested they would achieve greater economic efficiency and the diversion of through traffic out of residential areas, and reduce accidents. Although residential areas were avoided whenever possible, the road reservations in Sydney contained 10 000 — 15 000 inner-area dwellings (no exact count was ever made). Construction of housing in these areas, if allowed at all, required the agreement of the New South Wales Department of Main Roads (DMR).

In the early post-war years, scarce funds were used for upgrading existing main roads rather than for building freeways and expressways. These improvements were especially needed for inner Sydney roads, which were far narrower than those in inner Adelaide or inner Melbourne. Because of the post-war housing shortage and the cost of buying houses, only a small number of dwellings were lost to road construction; some were taken in the early 1950s along Military Road in North Sydney. In Sydney the DMR has relied more recently on the longer-term and cheaper strategy of road realignment, in which new developments must be set back enough to permit the road widening in the future.

The only major freeway in inner Sydney is the Warringah Expressway from the Harbour Bridge through North Sydney. From the late 1950s to 1974, the Expressway took over 600 dwellings. About 1500 people of varied socio-economic levels were displaced, mostly from old houses in single occupancy; the older areas near the bridge had more renters and low-income households.

Because these properties were compulsorily acquired rather than purchased privately, the DMR had an obligation to assist in the relocation of dislocated tenants. The DMR made a grant to the Housing Commission to cover the costs of providing alternative housing, and the displaced were given priority access to government housing. Although the DMR produced a number of reports throughout the 1960s to justify more freeways, the funds were unavailable and additional displacements caused by roads did not occur again until the 1970s (Chapter 9).

Few of Melbourne's many proposals for inner-city roadworks had been implemented before the 1970s. The 1964 Melbourne Transport Plan, approved in principle by the government in 1969, recommended 500 kilometres of freeways, leading mostly to the CBD. The MMBW (1971:71), which supported the plan, anticipated that up to 40 000 people would be displaced in the inner and middle suburbs. The Tullamarine Freeway and the South Eastern Freeway — the only major developments during the 1960s — took very little housing because they went along river valleys. They nonetheless brought in large amounts of traffic that subsequently filtered through many small residential streets. Since the mid 1960s, freeway proposals have met intense opposition from inner-city residents, on a wide variety of grounds (VCOSS, 1975:37-40).

One might expect less need for radial freeways in Adelaide: the City is much smaller, its CBD is relatively central, inner roads are wide, and many jobs are decentralised. However, the metropolis of Adelaide depends more heavily on the car than do the bigger cities, and much of the north-to-south traffic movement passes through or near the CBD. Throughout the 1950s, the South Australian Highways Department relied on a road realignment programme to improve existing main roads But with strong lobbying by city-centre interests, plans were developed for building, first, 160 kilometres of radial freeways (South Australian Town Planning Committee, 1962) and then an additional 300 kilometres (Deleuw, *et al.,* 1968). After a good deal of public controversy, the new Labor government in 1971 accepted the recommendation from another study for a ten-year moratorium on freeway construction in built-up areas (Sandercock, 1975:129-34). Very few dwellings had been taken for roads by 1971.

Employment Availability

From 1945 to 1971, 80 per cent of the increase of jobs in Sydney took place outside the inner city (Table 6.2). This reduced the inner city's share of total metropolitan employment from two-thirds to less than half. The suburbanisation of jobs, together with rising car ownership, has attenuated some of the journey-to-work difficulties for the rapidly decentralising residents. But inner-area employment still increased by over 100 000, while the number of resident workers dropped by over 33 000. The number of jobs per resident worker thus rose from 2.1 in 1945 (CCC, 1948:44) to 2.6 in 1961 and 2.8 in 1971 (Table 6.7). Melbourne and, to a lesser extent, Adelaide, have had similar trends. These rising imbalances have increased inner-suburban traffic and have heightened competition for inner-suburban housing.

The jobs per resident worker were initially greatest, and increased most for the white collar occupations (Table 6.7). Yet even for blue-collar workers (craftsmen, and manufacturing and transport workers), the inner areas have had an overall increase of jobs per resident worker. Later chapters will show that these changes have had a considerable impact on social status, and have produced other residential changes.

TABLE 6.7   *Changes in jobs and resident workers in inner Sydney, by occupation group, 1961-71.*

Occupational group [a]	Jobs ('000)			Resident workers ('000)			Jobs per resident worker		
	1961	1971	Change 1961-71	1961	1971	Change 1961-71	1961	1971	Change 1961-71
Professional, technical	48.4	61.2	+12.8	17.0	19.4	+2.4	2.9	3.2	+0.3
Administration managerial	39.1	40.7	+1.6	8.7	8.8	+0.1	4.5	4.6	+0.1
Clerical	124.3	151.6	+27.3	30.5	31.9	+1.3	4.1	4.8	+0.7
Sales	38.8	35.4	–3.4	12.2	11.2	–1.0	3.2	3.2	–
Transport and communication	31.9	32.1	+0.2	12.4	10.5	–1.9	2.6	3.1	+0.5
Craftsmen, etc.	197.4	153.4	–44.0	90.6	71.2	–19.4	2.2	2.2	0
Service workers	37.6	34.7	–2.9	22.7	19.1	–3.6	1.7	1.8	+0.1
Other	3.7	3.8	+0.1	6.3	2.2	–4.1	1.7	1.7	0
Not stated	4.3	20.3	+16.0	5.1	16.3	+11.2	.8	1.2	+0.4
Total	525.5	533.2	+7.7	205.5	190.6	–15.0	2.6	2.8	+0.2

[a] Location 'not stated' responses were allocated to the inner area in proportion to the stated responses.
Source: Based on analysis of unpublished tables and computer tapes of 'Journey to Work' Censuses, 1961 and 1971.

Summary

During the post-war years, Sydney, Melbourne and Adelaide have had far less suburbanisation of non-residential development than of residential development. Inner Sydney had an increase in jobs of a third, 40 per cent of the metropolitan investment in non-residential building (since 1969), increased real property values, and a considerable increase of land used for non-residential purposes. Offices have been most centralised, while retailing and manufacturing became more decentralised. The increases of non-residential land uses occurred because of the inner areas' increasing relative accessibility to the entire metropolis and the need to adapt old areas to cater for the increasing space demanded by modern developments. Melbourne and Sydney, both large and dense cities, experienced similar changes. Adelaide had fewer inner-suburban changes because of its smaller size and because of the location of the port and most manufacturing outside inner areas. Government office workers and institutional expansions added to the growth in all three central areas.

These non-residential developments involved considerable amounts of incursion into the existing housing. In inner Sydney, the losses were estimated at 15 000 dwellings, enough to house about 52 000 people (Table 6.8). Although this was a little less than the population losses associated with declining occupancy rates (fewer people per room; see Figure 5.4), non-residential incursion was responsible for the vast majority of forced moves. Commerce was the principle cause; industry and various public developments were also important. Many of the displaced were renters, old people and working-class families. Consistent with the concept of a transition zone, the greatest losses were in the areas near the CBD, which had some of the oldest and poorest housing in the metropolis. If it were not for the efforts of the Cumberland County Council and the City Council in Sydney, the losses would most certainly have been greater.

TABLE 6.8   *Estimated post-war housing and population losses caused by non-residential incursion in inner Sydney.*

Land-use incursion	Dwellings lost	Population capacity lost
Commerce	6 750	23 700
Industry	5 150	19 400
Roads and railways	1 800	3 800
Tertiary institutions	750	2 700
Schools	400	1 400
Hospitals	200	700
Total	15 050	52 000

See text for estimation methods. Estimates for commerce and industry are for 1947 to 1971; all others are for 1947 to 1976.

CHAPTER 7

Residential Development, 1947-61

The spatial models and the post-war plans suggested that losses and deterioration of inner-suburban housing were to be expected during the post-war years. But Chapter 5 showed there was growth and improvement. This chapter explains the major residential changes up to 1961; the improvement of 'slum' housing, suburbanisation, rising home-ownership, and limited public housing and private flat-building. Although most of the data is for Sydney, both Melbourne and, to a lesser extent, Adelaide have experienced similar developments.

The Slums

The acute housing shortage after the war was the legacy of almost two decades of depression and the war; by 1947, the problem had increased by demobilisation and the formation of new households.

In Sydney, as elsewhere, the inner-suburban housing market adjusted to these demands in a variety of ways. Except for North Sydney and parts of the City, most flats had been created cheaply by the subdivision of old houses. In 1947, boarding and rooming houses — mostly converted old houses — accommodated more than a quarter of the inner-suburban residents. Of the remaining houses, one of every twenty was shared by two or more separate households. Even the houses that were not shared or subdivided often included young couples living with parents, relatives or boarders, so that there was an average of almost two people per bedroom. Inner-area housing was used very intensively, especially in the areas closest to the city centre. During this time of universal housing shortage, the inner city was acting in the traditional role of adjusting the housing stock to provide smaller accommodation units within the reach of people on low incomes.

Inner-suburban housing, nonetheless, was often expensive and difficult to obtain. Almost three-quarters of the houses were tenanted, at rents that averaged over a third of the state's average male earnings and far more of the earnings of many residents. Landlords or tenants already in occupation could exact high 'key money' (informal and non-legal entrance payments) from new tenants. Moreover, dwellings were often dilapidated because of years of neglect. It is easy to see why so much of inner Sydney was considered a slum during the early post-war years.

During the mid 1930s and 1940s, special committees in Sydney, Melbourne and Adelaide all pronounced the inner suburbs 'slums' (Spearritt, 1974; Jones, 1972). It was expected that as the housing shortage was relieved and public housing was provided for the poor, the demand for these dwellings would reduce and values would fall. Inner-suburban housing, much of it over half a century old, was regarded as nearing the end of its useful life.

In 1947 the Cumberland Council estimated that 40 000 inner-suburban dwellings, a third of the stock, were so bad that they required immediate replacement (Table 7.1). Of the stock of Sydney's housing designated as substandard, the inner suburbs had 95 per cent. Taking into account other old dwellings expected to decline, the CCC was contemplating the need to replace three-quarters of the inner-area housing over twenty-five years — by 1972. In Paddington, 80 per cent of the housing was assessed as in need of immediate replacement and an additional 15 per cent by 1972. A study of houses requiring immediate replacement found the following problems: 45 per cent had badly cracked or damp walls, 45 per cent had sagging ceilings, 39 per cent had rotten floors, 46 per cent had no running water in the kitchen, and 48 per cent had no indoor bathroom (CCC 1948:68).

TABLE 7.1   *Dwellings judged to be requiring redevelopment in inner Sydney, 1947.*

| LGA [a] | Date of needed replacement | | | | | | |
| | Immediately | | Within 25 yrs | | More than 25 yrs | | Dwellings |
	no. ('00)	%	no. ('00)	%	no. ('00)	%	no. ('00)
City of Sydney	322	60	143	27	76	13	541
Leichhardt	34	20	117	72	12	8	162
Marrickville	18	8	139	63	63	29	219
Botany	7	10	47	67	16	23	71
North Sydney	9	5	43	25	122	70	174
Inner *Total*	390	33	489	42	289	25	1 167
Metro. *total*	423	12	796	21	2 518	67	3 737

[a] Local Government Areas are according to 1949-68 boundaries.
Source: Cumberland County Council (CCC *Expanded Housing Study,* 1947).

The Council diagnosed the problems as obsolescence of both houses and neighbourhoods:

Obsolescence in these areas is due, not to any natural defects in the land, but to outdated housing standards and dilapidation, while industrial penetration and lack of open space and other amenities have aggravated the condition. The existing street and subdivision patterns are so much below acceptable standards that rehabilitation of the areas is not possible without drastic clearance and the treatment of substantial areas at one time (1948:33).

This assessment had two essential applications. First, the housing had to be replaced rather than improved. Second, only public authorities had the ability to subsidise land acquisition, to compulsorily acquire small parcels for amalgamation, and to coordinate large-scale neighbourhood improvements. Another reason for public action was the need to ensure that low-income residents would benefit from the improvements.

The Council's proposed remedies involved both land-use planning and public housing. The innermost terrace housing was zoned for residential uses only, to stop further non-residential incursion and to reserve areas for medium-density redevelopment by the Housing Commission. Residential populations were still expected to drop by 15 per cent (the actual loss was 20 per cent by 1971) as crowding reduced and more land was used for parks, schools, and arterial roads. The inner areas just outside the terrace belt, which were diagnosed as having deteriorating housing but generally adequate neighbourhoods, were designated for medium-density redevelopment by private enterprise.

The Council believed that poor housing caused social problems and stressed the need for immediate action:

There can be no questioning the urgent need for ridding Sydney of its slums. If the cost to the nation, in the form of ill-health and premature death caused by the insanitary living conditions of these areas, of death or injury from accidents in their twisted streets, and of the vices and crimes which they have bred, could be assessed, there would be even greater cause for wonder that slum-clearance has been delayed so long and that it should have been subordinated to less important works. About a quarter of a million people live in conditions which are almost intolerable (1948:68).

Suburbanisation

By the late 1940s, Australia began to undergo the social change that had been delayed by the depression and the war. Sydney's metropolitan population increased rapidly, by 3.3 per cent per annum up to 1954 and by 2.3 per cent per annum from 1954 to 1961. Figures 7.1 and 7.2 show that Sydney had considerable increases in the number of middle-aged adults; many in the 1940s were refugees or assisted British migrants and more of those in the 1950s were southern Europeans. There were also large increases of young children, which resulted from the increases of adults in child-bearing years and sharp increases of marriage and fertility rates (Borrie, 1964:59). Given the Australian ideal of child-rearing in single-family dwellings (discussed in Chapter 4), population growth and the baby boom led to a rapid growth in demand for single-family housing, and suburbanisation away from the inner suburbs.

Yet suburbanisation and homebuilding on the urban fringe also required considerable economic resources. Young families were able to pay deposits from the sums saved during the war and while living with relatives afterwards. They were able to meet the repayments as the average earnings for males

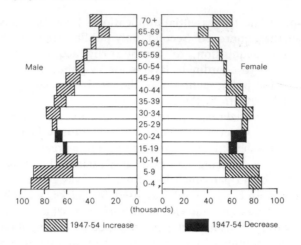

FIGURE 7.1.   Population changes, by age and sex, in Sydney, 1947-54
Source: Censuses, 1947 and 1954.

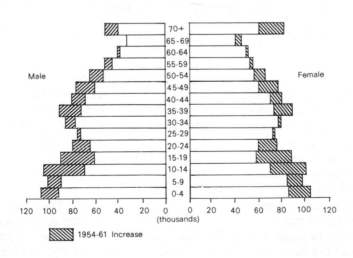

FIGURE 7.2.   Population changes, by age and sex, in Sydney, 1954-61
Source: Censuses, 1954 and 1961.

increased in real terms (the New South Wales average was deflated by the State's CPI) by 20 per cent from 1947 to 1954 and by a further 24 per cent to 1961. Home ownership was made easier by low interest rates and special loans for ex-servicement.

Suburban living had a number of attractions. First, the urban fringe during the 1950s was in the middle suburbs of today; a good deal of the new building was on land within the existing urban area left from earlier land booms. Second, the number of cars for every ten households in New South Wales rose, from one in 1947 to two in 1954 and to six in 1961. Third, most of the new jobs were by now outside the inner city.

Supply problems decreased throughout the metropolis as wartime controls were lifted, labour and materials became available, and the Housing Commission built large numbers of low-cost dwellings on the fringe. Almost 200 000 new homes were built in Sydney from 1947 to 1961, almost a fifth of them by the Housing Commission. With incomes growing and supply increasing, the number of years of average male earnings required to buy a house in Sydney dropped from 4.7 in 1950 to 3.6 years in 1955 and to 3.4 in 1960.[1] Home ownership had become a realisable goal for many families of modest means.

Falling occupancy rates in inner suburbs (Table 7.2), the major component of population losses during this period (see Figure 5.4), suggest that many people moved out to buy new homes. The greatest net losses were among young adults and children, who most needed single-family housing. On the other hand, there were absolute gains of older people, who were less likely to want or to be able to afford a move. Working-class residents were not left behind: manufacturing workers suburbanised only slightly less than others up to 1954 and at the same rate as others from 1954 to 1961.

TABLE 7.2   *Characteristics of occupied houses and flats in inner Sydney 1947-71*

	Houses			Flats		
	Owner-occupied (%)	People per room	Rent[a] (%)	Owner-occupied (%)	People per room	Rent[a] (%)
1947	27	.80	76	5	.70	100
1954	40	.72	78	7	.62	93
1961	63	.68	77	17	.60	83
1966	63	.64	78	18	.69	87
1971	61	.63	80	21	.66	92

[a] Private unfurnished average rent of inner-area tenancies as a percentage of the average for other areas.
Sources: Censuses, 1947-71.

This data does not show how many young, working-class Australians were leaving the area and how few were entering it. The Australian-born residents who moved to the outer suburbs were being replaced by large numbers of overseas migrants, a total of 25 000 up to 1954 and 28 000 more by 1961, of similar age and occupation. In the early post-war years, about 40 per cent of the migrants were from northern or central Europe (many displaced persons from Eastern-bloc countries) and another 40 per cent were from southern Europe (half from Italy and a third from Malta). From 1954 to 1961, three-quarters were from southern Europe. Map 7.1 shows that, in 1961, non-British migrants in the inner suburbs were heavily concentrated in the innermost transitional areas having the oldest and cheapest housing in the metropolis. The arrival of these people was a major reason why the demand for inner-suburban housing remained strong despite considerable suburbanisation.

The Housing Stock

Most of the net loss of 5500 occupied houses in the years 1947-61 occurred in the period 1954 to 1961 (Table 7.3). Most of these dwellings were lost to non-residential incursion, which took about 6 500 houses during these years. Some of the loss of occupied dwellings can be explained by increased vacancy rates, which returned to more normal levels from the very low levels of the post-war shortage.[2] These losses were partly offset by conversions of boarding houses and shared houses back to single households. Some of the old subdivided buildings were modified to provide fewer but more commodious units as the housing shortage eased.

TABLE 7.3   *Occupied dwellings, by type, in inner Sydney, (thousands)*

	Houses	Shared houses [a]	Flats (n.s.c.)	Flats (s.c.)	Non-private	Total	Unoccupied total [b]	Total dwellings
1947	74.5	8.6	8.9	19.1	5.7	116.9	-	-
1954	74.0	8.2	13.1	19.3	4.4	119.3	2.4	121.4
1961	69.0	5.8	12.2	24.1	4.1	115.2	4.8	120.0
1966	66.6	2.3	13.9	37.5	1.3	121.8	9.0	130.8
1971	68.7		12.5	48.9	1.3	131.7	12.3	144.0

[a] Shared houses and non-self-contained flats were combined after 1961.
[b] Figures for dwellings were unavailable for 1947.
Source: Censuses, 1947-71.

More importantly, there were almost 2000 new houses built in the years up to 1954 and 1300 more by 1961 (Figure 7.3). About half were built on vacant land in Botany, which was only then completing its first stage of development. In the eastern part of the LGA, building had been hindered in earlier years by swampy land, poor amenity, and remoteness from public transport. These modest houses provided for a net increase of almost 5000 residents, mostly blue-collar families with children. The other inner LGAs had considerable infill of new

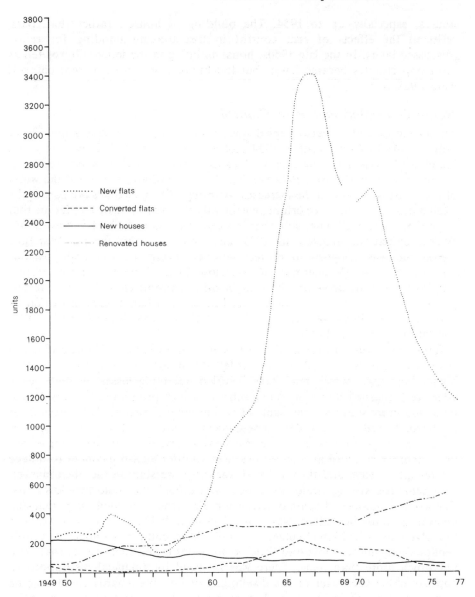

FIGURE 7.3.   Construction, conversion and renovation in inner Sydney, 1949-76
(Three-year moving averages. Paddington is included in inner Sydney only up to 1969.)
Source: Unpublished data from the Sydney Water Board.

houses, especially up to 1954. The building of houses, rather than flats, reflected the effects of rent control in discouraging building for rental (discussed later). In the late 1950s, house-building in the inner suburbs fell as infill opportunites became fewer; but flat-building increased as rent controls were relaxed.

Home Ownership and Rent Control

The proportion of owner-occupied houses in inner Sydney rose from 27 per cent in 1947 to 40 per cent in 1954 and 63 per cent in 1961. Even many old, dilapidated houses in unattractive localities were converted from rental to owner-occupancy (Neutze, 1972:84). The City of Sydney, which had the worst of the housing, shared in the increases. Although rising incomes are part of the explanation, the most important reason was the rent control legislation that applied to almost all inner-suburban houses in the late 1940s. The New South Wales legislation, enacted in 1939 and reinforced by federal War-time legislation, was designed to protect tenants during the war and post-war housing shortages (Vandermark & Harrison, 1972). Tenants could be evicted only as a result of property abuse or in other extreme circumstances. It also pegged rents at 1939 levels, which caused inner-suburban house rents to fall in real terms by almost 40 per cent from 1947 to 1954. Victoria had similar legislation (Johnson, 1972).

Rent control encouraged landlords to sell to sitting tenants. While ownership costs rose, rents were fixed and profits fell. Most hopes for profitable sales for higher land uses, which may have justified accepting losses on rents, were effectively quashed by the planning scheme, which prohibited non-residential incursion in most areas. The rights of sitting tenants also made it difficult for landlords to sell on the wider home-ownership market. The owner's options were to keep the property and receive a small return; to sell to the sitting tenant or to another landlord at reduced price; or to offer a cash payment to induce the tenant to leave and then sell with vacant possession on the open market.

Tenants had strong incentives to buy even though they paid very low rents. The average number of years of average male earnings needed for purchasing an average house in Redfern was only 1.6 years in 1947 and reached a post-war low of 1.1 years in 1956 (Neutze, 1972:110). Most could buy under favourable vendor financing that involved little or no deposit, and repayments that were not much more than rents. There was no need for financial institutions to approve either the buyer or the dwelling. Low-income tenants could become owners without having to move house or away from nearby jobs or familiar neighbourhoods.

The effects on the residential property market were sweeping indeed. After virtually no sales during the war, the proportion of houses sold annually rose quickly to 5 per cent in Paddington in 1953 (Roseth, 1969:144) and to 7 per cent for terrace houses in Redfern from 1949 to 1953 (Neutze, 1972:114). Johnson (1972) has recorded that North Melbourne, which was covered by similar legislation, also had large increases of sales during this period (p.59), mostly to sitting tenants (p. 61). Mainly as a result of rent control, landlords in North Melbourne received prices that were a third less than those paid to owner-occupants, who offered vacant possession (p. 52). Similarly, the average prices for houses bought by individuals declined in real terms in both North Melbourne and Redfern during the early 1950s (Johnson, 1972:182; Neutze, 1972:110).

Rent control in New South Wales benefitted all renters with tenancies dating from before 1954. Home ownership brought improved maintenance and many building improvements (Figure 7.3) which had been discouraged by rent control. The major losers in these changes induced by rent control were the landlords, not all of whom were wealthy, and anyone seeking dwellings in a shrinking rental market.

In South Australia, the rent control legislation also limited rents but provided less security of tenure to sitting tenants. If a landlord certified that he planned to sell the dwelling, he could serve the tenant with a notice to quit the premises. Unlike the situation in inner Sydney and inner Melbourne, rising home ownership in inner Adelaide involved the forced displacement of considerable numbers of poor tenants.

Home Ownership and Migrants

From the mid-1950s, non-British migrants replaced sitting tenants as the chief buyers of formerly rented houses in the inner suburbs. In North Melbourne, Johnson (1972) has recorded that more than half of the home buyers by 1954 were migrants (p. 59; they owned more than a fifth of the houses by 1955 (p. 56). In Redfern, the proportion of homes owned by non-British migrants (mainly Greeks) rose from 2 per cent in the early 1950s to 5 per cent in 1954, 10 per cent in 1956 and 26 per cent in 1961. Paddington had parallel increases of non-British ownership, mostly Italians (Roseth, 1969:136). Although most purchased the cheap terrace houses near the CBD, some had, by 1961, started buying more expensive, slightly more distant, semi-detached and detached houses (see Map 7.1). Consistent with the invasion/succession of the zonal model, migrants were becoming owners and moving outward after brief periods of adjustment and saving while living in rental accommodation near the city centre.

Migrants overcame formidable obstacles to make these purchases. Not being sitting tenants, they had to pay full market value. When landlords paid sitting tenants to vacate, migrants were usually paying the higher price and effectively subsidising the former tenants, which helped some to buy outer-suburban homes. Access to finance also presented problems, because banks were reluctant to make loans on slum housing or to people with little savings. Accordingly, landlords could often exact higher purchase prices from migrants by making vendor finance available at what was at the time usurious rates of around 10 per cent interest. Migrants were further disadvantaged by their lack

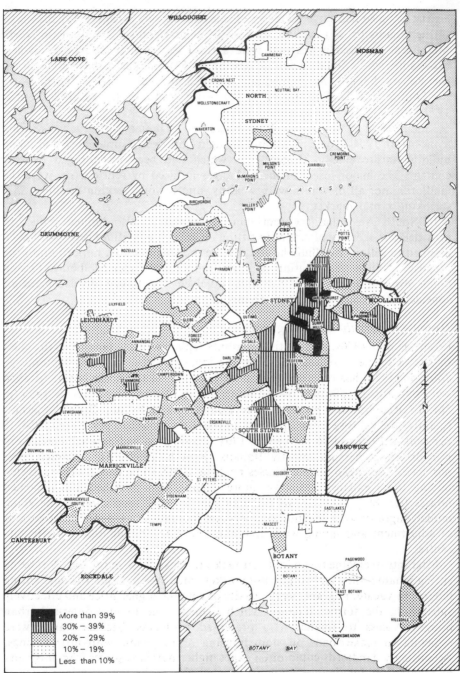

MAP 7.1.   Distribution of non-British-born migrants in inner Sydney, 1961
Source: Based on analysis of unpublished 'CD' Census data, 1961.

of familiarity with the local market. For all these reasons, they paid more than native Australians for equivalent houses. In North Melbourne, Johnson reported that: 'in 1955, at the peak of the migrant buying, an Australian buying for owner occupancy paid $2600 on average when a migrant paid $4700 — a difference of $2100' (1972:184).

To make these purchases involved considerable hardships. Husbands took multiple jobs, wives with children went to work, and crowding was often severe. The strong motivation is partly explained by the migrant's determination and his drive for economic advantage. Rapid family formation and the security of home ownership were added incentives. Discrimination in the private rental market, and ineligibility to apply for public housing, were additional reasons for buying.

The strong demand by migrant purchasers had a considerable impact on the property market. From the early to the late 1950s, annual sales rose from 8 per cent to 13 per cent in both Redfern and Paddington. House prices in Redfern rose at a compound average rate of 14 per cent annually from 1953 to 1961 and doubled in real terms from 1957 to 1961 (Neutze, 1972:110). Prices in Paddington (Roseth 1969:150) and North Melbourne (Johnson, 1972:184) had similarly large increases over this same period of time. Capital gains through the 1950s were so great that owner-occupants in effect had free accommodation and showed considerable returns on their investments (Neutze, 1972:113). Migrants fared less well than sitting tenants because they paid so much more for their houses but received about the same amounts when they sold them later (Johnson, 1972:184). The rates of increase, which were considerably above those of the rest of the metropolis, reflected the growing confidence about the future and desirability of old residential areas.

Part of the increased value of the properties resulted from improvements by the new owner-occupants. During the late 1950s, the number of houses that were renovated increased further (see Figure 7.3). Even poor owners, who could not afford the major alterations and additions shown by these figures, did a considerable amount of cleaning up, repainting, and repairing of roofs and plumbing. Because they were satisfying their own needs rather than making an investment, future market expectations and the risks to capital were of little concern to them. Most of them probably expected to remain in their houses indefinitely and few could afford to move elsewhere anyway. Because the old dwellings were brick and structurally sound, the deterioration resulting from years years of neglect could be made good. The availability of jobs and rising real incomes, even for unskilled workers, made it possible for the residents to afford improvements. The strong attraction of centrally located jobs was a further factor encouraging residents to stay and renovate rather than move on.

Private Flats and Rental Accommodation

Rent control and the demand for home ownership considerably retarded the private development of flats. In Sydney, rent control applied equally to new and established dwellings until 1954. Accordingly, in the inner areas, despite its considerable accessibility advantages, there were more private houses built than private flats from 1947 to 1954. Nearly all of the 1100 privately developed flats that were built were in North Sydney, mostly in Neutral Bay. They were sold under company titles; that is all the members holding shares in the company were owner-occupants of flats in the block.

In 1954, the Landlord and Tenant Act was amended to free from control any new tenancies after an owner had obtained vacant possession; a similar change was made in Victoria in 1956.[3] These changes, together with greater competition for the rapidly shrinking stock of rented housing, caused the real cost of house and flat rents to rise by 27 per cent from 1954 to 1961 in the inner suburbs. Moreover, there was considerable demand from increasing numbers of young adults (Figure 7.2) throughout Sydney during the late 1950s. Their rising incomes enabled many of them to leave home and set up house for themselves. These changes, together with the increasing number of inner-city, white-collar jobs, considerably increased incentives for the building of flats in the inner suburbs.

Between 1954 and 1961, there was a net increase of over 3000 private flats in inner Sydney. Because the flat boom started late in the intercensal period (Figure 7.3), few new flats were counted in 1961, although large numbers were under construction or awaiting tenants. Almost all were in the most attractive inner-suburban areas. Two-thirds were in North Sydney, mostly in Neutral Bay along the slopes overlooking the harbour and within easy access to the city centre, often built on the large sites of old houses. Others were in the former gardens of large mansions in Potts Point, near the harbour and CBD, or on land near parks and railway stations, in the southwest of Marrickville.

Investors were at first cautious about building rental flats because they feared reinstatement of rent control and were uncertain about the future demand. One way to minimise the risk was to increase densities by converting existing houses into flats, which saved considerably on construction costs. It appears that at least a third of the increase of flats from 1954 to 1961 were provided in this way.[4] The largest numbers of conversions took place in the City of Sydney, Leichhardt and Marrickville. At that time, few parts of these areas could attract new flats and there were many rooming houses that could, with a few plumbing changes, be converted into 'self-contained flats' providing higher returns. Old mansions in relatively poor living areas were also prime targets for conversion into flats. In 1961, nearly all the private flats in Redfern were house conversions (Neutze, 1972:7-8). These conversions, and the lingering effect of rent control, probably explain why private flat rents in the inner suburbs did not increase as much as those in other parts of the metropolis during the 1950s (Table 7.2).

By discouraging the building of flats and reducing the stock of rented houses, rent control encouraged the market for accommodation in shared houses, houses let on a single-room basis, and boarding houses. Some people who could have afforded new flats were probably forced into these kinds of housing.

The number of people living in this accommodation nonetheless declined considerably (Figure 5.2) as did the accommodation (Table 7.3). The numbers of non-self-contained flats increased up to 1954 only because boarding houses and old hotels were converted into many single-roomed dwellings.

In the City of Sydney there were moderate net losses of non-self-contained accommodation, caused mostly by non-residential encroachment, which were balanced by moderate net gains from the conversion of houses to multiple occupancy in Leichhardt and Marrickville. To a limited degree, land-use succession was following the theoretical pattern of radiating outwards from the city centre.

Government Housing

Despite the post-war plans for massive public redevelopment, the New South Wales Housing Commission had built less than 1500 new units in inner Sydney by 1961. The Commonwealth/State Housing Agreement, which provided most of the funds, made no provisions for the added acquisition costs of slum clearance. In the early post-war years, land prices for the dense, dilapidated dwellings were high because of the lingering expectations of sales for non-residential use. The Commission also found it difficult to justify the demolition of existing housing, however bad, when there was an acute accommodation shortage. At a more practical level, the Housing Commission did not have enough inner-suburban units to temporarily house those displaced by redevelopment. Most of the Commission's efforts were devoted to fringe development which increased the overall supply of housing in the metropolis.

The New South Wales Housing Commission nonetheless went ahead with some limited clearance plans. In its loan programme for 1947-48, the state government provided $2.5 million to help with acquisition costs, a tenth of the amount needed for small clearance projects proposed in Waterloo, Redfern and Paddington.

By 1954 the Housing Commission had built 309 flats in Milsons Point in North Sydney, 175 in Balmain, 217 in Redfern, and lesser numbers in Surry Hills, Glebe, Erskineville and Waterloo. All but the first two were slum-clearance programmes, which explains why there was nearly one family displaced for every unit. built. The existing housing in these areas was poorly built and severely deteriorated. Nearly all, the displaced people were low-income, Australian-born renters.

Consistent with planning goals, the projects added open space (up to the standards set by the Cumberland County Council) and reduced densities, from about thirty-two to about twenty persons per gross hectare in the Redfern sites. Although most of the projects had a mixture of housing types, the emphasis was on three-storey, walk-up flats. This was the only way to provide more open space and still be able to rehouse all the existing residents. Reflecting the attitudes of the time, most of the rehoused residents nonetheless chose to move to suburban cottages provided by the Commission rather than to return to their former localities. Many of them chose to move to Botany.

The development of public housing plodded along at the same pace during the mid and late 1950s. Although waiting lists for public housing increased, funding remained scarce and the case for slum clearance diminished as owner-occupancy rose and dwellings were better maintained. Of the 750 or so government flats that were built during the period, most were extensions, at slightly higher densities, of the earlier slum-clearance projects in Surry Hills and Redfern. Smaller projects of walk-up flats in Paddington, Glebe, Marrickville (for the elderly), and elsewhere in the inner areas, were more like private development of flats at the time. By 1960, some additional clearance and construction had begun in Redfern and Waterloo. The Housing Commission also built several hundred new houses in Botany. But the number of inner-suburban government houses nonetheless declined considerably because of the policy of allowing sitting tenants to buy on generous terms.

Summary

The dominant pressures on post-war urban development have been more affluence, the baby boom, and rising car-ownership — all of which contributed to rapid suburbanisation of inner-area residents. However, unlike in the United States, the slum syndrome of falling values, deterioration, and abandonment never eventuated. Suburbanisation enabled the remaining residents to be housed more adequately and freed accommodation for migrant arrivals and for those displaced by non-residential incursion. In broad terms, these trends are consistent with both the zonal model and the filtering down process of lower-income residents moving into housing vacated by slightly more affluent occupants.

The increase in supply outside the inner city, together with the economic advancement of even the lower-income households, allowed inner-area housing conditions to improve along with those of the rest of the metropolis. The number of cheap rooming houses and other kinds of subdivided accommodation fell. If rent control had not discouraged the private development of flats, these losses would have been more rapid. Home-ownership levels rose markedly, partly because of rent control, but also because rising real income enabled poor tenants and new migrants to buy their own homes. Once they owned their dwellings, they began to make up for the years of neglected maintenance and reverse the long trend of inner-area housing decline. The improvement of housing that had long been regarded as slums was, therefore, not usually at the expense of the poor. Because of the limited amount of public or private development of flats, residential developments during the 1940s and 1950s dislocated an insignificant number of people; most of the displacement was a result of non-residential incursion.

CHAPTER 8

Residential Development, 1961-1971

This chapter describes residential developments from 1961 to 1971 more fully than those that deal with the earlier years. More data is available and the findings have greater implications for current policy. Some of the issues also changed considerably. As fewer tenants were protected by rent control, landlords were encouraged less to sell, and conversion from rental to owner-occupancy of houses became less frequent. The main features of the 1960s were the continued purchase of housing by migrants, moves by affluent households into renovated old terrace housing (gentrification), the boom of private flat-building and the public redevelopment in the form of high-rise flats, and increased vacancy rates. The examples and data given are primarily from Sydney, although Melbourne and Adelaide experienced some similar kinds of inner-suburban change.

Houses

The number of occupied houses in inner Sydney remained remarkably stable during the 1960s. There was a net loss of only 300 (Table 7.3) despite estimated gross losses of over 6000 as a result of increased vacancy rates,[1] non-residential incursion, and public and private redevelopment for flats. More than 5600 additional houses became available during the 1960s. Map 8.1 shows the location of areas in inner Sydney that had net gains or net losses of houses. Considering the rising land costs and pressure for redevelopment, the gains of houses is a striking finding that requires further explanation.

The gross increase of houses occurred partly from the 2000 built during the 1960s, slightly less than during the 1950s (Figure 7.3). Some were infill of detached houses in still loosely developed areas like Botany. Especially in Leichhardt and Marrickville, they were built in the backyards of houses with large lots, or replaced badly deteriorated old houses or sheds. Not all of these resulted in net increases. About a quarter were medium-density town houses (villa units), which were generally expensive and used land relatively intensely.[2] Most town houses were in North Sydney but one of the largest was the Wyldefel Gardens on the harbour slopes of Potts Point.

More of the additional houses resulted from conversions. To assume that two-thirds of the large losses of shared houses (Table 7.3) were conversions back to single-family housing would explain about 2000 of the house gains.

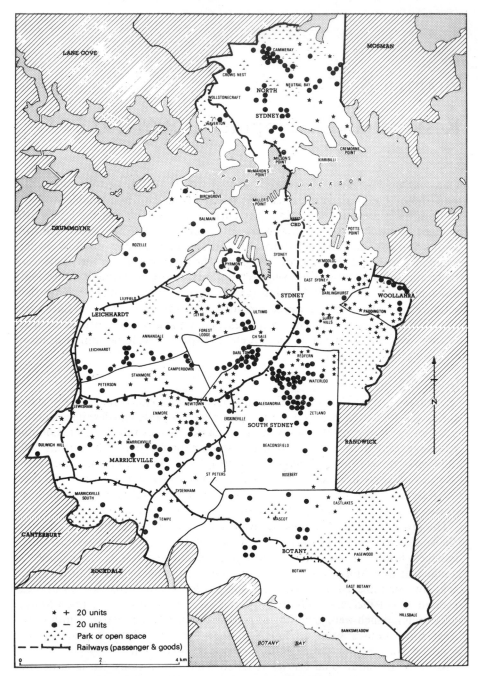

MAP 8.1.   Changes in numbers of occupied houses in inner Sydney, 1961-71
Source: Based on analysis of unpublished 'CD' Census data, 1961 and 1971.

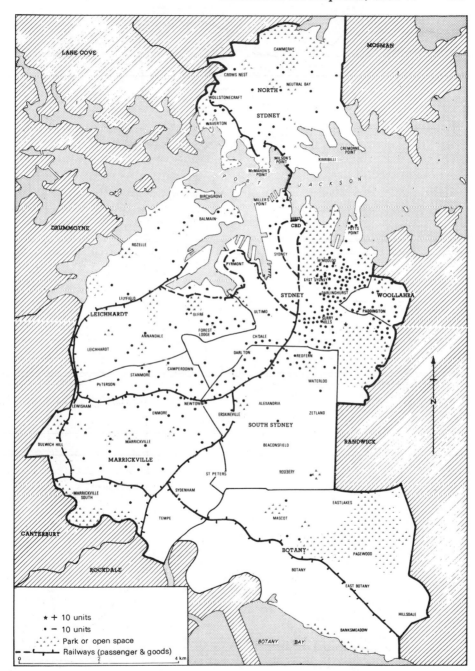

MAP 8.2.   Changes in numbers of occupied, non-private dwellings in inner Sydney, 1961-71
Source: Based on analysis of unpublished 'CD' Census data, 1961 and 1971.

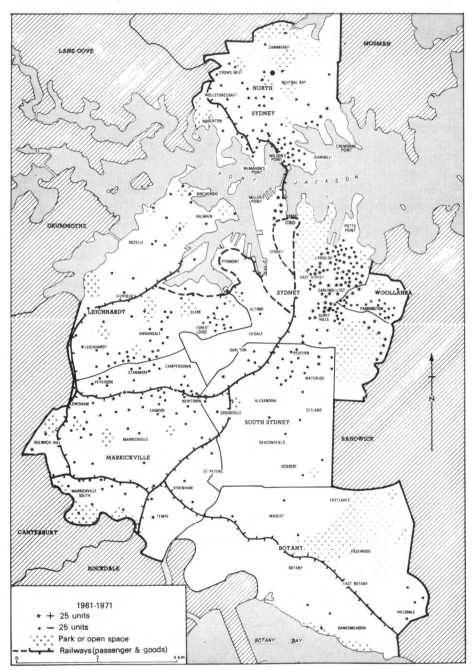

MAP 8.3.   Changes in numbers of non-self-contained flats in inner Sydney, 1961-71
Source: Based on analysis of unpublished 'CD' Census data, 1961 and 1971.

This leaves a gain of several thousand more houses that probably had previously been used for boarding or rooming houses, or as combined house/shops. At least one out of every twenty houses in 1971 had been either newly built or converted from multiple occupancy since 1961.

Numbers of houses generally increased most where non-private units and non-self-contained flats declined most (compare Maps 8.1, 8.2, 8.3). In the 'transitional' areas of old terrace housing, most of these additional houses were converted from buildings previously used as boarding houses or let as single rooms. The gains of houses in Leichhardt, Marrickville and other more distant areas resulted more from amalgamations of shared houses. This evidence further suggests that the 'filtering down' process involving subdivisions of old houses — a dominant force since the turn of the century — had been reversed. The explanation lies in the changing nature of inner-suburban demand discussed throughout this chapter.

Migrant Buyers

Part of the strengthening demand for inner-suburban houses resulted from the continuing increases of non-British migrants. Although some groups who had arrived earlier (notably Italians) were moving outwards, the numbers of Greeks, Yugoslavs, Turks and other more recently arrived groups continued to grow. Many were women joining men who had settled earlier (Burnley, 1972:72). From 1961 to 1971, the number of non-British migrants in inner Sydney rose by 28000 and from 19 per cent to 27 per cent of the inner-city population. Family formation and economic advancement encouraged increasing numbers of migrants to buy their own homes.

Especially in the early 1960s, migrant buyers were most active in the innermost terrace areas that had the cheapest housing. In Paddington, Roseth reported (1969), they comprised two-thirds of the owner-occupant buyers between 1959 and 1962 and almost half between 1963 and 1966 (p. 179); the majority were Italian families with children, headed by blue-collar workers (p. 181). In Redfern, over half of the owner-occupant purchasers in the mid 1960s were non-British migrants (mostly Greeks); non-British migrants comprised 41 per cent of the owner-occupants in 1969.

As a result of this strong demand from migrants, house prices in Redfern rose by 67 per cent from 1960 to 1966 (Neutze, 1972:110). This was substantially above the 29 per cent increase in the middle suburb of Bankstown (Neutze, 1971a:85), and was equal to the 67 per cent increase in the eastern suburb of Randwick, which experienced price inflation because of flat development (Neutze, 1971b:80). Figures from Melbourne over the same period show that the price increases in the inner areas of North Melbourne, an area of heavy migrant settlement, exceeded those of other parts of the metropolis (URU, 1973:157).

By the late 1960s, increasing numbers of migrants were making second-stage moves outwards into bigger and better housing in Leichhhardt, Marrickville and Botany (compare Maps 7.1 and 8.4). In general, the innermost areas had

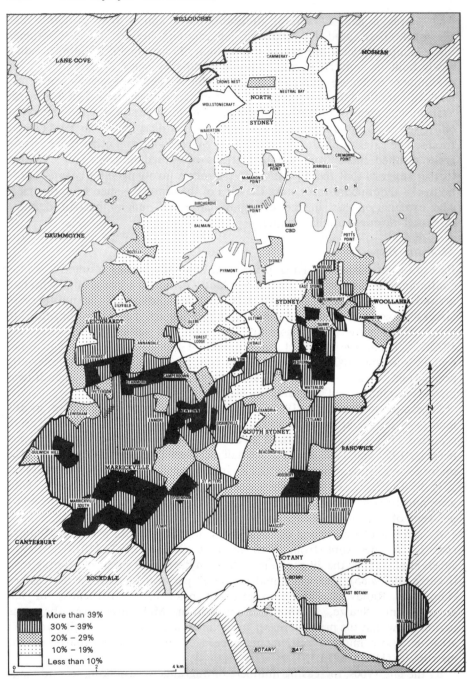

MAP 8.4.   Distribution of non-British-born migrants in inner Sydney, 1971
Source: Based on analysis of unpublished 'CD' Census data, 1961 and 1971.

continued gains of young, adult migrants and losses of migrants in the middle-age group; areas a bit further out had gains in both age groups (Burnley & Walker, 1977:18-19). In these parts of the inner areas, the proportions of blue-collar workers remained fairly stable, occupancy rates generally rose, and the proportions of children and, to a much smaller extent, young adults, increased. As the migrants assimilated economically and socially, they were generally following the Burgess model of spatial succession outwards into better housing formerly occupied by older Australians.

Gentrification

In the later part of the 1960s, the settlement of migrants in some of inner Sydney's terrace housing areas tapered off sharply, partly because of rising competition from young, middle-class Australians. From 1966 to 1971, the proportion of blue-collar workers in the labourforce in these areas fell dramatically, by up to 15 per cent compared with 5 per cent for the whole metropolis. The percentage of professionals and other higher-status, white-collar workers rose by .5 per cent metropolitan-wide but by 7 per cent in Paddington, 6 per cent in Balmain, 5 per cent in Glebe and 3 per cent in Chippendale. These innermost areas also had sizeable losses of children, large gains of young adults aged between sixteen and twenty-five, and small losses of the aged. As the young, middle classes replaced working-class families with children, occupancy rates in houses dropped sharply (Roseth, 1969:124).

This 'filtering up' of the old houses, radiating from the innermost areas outwards, resulted from the complicated interrelationship of a variety of developments. As the baby boom came of age, young people were establishing their own households (Figure 8.1) and securing white-collar jobs, which had been growing rapidly throughout the 1950s and 1960s in the CBD and inner city. Households with two income earners increased as participation by women (aged fifteen to sixty-four) in the labourforce rose rapidly in Sydney, from 40 per cent in 1961 to 48 per cent in 1971. There was a considerable minority of young adults — more than in earlier generations — who were postponing child-bearing and leading the career-and consumer-oriented life-styles well suited for inner-suburban living. Many openly rejected the image and life-styles of outer-suburban living.

The childless, young adults had less need for large houses and gardens in the outer suburbs. Despite continued rises of real income (by about 1 per cent per year through the 1960s — a third of the 1950s rate), increasing numbers were encouraged to buy cheap, inner-city houses, rather than more expensive houses elsewhere in the city, as interest rates rose and the number of years of average earnings needed to buy an average house in Sydney rose from 3.4 in 1960 and 1965 to 3.9 in 1970. Although car-ownership rates climbed to one per household by 1971, new houses were increasingly distant from the jobs and attractions of the city centre. For all of these reasons, houses in the inner suburbs became increasingly attractive for some middle-income households.

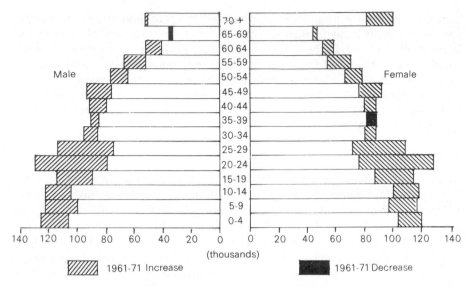

FIGURE 8.1.   Population changes, by age and sex, in Sydney, 1961-71
Sources: Censuses, 1961 and 1971.

Another interesting question is why some affluent, childless, young adults, who wanted to live in the inner suburbs, chose old houses instead of new flats. Terraces offered some outdoor space and were usually more commodious. Migrants had already reversed much of the slum image and social attitudes to terraces now changed: young, middle classes made it into a fashion symbol of urbane life-styles, community diversity, architectural charm and historical significance — a rejection of the suburban stereotype. Renovating an old terrace house presented a different image from buying a home unit and opportunities for self-expression. This turn-around was facilitated by the solid construction and favourable locations of many of the terrace houses.

Paddington exemplifies this 'gentrification' phenomenon throughout Australia; a detailed case study is available of its post-war development (Roseth, 1969). Located only three kilometres east of the city centre, Paddington has many outstanding residential features, acknowledged even by the post-war planners who had declared it a slum. The terrain slopes down from a central ridge, providing may harbour views. It is located near the high-status Woollahra area to the east and has little intrusive industry. Unlike many of the terraces in other areas, those in Paddington were designed for middle-class businessmen and professionals. Built in the 1880s, they have two, three and sometimes even four storeys, fairly wide (five-metre) frontages, and elaborate cast-iron balconies and other attractive ornamentation. It is hardly surprising that Paddington was the first inner area to experience gentrification.

The trend-setters — the first of the middle-class arrivals — were a few artists, journalists and other white-collar workers during the early 1950s. The movement became more widespread in the late 1950s and accelerated in the mid 1960s. White-collar workers were 14 per cent of the buyers from 1959 to 1962 but 40 per cent from 1963 to 1966. They were almost entirely young and Australian-born, mostly married couples but some single people. In sharp contrast to the migrant buyers, only a few had school-age children. Their individual incomes were about the metropolitan average but many households had two incomes. Although most had been raised outside the inner suburbs, almost all were first-time buyers moving from inner or eastern suburban flats. Only 3 per cent even considered buying a flat or unit.

Gentrification also spread to other inner suburbs. Of those purchasers in Paddington who considered buying dwellings in other areas, almost all considered terrace houses elsewhere in the inner city, mostly in Surry Hills, Glebe and Balmain (Roseth, 1969:236). Most of these same areas had large increases of houses as a result of conversions (Map 8.1). Although Surry Hills had poorer-quality terraces, there were many, especially in the east, that were free of intrusive industry or flats and were located on handsome, wide, tree-lined streets. In Glebe, there were very large and good-quality terraces, many previously subdivided into single rooms, located near the University. Balmain, like Glebe and Paddington, had an attractive village atmosphere and little intruding industry. Further attractions in Balmain were the spectacular harbour views from the hill slopes and the short ferry trip to the city centre. The young, middle-class buyers entered these areas later than they did Paddington, generally from the mid to late 1960s onwards, partly because, by then, prices in Paddington had already become quite high.

The terrace housing also experienced considerable 'filtering up' in terms of the housing quality. Unlike the migrant and sitting-tenant buyers of the 1950s, the young 'trendies' had relatively high incomes. They were able to pay, soon after moving in, for major alterations and additions, which often made the dwellings even more attractive than when they were new. Of the Paddington owner-occupants who bought during the early 1960s, 43 per cent had, by 1966, made some structural changes and rebuilt both the bathroom and the kitchen; 70 per cent had rebuilt the bathroom (Roseth 1969:216). Only 5 per cent had done nothing and only 13 per cent only painted and cleaned but had made no major repairs. Typical renovations cost between $2000 and $3000 — about a third of the purchase price of the dwellings. Tenant purchasers and southern European buyers also made repairs, but the value of these was far less. In 1966, there was one official building application for renovation for every fifty houses in Paddington; by then, many other houses had already been rehabilitated or were being improved without permits.

The number of major alterations and additions throughout the inner suburbs started to increase sharply from the late 1960s onwards (Figure 7.3). In Surry Hills, levels of renovation by 1970 were as extensive as those in Paddington in the mid 1960s (Ogilvie, 1969:55-6). Even in Redfern, an area that attracted few middle-class residents, many houses were renovated (Neutze, 1972:109) or reconverted from multiple to single occupancy (compare Maps 7.1, 7.2 and 7.3). Although improvement was most intense in areas of middle-class invasion, established migrants and working-class families in other areas were also making substantial, if less visible, improvements.

In Paddington, and probably elsewhere in the inner city, the renovations were made almost entirely by owner-occupants during the early years. The market was too uncertain for renovation by investors for either sale or rent. Banks were reluctant to give loans in former slum areas and many renovators used their own funds, or borrowed at high interest rates. Despite doubts about future market values, owners were conscious of investment values. Roseth (1969) reported that four-fifths of the renovators in Paddington expected property-value increases by at least as much as was spent on improvements. By the mid 1960s, the steadily rising property values made it easier to borrow for renovations (p. 227) and renovation by landlords and speculative purchasers increased (p. 110).

The heightened demand of middle-class purchasers, together with the housing improvements, considerably raised sale prices of houses. Although prices in Redfern and Paddington were similar up to 1960, during the next five years they rose by 207 per cent in Paddington (p. 207) compared to 67 per cent in Redfern (Neutze, 1972:110). The relatively rapid price-rises in all inner areas, and higher interest rates, meant that fewer low-income people could buy them. The number of years of average earnings needed to buy an average house rose in Redfern from 2.0 in 1960 to 2.5 in 1967, and by much more in Paddington. Low-income owners were not forced out and many made capital gains. Although owner-occupancy rates did not rise, there were some rented houses sold and the tenants, seldom protected by rent control, were forced out.

Rising house-values also made redevelopment increasingly less attractive than renovation. In Redfern, figures from the Valuer-General show that from 1963 to 1969 the value of the houses, despite their age and condition, rose faster than the value of their sites. The improvements in and growing popularity of the areas provide part of the answer. Another explanation is that redevelopment potential was limited by the costs of amalgamating the small sites.

The main difficulty for low-income tenants was the rising demand for and diminishing stock of rented houses in the inner suburbs. As house prices and interest rates rose relative to earnings throughout the metropolis, more families were forced to rent. Many young students and white-collar workers rented houses instead of flats, by forming groups that jointly could better afford to pay high rents. These demands made it profitable for landlords to improve their premises and to increase rents. For example, a group of old terrace houses in Redfern were renovated at a capital cost that could be recouped by higher rents within only eighteen months (Vandermark & Harrison 1972:23). These renovations and rent rises, and amalgamations of formerly subdivided houses, undoubtedly dislocated a number of tenants.

All the inner LGAs had sizeable increases in house rents, greater than those outside the inner suburbs. The rises were especially sharp in Leichhardt LGA, which contains such increasingly popular suburbs as Balmain and Glebe. Inner-suburban house rents remained at about 18 per cent of average male weekly earnings, despite sizeable increase of real incomes and slight falls in the percentage of earnings paid in rent in the rest of the metropolis. Even if existing tenants were not directly displaced, they were forced to pay more for the increasingly popular and scarce rented houses.

Gentrification has also wrought major changes in inner Melbourne. Although having more timber housing — a factor encouraging redevelopment rather than renovation — the City of Melbourne in particular had a well-planned system of wide streets and parks that enhanced its residential potential. A major reason why gentrification was slower in Melbourne was the very real threat up until the early 1970s of redevelopment by the Victorian Housing Commission, even in the more attractive inner areas.

The first areas to be gentrified in inner Melbourne were generally near middle-class employment centres, like East Melbourne near the CBD, and Parkville and Carlton near the University and hospitals. Nodes of better housing in elevated areas, frequently built initially for professionals and which subsequently 'filtered down', have also been at the fore of the gentrification process. More than in Sydney, the rejuvenation started from particularly attractive streets and then spread outwards. During the late 1960s, almost all suburbs in the City of Melbourne had increasing numbers of middle-class residents in old houses (VCOSS, 1975:45-6). Even the working-class, industrial areas of Port Melbourne had a small but growing invasion of young, white-collar workers (City of Melbourne, 1974).

Public policy had relatively little influence in the rejuvenation of inner suburbs. Although zoning had limited incursion by non-residential uses, market pressures explain the small amount of intrusion by flats in these areas. Indeed, policies designed to preserve and improve these areas generally came after the gentrification process had been firmly established. For example, Paddington was zoned as a conservation area in 1968, ten years after the middle class started to move in. The successful fight against road expansion in Paddington and Leichhardt, and against flats in Centennial Park, also occurred only after the vocal middle classes had arrived. Evidence of these new political pressures is reflected in the fact that the proportion of new Paddington owner-occupants that were concerned about flats destroying the character of the area was about two-thirds for both the white-collar workers and the Australian-born but only one-third for both the blue-collar workers and the European-born (Roseth, 1969:204). Local government policies may have been encouraging gentrification but they have not been the main cause.

Private Flats

The net increase of more than 22 000 private flats in inner Sydney was one of the most important residential developments of the 1960s (Table 7.3). Although conversions of houses to flats increased from the 1950s levels (Figure 7.3), more than 90 per cent were newly constructed. Because they were generally small and of only modest quality, the rents of inner-suburban flats were becoming much cheaper relative to both average earnings and private house rents.

The boom in flats occurred for some of the same reasons as gentrification did, although the former was not an entirely new phenomenon. Rising incomes enabled many people — especially the rising number of Sydney's young adults (Figure 8.1) — to maintain their own households. Relaxation of rent control, and the shortage of rental accommodation that it had caused, were perhaps equally important contributing factors. The inner areas attracted a quarter of the metropolitan increase of flats — the developers' response to the increasing demand for housing near the jobs and services of the city. The availability of under-utilised land in the inner suburbs was another important factor. While local govenment had discretionary powers over approval for development, there was little restraint on the building of flats. The building regulations permitted generous numbers of small flats to be built on minimal lots with very little parking and open space. Many local councils approved of flat-building in the inner suburbs because it could replace deteriorated houses, increase populations, raise values and increase the revenue from local property taxes. More importantly, most property owners opposed any constraints on their ability to make profitable sales. It was not until the 1970s that some local councils and their rate-payers had second thoughts.

In contrast to the earlier years, private development of flats during the 1960s was fairly widespread (Map 8.5). North Sydney LGA developed 6000 flats, which was a third of the total number for the inner area and three times as many as during the 1950s. The reasons remained much the same: harbour views, north-shore status and the availability of relatively large sites. To the west, in Wollstonecraft, the flats were near the railway station, minutes from the CBD. By 1971, flats outnumbered houses throughout North Sydney by two to one. North Sydney flats remained on average more expensive than those of any other inner LGAs.

Marrickville also had many more flats built during the 1960s. Most were in the far southwest, on large house sites that were near railway stations and parklands and protected from industry. Other areas of flat-building in Marrickville had many of the same advantages. Although Leichhardt had considerable residential attractions and plenty of old, weatherboard houses for redevelopment, it saw much less, far more scattered, flat development; the dense buildings on small parcels were expensive to acquire and amalgamate. In both Marrickville and Leichhardt, more than 10 per cent of the new flats of the 1960s were actually converted from another residential use, mostly shared houses.

Botany, which had only a few hundred flats in 1961, had more than 3000 new ones built privately by 1971, largely because of the availability of large tracts of vacant land. About 1000 were built on the site of the former Rosebery

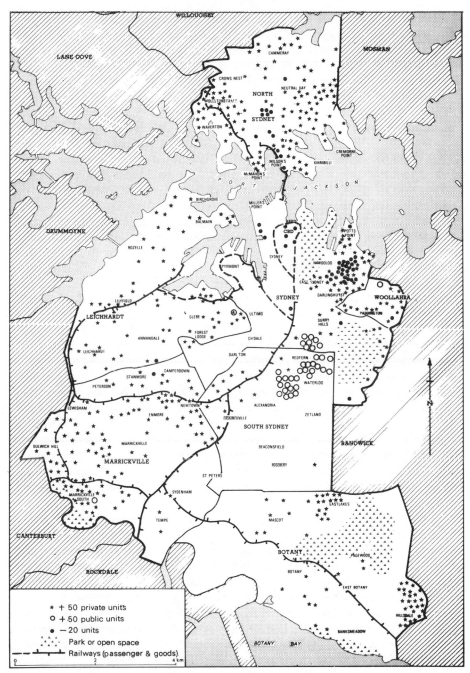

MAP 8.5.   Changes in distribution of self-contained flats in inner Sydney, 1961-71
Source: Based on analysis of unpublished 'CD' Census data, 1961 and 1971.

racecourse. Another 1500 were built in Hillsdale, mostly on land that had been kept vacant in the hope of eventual industrial development. Once the residential zoning of these areas was assured, the accessibility attracted the development of walk-up flats, despite the nearby heavy industry. Although they were of modest quality, they were new and relatively large, and therefore their average rents in 1971 almost equalled those in North Sydney.

Closer to the city centre, Potts Point had large parcels and sufficient amenities to warrant the construction of high-rise blocks which could overcome high land costs. Within the less expensive, southern part of the CBD, a few large, expensive home-unit complexes were built, most notable the thirty-seven-storey Park Regis development. The transitional areas east of the CBD had considerable gains as older hotels were converted to small, bedsitter flats.

Relatively few flats were built in areas of terrace housing. Of those that were, most were high-density, walk-up blocks of very small flats, located in particular areas where land was relatively easily assembled. For example, in Paddington almost all the construction of flats took place on parcels of vacant land (Roseth, 1969:129). In addition to scattered new construction, these areas continued to have conversions of relatively large houses, on those sites too small for flat redevelopment, into two or more flats (Vandermark & Harrison, 1972:26).

Private development of flats near the city centre was restrained mainly by high land values, although lack of residential amenity was also important. Data from inner Melbourne show that, as a land use, flats at that time competed poorly with both manufacturing and terrace housing (URU, 1973:21). In North Melbourne, the value of sites used for manufacturing in 1961 was 60 per cent higher than those used for flats. Moreover, there were few opportunities for infill in areas of terrace housing, and redevelopment was very expensive. Usually several parcels of land had to be amalgamated in order to accommodate new blocks of any size. Site values per square metre for small houses in North Melbourne were roughly comparable to those of flats a bit farther out in St Kilda. Finally, terrace houses were valued for their own sake and covered more of their sites than detached houses.

It is difficult to know how many residential buildings were demolished to make way for the building of flats. However, estimates can be made by examining changes in the number of different types of housing in areas where most of the private flat-building took place from 1961 to 1971 (Table 8.1). These were CDs with a net increase of twenty-five or more flats and total increases of both dwellings and population; areas of public redevelopment were excluded. Three-quarters of inner Sydney's privated flat-building during the 1960s was in these areas. Unexpectedly, they also had an increase of a thousand houses. Losses of houses due to the incursion of flats was more than offset by new construction and conversion. Shared houses (counted as non-self-contained flats) and boarding houses (non-private dwellings) were converted back to single occupation.

Making some assumptions, it can be crudely estimated that an average of

TABLE 8.1   *Estimated housing changes in inner Sydney CDs having private development of flats, 1961-71.*

LGA[a]	Housing types (net change)					Est. flat gains per res. building lost.[b]
	Houses	s.c.flats	n.s.c.flats	Non-private	Total	
Sydney	+115	+2324	-173	-175	+2091	9
North Sydney	+142	+4634	-392	-122	+4262	16
Leichhardt	+195	+791	-246	-23	+717	7
Marrickville	+435	+3714	-882	-172	+3095	12
Botany	+113	+3928	-134	-17	+3890	30
Total	+1000	+15391	-1827	-509	+14055	17

[a] Local government areas are for pre-1968 boundaries.
[b] See text and Note 3 for method of estimation and criteria for *CDs* covered.
Source: Based on analysis of unpublished *CD* data of Censuses 1961 and 1971.

one existing building was taken for every seventeen new, inner-area flats.[3] If this average applied for all additional private flats built during the 1960s, then about 1300 existing residential buildings were either redeveloped or converted for this purpose. Even allowing wide margins for error, it is clear that private development of flats was responsible for the loss of a considerably smaller number of houses than either business or industrial incursion.

One reason why losses were relatively small was that the regulations for flats required little parking or open space and sites could therefore be used more intensively. A two-storey building of twelve single-bedroom and two-bedroom flats could fit on the 45-by-15 metre site of an old dilapidated cottage in Redfern (Vandermark & Harrison 1972:36). In St Kilda in inner Melbourne, and in Randwick in eastern Sydney, two-to four-storey buildings provided ten to fifteen new flats on single-house sites (URU, 1973:55; Neutze, 1971b:11). Similar figures have been reported in an Australia-wide study (Department of Housing, 1968:15). High-rise flats, mostly in better areas and with larger sites, probably yielded a far higher ratio of new flats per old house demolished; areas where conversions predominated probably had far lower ratios.

Another explanation was the availability of vacant or underdeveloped land. Some developers used industrial land with minimal buildings in residential zones (Neutze, 1971b:33; 1972:119). Others took houses on large, awkward sites, or else the combination of a single house and the backyards of adjacent properties. Developers could frequently use these kinds of sites and councils were complacent because only one or two house sites were needed and owners were willing to make profitable sales.

These various ways of finding and using sites explains why the number of new flats per house demolished varied considerably between different inner areas. At one extreme, there were only seven new flats per dwelling lost in Leichhardt. This LGA had very dense existing housing, few opportunities for infill, and many conversions of houses to flats. Despite having many of the same limits, the city of Sydney had fewer dwellings lost per flat because of more high-rise construction and conversions of a few old hotels into many bedsitter flats. Marrickville, and more especially, North Sydney, gained considerably more flats per dwelling lost because the land parcels available were larger. The ratios were higher in North Sydney because of the intensive development and, in Botany, because of the extensive use of vacant land.

That private flats took relatively few houses has a number of implications. First, flat construction could not have replaced much deteriorated housing — one goal of the Cumberland County Plan. In fact, of the dwellings that were taken, most were probably sound, owner-occupied structures on large land parcels in areas of high amenity. Second, profitability was so sensitive to the cost of purchasing existing houses that relatively few people were displaced compared to the number housed in the new flats.

Enough housing to accommodate about 5000 people was lost to private development of flats. Of these, many were probably owner-occupants who willingly made profitable sales. A few were undoubtedly poor tenants who were forced out, especially in the innnermorst areas like Redfern (Vandermark & Harrison, 1972:38), but the population change caused by flat development, shown on Table 8.2, depended more on the tens of thousands of people who moved into the new units. Other influences on the population change in these areas were the declining occupancy rates and the invasion of migrants into the remaining houses. The latter tended to lower socio-economic status and increase the numbers of children in the area.

TABLE 8.2   *Population change in inner-Sydney CDs having private development of flats, 1961-71*

	Population Selected age groups				Labour-force Selected industries		
	Total	0-15	20.34	65+	Total	Manuf.	Fin. & Prop.
1961	102 968	18 653	22 085	13 045	51 926	18 763	2 149
Change:							
1961-71	+28 741	+7 543	+15 526	+550	+16 235	+1 032	+4 862
% change	+28	+40	+70	+4	+31	+6	+226

See text and Note 3 for the criteria for CDs covered.
Source: Based on analysis of unpublished CD Census data, 1961 and 1971.

The areas most affected by the development of flats had a very large net population increase, approaching 30 000 people, despite declining occupancy rates in the houses. As expected, the increases were greatest for young adults and for workers in the higher-status finance and property industries. However, the number of children also increased in areas of flat development in all LGAs except North Sydney. Although much of this was due to child-bearing by migrants in nearby houses, children also increased in areas of flats that had stable or falling migrant populations. Similarly, the number of manufacturing workers in these areas increased slightly (mainly because of the large gains in Botany), even though the inner city as a whole lost manufacturing workers. The boom in flats contributed mostly to increases in numbers of young, white-collar workers, but it also provided housing for blue-collar workers with children and appears to have displaced few of them.

Non-self-contained Flats and Non-private Dwellings

The number of inner-suburban dwellings subdivided or used for multiple occupancy dropped sharply during the 1960s (Table 7.3). From 1961 to 1966 alone, the number of shared houses was halved and the number of non-private dwellings was reduced to one-third. During the late 1960s, there were further losses of non-self-contained flats. Chapter 5 showed that the losses of these dwellings, and reduced numbers of people in those that remainded, were the major components of the population losses of the inner suburbs during the 1960s.

A possible reason for losses of these dwellings is commercial encroachment, as predicted by the ecological succession developed in the zonal model. In fact, most of those lost were in the old, transitional areas near the CBD (Maps 8.2, 8.3). However, the majority, even in these areas, were apparently converted back to less intense residential uses. Many were converted to use as single-family houses, and many old hotels and boarding houses were let as single rooms. These areas were 'filtering up' from the innermost areas outwards. Although the overall demand for inner-city houses was rising, the demand for cheap housing was falling. Fewer people needed such minimal housing because of the increased affluence of the young adults, and the greater availability of flats. As part of the general housing improvement, many people wanting transitory accommodation were living in flats instead of subdivided houses. Those seeking single rooms could, as a group, outbid ordinary families wanting a dwelling for use as a single residence.

Vacancy Rates

Unlike most indicators of the housing market, rising vacancy rates — 7 per cent in 1961 to 10 per cent in 1971 — could suggest a weakening of demand. However, the 1971 Census figures (Table 8.3) provide no support for this interpretation. A third of the vacant dwellings had occupants who were only temporarily away, for work or holiday purposes. This was probably a substantial component of the

TABLE 8.3   *Reasons given for vacancies of various types of dwellings in Sydney, 1971 (percentage of total dwellings of each type)* [a]

Dwelling type and area	Reason for vacancy					Total
	Sale/ To let	New	Under repair	Temp- orary absence	Other/ Not stated	
Houses						
City of Sydney [b]	3.0	-	2.0	2.8	4.8	12.7
Inner area	1.7	.1	1.1	2.1	2.0	6.9
Metro.	1.0	.4	.3	2.5	1.2	5.5
Flats						
City of Sydney [b]	6.5	.9	.7	6.0	2.5	16.6
Inner area	3.8	1.1	.4	3.7	1.2	10.2
Metro.	3.8	1.3	.3	3.2	1.0	9.7
Other Private [c]						
City of Sydney [b]	8.9	-	.3	3.8	1.9	14.8
Inner area	6.1	.2	.2	3.2	1.3	11.0
Metro.	4.4	.5	.3	2.8	1.1	9.2
Total [c]						
City of Sydney [b]	5.9	.4	1.0	4.5	3.1	15.0
Inner area	3.6	.6	.9	3.4	1.9	10.4
Metro.	1.8	.6	.3	2.0	1.1	5.9

[a] Figures on the percentage of total occupied and unoccupied dwellings.
[b] 1971 Sydney City boundaries.
[c] Excludes non-private dwellings.
Source: Census, 1971.

vacancy increase, as the number of young adults in white-collar jobs increased considerably during the 1960s. Of the rest, a fifth of the dwellings were either new and not yet occupied, or old and being repaired — both signs of strong demand. Less than 4 per cent of the total dwelling stock, well under half of the vacant stock, was vacant awaiting sale or rent. This is close to the minimum level necessary for normal turnover in highly transient areas. The remaining third of the vacant dwellings, where no reasons were given for vacancy, included units awaiting demolition or conversions. Inner-suburban vacancy rates were almost twice the metropolitan average, mainly because they had more of the rented dwellings that house people who move and travel frequently.

Vacancy rates in inner-area houses were fractionally higher than in other areas, possibly because the former had more vacant for 'other and not stated' reasons (which would include vacancy prior to non-residential incursion), and a higher proportion vacant for the reason they were 'under repair'. Less than 2 per cent of houses were vacant for sale or rent, despite the greater turnover among rented houses, and perhaps also among owner-occupied houses in inner areas. The City of Sydney had an especially high vacancy rate, because of even more frequent turnover, more alterations and additions, and more vacancy prior to non-residential incursion. Almost all the areas having vacancy rates of more than 15 per cent were either undergoing non-residential incursion, including Pyrmont, Woolloomooloo, Darlinghurst and Kings Cross, or were experiencing residential renovation, like Paddington and Glebe.

Less than 4 per cent of the inner-suburban flats were available for rent or sale, the same figure as for the rest of the metropolis. Although the City of Sydney (1971 boundaries) had very high vacancy rates for flats, less than 7 per cent were available for sale or rent. High turnover rates, many temporary absences and vacancies prior to redevelopment are again probable explanations, and the same reasons probably apply, to an even greater extent, to the vacancies in other private dwellings.

The New South Wales Housing Commission

Despite the considerable improvement of many inner-suburban houses, public redevelopment increased considerably during the 1960s. Of the gain of 3100 publicly owned dwellings (a 160 per cent increase), about two-thirds occurred in slum-clearance programmes. The New South Wales Housing Commission (NSWHC) was not entirely unaware of the extent of private rehabilitation, rising owner-occupancy, and other indications that few if any inner areas were still slums. It concentrated attention on the areas of very poor housing that had the least potential for renovation. The NSWHC also advocated clearance and high-rise construction with maximum number of dwellings in order to meet the long waiting list for inner-area public housing. Inner-area, high-density redevelopment was also advocated in order to make use of spare services capacity, to help reverse inner-area population losses and minimise urban sprawl, and to include improvements to streets and neighbourhood facilities.

The slum-clearance projects of the 1950s continued in Surry Hills, Redfern and Waterloo (Map 8.5). In the early 1960s, the NSWHC built 430 high-rise units in Surry Hills, 280 in Redfern and, a little later, 580 in Poet's Corner, Redfern. By 1971 nearly 800 more had been built, most in nearby Waterloo. Other developments were a number of smaller buildings in Glebe and Paddington, units for the aged throughout the inner suburbs, and 630 flats and aged persons' units on part of the former site of the Rosebery racecourse in Eastlakes. Virtually no houses were being built because of the high land costs in the inner areas.

The slum-clearance developments in the 1960s were built at very high densities, approaching 100 people per hectare. This was twice the existing density and four times that of the early NSWHC redevelopments. There were two major reasons for this policy change. First, acquisition costs had risen so much that, despite special state subsidies, clearance and low-density construction were no longer economic solutions. Second, the Commission acknowledged that private improvements, together with the destruction of much of the worst housing by non-residential incursion, had lessened the need for the clearance. A 1965 survey of property-value records showed that less than 4 per cent of the 128 hectares of sites examined in inner areas were actually 'ripe for redevelopment' (Jones,

1972:75). By the end of the 1960s the primary justification for inner-suburban redevelopment in Sydney had become the provision of additional, low-cost units to compensate for the losses caused by rising home ownership, private rehabilitation and redevelopment, and rising rents and prices.

From the second world war until 1970, the NSWHC had cleared 30.3 hectares of inner-suburban housing (Table 8.4). This was less than 1 per cent of the area that had been designated for clearance in 1948 by the Cumberland County Plan. The Commission took 1430 dwellings — about the same number taken by private development of flats during the 1960s. Because the public development aimed to·replace dilapidated old houses, it demolished one existing dwelling for every two-and-a-half new flats built, about eight times the ratio estimated for private development. Another difference was that public development provided a good deal of additional open space and community facilities. Of the 1800 displaced families, four-fifths were rehoused by the NSWHC. The Commission considerably increased ópportunities for low-to moderate-income people to live in the inner city. From 1961 to 1971, inner areas redeveloped by the Commission had a population increase of 85 per cent, over 9000 people. Moreover, the increase in the numbers of children (106 per cent) and the aged 82 per cent) shows that the most vulnerable life-cycle groups benefited as much as anybody. The labourforce increased at a slightly lower rate (78 per cent) than the total population because many children and pensioners were housed. These areas also had a 46 per cent increase of manufacturing workers, despite an overall loss of them throughout the inner city (partly as a result of a classification change). The Commission tenants in inner-area flats paid rents of only $9.58 per week in 1971,

TABLE 8.4   *Position at 30 June 1970 of NSW Housing Commission's slum-clearance programme for inner Sydney.*

Position	Red-fern	Water-loo	Surry Hills	Glebe	Padd-ington	North Sydney	Bal-main	Total
[Acreage of site]	[24.09]	[30.84]	[10]	[7]	[1.7]	[.33]	[.125]	[74.1]
Residential dwellings demolished	473	549	254	138	5	-	5	1 424
Shops demolished	48	17	6	2	-	-	-	73
Commercial buildings demolished	50	13	30	8	-	1 (hotel)	-	102
Dwellings erected, or to be erected by Commission	1 403	1 293	592	84	53	24	6	3 455
Families originally resident	665	689	288	162	5	3	11	1 823
Families re-housed by Commission	555	468	285	148	5	2	9	1 472
Families providing own accommodation	110	221	3	14	-	1	2	351

Source: NSWHC, *Annual Report*, Annexure F, 1970.

compared to rents of $20.84 paid for private flats. Public redevelopment in New South Wales has clearly brought substantial financial and locational advantages to thousands of poor and disadvantaged families.

The Victorian Housing Commission

Redevelopment by the New South Wales Housing Commission is modest when compared to the massive clearance programme of the Victorian Housing Commission.

The VHC had by 1970 cleared almost four times as much inner land (111 hectares), demolished two-and-a-half times as many existing houses (3788) and built two-and-a-half times as many new flats (8635) as had the NSWHC (Jones, 1972:72). Most of the VHC activity took place during the late 1960s, by which time the NSWHC had greatly reduced its slum-clearance programme. In 1970, replacement housing in clearance areas accounted for only 9 per cent of the metropolitan, public-housing buildings in New South Wales, but a startling 75 per cent in Victoria (Jones, 1972:72).

Unlike the medium density of some of the inner-Sydney developments, the VHC housing in inner Melbourne consisted almost entirely of massive high-rise flats, of concrete panel construction, made by the Commission's own factory for prefabricated concrete housing. Thirteen per cent of the VHC's slum-clearance areas were sold for expensive, private developments at only 44 per cent of the acquisition costs; the purpose was to remove slum housing and to increase inner-area populations. About 550 houses occupied by low-income people were demolished in these areas and population gains were small. By ordering the repair or demolition of sub-standard private housing, under the Housing Act of 1958, the VHC has further reduced the stock of poor-quality but low-cost inner housing. In sharp contrast to the NSWHC, the VHC, throughout the 1960s, believed that much of the inner areas were slums that must be replaced by high-density flats, regardless of the other effects.

These clearance activities have displaced, often harshly, more than 10 000 people. Most of the clearance took place during the late 1960s, when about two-thirds of the displaced were owner-occupants and half were migrants (Jones, 1972:81). Few owners or southern Europeans were willing to accept alternative accommodation from the Commission. Because of moving costs and the depressing effect of slum-clearance threats on market values, compensation at market values for their properties was seldom sufficient to secure comparable housing elsewhere. Many of the displaced people relocated considerable distances away from their old dwellings and their journeys to work lengthened accordingly (Holdsworth & Brooks, 1971). These inequities, the rising number of middle-income owners, and growing opposition to high-rise development, led to intense opposition to the clearance programmes. Since the late 1960s, the VHC programme has been blocked by court battles, black bans, opposition from local councils, residents refusing to obey eviction orders, and street demonstrations (Hargreaves, 1975).

The South Australian Housing Trust

In Adelaide there has been little public redevelopment, despite the fact that several reports of the 1960s had urged against the slums. O'Reilly reported that, by the early 1970s, there had been only very small redevelopments, such as in Parkside and Gilberton, which had displaced, in total, little more than a hundred old houses (1977:9). Most of the new units, built with the intention of replacing old housing without further urban sprawl, were walk-up flats. A proposal was made in 1968 to replace sixty-nine old houses and 150 residents in Hackney with high-density residential development to house 1000 people (Sandercock, 1975:136). However, a final decision on the project was delayed until the early 1970s.

In Adelaide the main device for dealing with poor housing has been the Housing Improvement Act, which enables the South Australian Housing Trust (SAHT) to apply rent controls or order demolitions for any dwellings considered substandard. Unlike the VHC's actions under similar legislation, the South Australian emphasis has been on advising owners on rehabilitating the structures, and therefore fewer have been demolished. Although the programme is sensitively administered, it is possible that it has nevertheless encouraged housing losses and rent rises that strain the budgets of the poor.

Summary

Since the early 1960s, residential demand in the inner suburbs has increased considerably. In the early years, many recently arrived southern European migrants were purchasing homes in inner areas. Especially in the late 1960s, more young, Australian-born, white-collar workers have rented flats, or rented houses or bought and renovated them in these areas. Rents and prices have risen faster in inner than in other areas. These trends have been reinforced by the continued centralisation of white-collar jobs and other city-centre attractions and the increasing cost and relative inaccessibility to the CBD of housing elsewhere in the metropolis. Despite the spontaneous improvements, the Housing Commissions, most notable the VHC, persisted in their slum-clearance programmes.

By almost any available measure, the inner suburbs have been 'filtering up' in a wave action moving from the innermost areas outwards. Unlike the 'filtering down' in the American inner city, owners could sell and make considerable capital gains, and owner-occupants were encouraged to stay in improved neighbourhoods. However, tenants were forced to pay higher rents or were otherwise induced to move. SATS data shows that, of the low-income people who moved from the inner suburbs of Sydney during the late 1960s, half moved to another inner-city location, 15 per cent moved to an outer suburb and the rest moved to middle suburbs. Few were forced to the fringe.

The problems of low-income tenants have been only partly relieved by the massive boom in flats, the provision of public housing, and some slight 'filtering down' in the middle suburbs. The inner-middle suburbs in both Sydney and Melbourne during the 1960s had relatively lower rent rises, smaller gains of upper-status white-collar workers, smaller losses of blue-collar workers, and gains of Greeks and Italians.[4] The rapid loss of non-self-contained flats and non-private dwellings suggests that the overall losses of the supply of low-cost housing resulted largely from decreasing demand for it. However, other changes of the inner-area housing stock have considerably dislocated or disadvantaged large numbers of poor tenants, very few of whom remained under the protection of rent control.

CHAPTER 9

Non-residential Development and Policies in the 1970s

This chapter, and the next, review inner-suburban developments in the recent past, and assess future prospects. Although earlier chapters have policy implications, these concluding ones make a number of explicit policy judgements and recommendations. These evaluations are made from a residential point of view and are based on two basic metropolitan-wide goals: (1) maintaining an adequate stock of low-cost housing of reasonable quality, and (2) minimising the difficulties of journeys to work and to urban facilities, especially for low-income households. It is assumed that both these goals would be furthered by the decentralisation of the growth of jobs and urban facilities to selected suburban nodes throughout the metropolis. This would reduce the losses of low-cost, inner-suburban housing and the dislocations of the poor, caused by redevelopment and by occupancy by higher-income households who want to live near jobs and services. Decentralisation could also ease the accessibility difficulties of people living in outer areas. These policy objectives will be especially important when the real price of petrol rises.

The issues of the 1970s should be viewed in the context of findings from the earlier chapters. During the post-war years, the inner suburbs have avoided the widespread decay of North American cities and have experienced considerable non-residential development. The total number of jobs increased by 25 per cent up to 1961, and the number of white-collar jobs, especially in government, continued to increase during the 1960s. The expansion of non-residential uses had by 1971 taken more than 15 000 dwellings, occupied mostly by people on low incomes. Most of these losses were caused by commercial and industrial development, although incursion by public institutions and roads have also been important.

During the early 1970s, inner-suburban, non-residential development followed, but at a slower rate, the patterns of the 1960s. Since 1974, the growth of commerce and industry has virtually stopped in inner Sydney and inner Melbourne. In manufacturing industry at least, employment has fallen dramatically. This chapter argues that the current malaise in commerce and industry in inner areas has resulted more from the economic downturn than from suburbanisation. Although the impetus for urban growth has diminished, there already is a large centralisation of inner-area jobs. If the economy improves, there will be renewed pressure for non-residential development. This could increase the number of jobs and take many of the several thousand homes remaining in areas in inner Sydney zoned for non-residential uses in 1971.

Office Development

The office boom extended into the mid 1970s. Although completion of office buildings will continue into the 1980s, there have been few projects commenced since 1974, because of the oversupply that emerged around then and the slow growth of jobs during the current economic recession. The amount of vacant office space in the Sydney CBD rose from 200 000 square metres in 1971, to 929 000 in 1976 with 420 000 square metres more were then being built (City of Sydney, 1978). Oversupply also is apparent in North Sydney and in the Melbourne CBD. City-centre property values fell in Sydney by 25 per cent in 1976 and then by another 25 per cent in 1977 (City of Sydney, 1977). The collapse of the CBD office boom did not result from decentralisation; almost 90 per cent of Sydney's investment in office accommodation in 1975 was still in the inner city.

In order to attract the votes of residents, the Sydney City Council has claimed credit for the decline of CBD development (City of Sydney, 1977:10). The 1971 Plan, which reduced allowable floor-space ratios and limited the CBD spread, limited incursion into residential areas but allowed for almost a 100 per cent increase of CBD employment (City of Sydney, 1971:82). The Strategy Plan released for the 1974 City Council elections called for further constraints but suggested a preferred CBD development from 1974 to 1985 of 700 000 square metres more office space and 31 per cent more employment (City of Sydney, 1974*b*:18). After the election, even these modest constraints were dropped. Proposals that do not conform to the Plan have been approved, and consideration is being given to the 'Boulevard' scheme for more offices along Oxford Street. The 1972-5 federal Labor government's plans for office decentralisation, which included a major Commonwealth office centre at Parramatta, have lapsed and neither the Labor state government nor the Liberal federal government has any dispersal programme. In 1976, the main occupiers of office space in the CBD were still government (City of Sydney, 1978).

Office development elsewhere in inner Sydney has been controlled. The New South Wales government's massive 'Rocks' plan (discussed in Chapter 6) was halted by a Builders Labourers Federation (BLF) 'green ban' until the plans were modified to reduce the commercial development, to preserve historic buildings and to provide government housing. In Woolloomooloo, intense office development was thwarted by a BLF green ban and opposition from all levels of government. In 1975, a tripartite agreement was reached between the city, state and federal governments. The plan provided for residential renovation and redevelopment by the Housing Commmssion (discussed in Chapter 10). Finally, an 'anti-development' Council in North Sydney, elected in 1972, stopped earlier redevelopment plans (discussed in Chapter 6) and sharply reduced permissable development in the commercial centre at Milsons Point and in old mixed-use areas like McMahons Point.

The City of Sydney has recently been limiting non-residential development outside the CBD by zoning some areas for residential uses. In the more developed areas east of the CBD, the residential zoning prohibits office building but still allows other activities that displace residences and provide jobs. These areas have experienced steady incursion, especially in the early 1970s, often by small professional offices, boutiques, and other commercial uses that can use existing houses. Similarly, old terraces in The Rocks area are being converted to non-residential use (City of Sydney, 1976*b*:18). In the residential zones in other parts of the city, these uses are prohibited (City of Sydney, 1976*a*) but incursion and job growth has still occurred. There is little opposition to these housing losses because the appearance and amenities of the areas seldom change, diversity is increased and property values rise. Recent action plans have proposed more stringent controls, but enforcement will be difficult.

Changes of rating policies, a topic of considerable controversy, are unlikely to affect the kind or location of inner-suburban development, because rates are low and vary little between LGAs (Woodruff & Ecker-Racz, 1969:173). Nonetheless, there are strong arguments for shifting the rate burden more toward non-residential users. They have a greater capacity to pay and if they paid more, the councils could ameliorate more of the traffic and pollution problems they generate. Also, the costs of rates, especially on residential property in areas zoned for higher uses, are often borne by aged home-owners or passed on to low-income renters.[1] For these reasons, the City of Sydney in 1977 proposed differential rating for non-residential properties. Since rates in Sydney are based on unimproved values, down-zoning (reducing the permitted development potential) would further lower the liability of those living in non-residential zones. Rate burdens on residents could also be eased by taxing state and Commonwealth government properties and by seeking state payment for city services used by the entire metropolis (Anglim *et al.*, 1975).

Few controls have been placed on office development in Melbourne. The Melbourne Strategy Plan (City of Melbourne, 1974), adopted in a modified form in 1978, sought to limit high-density offices to the CBD. However, the Council has been reluctant to enforce the plans, claiming that property-owners could seek compensation for lost development potential (Bayne, 1977). Contrary to the 1974 plan, the City Planner in 1977 recommended that offices should be allowed in mixed-use areas, containing a considerable number of dwellings, on the CBD fringe and along St Kilda Road and Royal Parade (Ogilvy, 1977). Amendment 96 to the Melbourne and Metropolitan Planning Scheme, on exhibition in 1978, would permit this development. Similarly, a June 1976 Interim Development Order, requiring Council approval for CBD demolitions, was dropped within five months. Plans for the decentralisation from the CBD of some Commonwealth office workers to suburban centres were abandoned after the change of federal government in 1975. The nearby St

Kilda Council has been encouraging redevelopment of dwellings for high-density offices along High Street (CURA, 1977: 45-7).

In Adelaide, the office building boom was more modest and has declined far less. Moreover, office development in central areas probably presents fewer commuting problems and generates less additional competition for inner-suburban housing than in the larger cities. If governmental policy were able to keep the offices in Adelaide from further spill-over from the CBD, this would limit the incursion of offices into nearby housing and would encourage the use of public transport. The South Australian Labor government supports office centralisation and in 1972 had established the City of Adelaide Development Committee, which had representatives from both the state government and the local council, to control major development. In sharp contrast to earlier policies of the City Council, the Committee firmly stated that 'Land in residential use, or whose last use was residential, may not be made over to other uses, except where no possibility exists of restoring a tolerable residential environment' (City of Adelaide Development Committee, 1972:9).

Outside of the city centre, large houses in areas zoned for medium density residential development have been converted to offices (Lewis, 1977:9). Additional houses along major arterial roads have been redeveloped or converted for use for commercial purposes. From 1971 to 1976, inner Adelaide had a loss of 380 dwellings in CDs zoned primarily for non-residential uses (Lewis, 1978:7). Although all local councils in inner Adelaide had adopted planning schemes during the early 1970s, those outside the City still were allowing, either through consent or lack of enforcement, small amounts of commercial incursion into residential areas.

In summary, private developers, with scant regard for substantive demand, have created an oversupply of office building in the inner areas. Recently imposed planning restrictions limit allowable incursion but will do little to limit further growth of office jobs in inner areas whenever the demand for more office space again develops. If the large metropolitan areas are to achieve the benefits of more decentralisation, the allowable areas and densities for office development should be further reduced, and infrastructure should be provided for them in suburban centres (Alexander, 1978). However, there would be intense opposition from property interests; the only feasible policies would probably be to limit incursion in CBD fringe areas but not to reduce the total amount of office space permitted. Decentralisation of government office-workers is possibly the only feasible way to offset some of the problems of any further increase of non-government office-workers.

Industrial Development

Since 1971, inner industrial areas have continued to decline in most respects but generally remain valuable and important. Prices of industrial sites in inner Sydney rose more slowly than those in outer areas during the early 1970s, and have declined slightly since the economic downturn in 1974 (PLI, 1976:142;

AIUS, 1975:61). Nonetheless, land prices per square metre in inner Sydney and inner Melbourne in the mid-1970s still were about twice those in middle suburbs and three or more times those in outer areas (AIUS, 1975:88; 1977:5). The little evidence available suggests that few inner-city firms want to relocate (City of Sydney, 1976a:13-18). There has been continued industrial incursion, including in Sydney, the expansion of Colonial Sugar Refinery in Pyrmont and textile factories in Surry Hills. The claims of 'blighted' and abandoned industrial land (for example, Quinn, 1974:31) have been contradicted by surveys showing little vacant industrial land in inner Sydney or inner Melbourne (EHCD, Studies Bureau, 1976b; AIUS, 1975, 1977). The most extensive and recent study of inner-area industrial land (PLI, 1976:157) concluded that 'there is ample evidence that inner Sydney still attracts new enterprise. Its relative decline in the expanding metropolitan milieu, and short term fluctuations in demand, should not be allowed to obscure operation of broadly industrial economic activity'.

In the future, there will probably be renewed pressure for industrial incursion into housing in areas zoned for residential uses, despite the decline in manufacturing. Offices and related services have been increasingly trying to locate in old industrial areas like McMahons Point in North Sydney and Surry Hills in the City of Sydney. Transport and storage activities, which already use a third of the zoned industrial land, will probably expand when the new port in Botany is established and if the airport is upgraded (Kendig, 1976c). Under the planning schemes in effect in 1971, at least 1500 dwellings in inner areas were zoned for industrial use. Similarly, in inner Adelaide, a quarter of the industrially zoned land is still used for housing (Lewis, 1977:9).

To limit further incursion, local councils have recently been reconsidering their previous policies of allowing industrial expansion into housing areas in the industrial zones. For example, the 1974 Botany plan rezoned a substantial area from industrial to residential use and the South Sydney Council in 1975 determined to rezone to residential use small pockets of dwellings in the industrial zone. Similarly, the City of Sydney's Action Plan for Surry Hills, approved as an interim development order in 1976, has rezoned some housing areas from industrial to residential uses. The housing in these areas provides an important pool of low-cost housing.

If further increases of employment in the inner city are to be prevented, offices in industrial areas would have to be discouraged even when no housing is taken, for example, the proposed development of a fifty-storey office block on the old Toohey's brewery site in Surry Hills. Moreover, as is discussed in the section on the development of flats in the next chapter, rezoning selected industrial sites to residential uses could encourage the growth of the inner-suburban housing stock.

Road development

In the early 1970s massive freeway systems were proposed for Sydney, Melbourne and Adelaide. In Sydney, a major study reaffirmed the need for the radial freeways (SATS, 1974), and the New South Wales Department of Main Roads (DMR) made a number of acquisitions for inner-area roadworks (shown on Map 6.3). The Kings Cross Tunnel took about 800 dwellings (about a hundred properties), mostly old, low-rent tenements housing about 1200 people. To make way for the Northwestern Freeway, the DMR acquired about sixty dwellings in Pyrmont and eighty in Glebe. By late 1977, about ninety of them had been demolished, thirty were derelict and twenty were occupied by either squatters or people renting from the DMR. About 170 additional dwellings, mostly flats and rooming houses, accommodating about 400 people, were acquired for the William Street Underpass for the eastern distributor road just east of the CBD. Thirty or so of the dwellings have been demolished and most are empty and derelict.

Opposition has mounted as the DMR began these acquisitions. Since 1972 there have been bitter demonstrations and black bans by the Builders Labourer's Federation against the Northwestern Freeway and the eastern distributor. The Leichhardt Council has protested strongly against both the Northwestern and Western Freeways and the Sydney City Council's action plans have advocated road widenings and upgrading of arterial roads rather than construction of freeways. The federal Labor government also opposed inner-city freeways. A Commonwealth Bureau of Roads report (1973) argued against inner-city freeways and the federal government threatened to withhold a $43 million road grant from the DMR unless the demolition for the Northeastern Freeway were halted. The federal government also bought 700 houses for rehabilitation in Glebe that were in the path of the western distributor (Chapter 10).

As a result of these various pressures, the New South Wales Urban Transport Advisory Committee (1976) made recommendations against the proposed inner-area freeways, except for short sections of the eastern distributor and Northeastern Freeway. The newly elected New South Wales Labor government accepted these proposals late in 1976 and postponed a decision on the Northwestern Freeway. The eastern distributor, which is still planned between Bourke and Palmer Streets, would require the demolition of 300 dwellings. Recent amendments to the proposed widening of King Street, Newtown, would take several hundred homes along the railroad lines. Opposition to these proposals remains intense.

In Melbourne, the 1969 freeway plans also aroused widespread opposition. Just before the 1972 state elections, the Liberal premier announced the abandonment of the inner-city parts of the plan (Sandercock, 1975:159). The housing taken by road development in the inner areas thus far has resulted from road widenings, such as Hoddle Street in Collingwood and High Street in St Kilda. There is a good deal of controversy surrounding the F.19 Eastern Freeway, which bisects the community of Fitzroy, and adds to local through traffic without destroying dwellings (CURA, 1977). The biggest transport development in Melbourne, the $800-million-dollar underground railway loop project, could ease accessibility problems to the CBD — and thus reduce through car traffic and housing competition in the inner suburbs. However, given the current lack of firm planning controls on office development, the rail loop will probably encourage further central growth and incursion by non-residential uses. The Westgate Bridge may also encourage more non-residential development and will increase road traffic in inner suburban residential areas.

In Adelaide, the freeway proposals of the 1960s were drastically cut back in 1971 by the new state Labor government. In Hindmarsh, the planned hub of the proposed highway system, the Highways Department in 1975 still owned 5 per cent of the land (most of which was used or zoned for industry) and was buying more; by 1978, it had bought 170 dwellings in the area, fifty of which have been demolished. The Highways Department in 1978 owned 800 dwellings throughout Adelaide, many of which are in the inner suburbs. A large proportion of these are under-maintained and others have been demolished. The Adelaide City Council also has acquired several hundred dwellings for road widenings: but some plans have been dropped and houses have been sold by the Council to the Housing Trust for rehabilitation or redevelopment. Although plans for the North/South Freeway are still being considered, it is unlikely that much inner-area housing will be taken for roads in the foreseeable future.

The future demand for inner-suburban freeways can be limited by limiting the number of inner-city jobs. Better transport to the inner city for the existing jobs can be provided by rail and buses, which also serve those who do not own or use cars. From a residential point of view, there still is a strong case for improving the arterial road systems, even if road widenings take some housing, because the diversion of traffic can improve residential areas. Better environmental traffic management of existing streets could also improve access, with only beneficial effects for inner-suburban housing.

Public Institutions

The expansion of public facilities remains a major threat to inner-area housing, especially in inner Sydney. Proposals for further expansion by Sydney University have faced local protests, a moratorium imposed by the Australian Universities Commission, and opposition by both the City of Sydney and South Sydney Councils. However, the University has continued to purchase land outside the approved expansion area, using unrestricted funds from its investments and private donations. A total of 300 additional dwellings would be taken if the state Minister for Planning and Environment approves an extension of the special-use area in Darlington.

In the same area, Sydney Teachers College had planned to take 300 dwellings (City of Sydney Resident Action Group Committee, 1977:16). Opposition from local residents and the City Council has at least temporarily stopped the plans but the College still owns properties in the proposed expansion area. If the developments planned for the Sydney Technical College and the New South Wales Institute of Technology proceed, the number of tertiary students in the

City of Sydney could rise from 65 000 in 1971 to 80 000 by 1990 (City of Sydney, 1974*b*:50).

Hospitals are also expanding and taking inner-area houses. Many of the hundreds of acquisitions shown on Map 6.3 took place in the 1970s. The Royal Prince Alfred and St Vincents Hospitals own adjacent properties and together they have plans to take 175 more dwellings. Only the few houses used as clinics under the Community Health Programme have provided direct benefits exclusively to inner-suburban residents.

Further expansion of these central-city institutions would take housing and bring in students and workers who drive up housing costs; few of them provide unique services to the entire metropolis, which is the primary justification for central locations. Decentralisation of any further grcwth of these facilities would preserve housing and improve accessibility elsewhere in the metropolis.

Employment Availability

Changes of total employment in inner areas during the 1970s will not be known until the 1976 Census results become available. However, planning authorities in Sydney and Melbourne have estimated that the number of inner-area jobs has probably remained stable or has fallen slightly since 1971. Employment in the CBD has probably fallen slightly while, elsewhere in the inner city, large losses of manufacturing jobs have probably been offset by small gains for office, transport and service workers. Since inner-suburban populations have fallen rapidly (Chapter 10), the number of inner-city jobs per resident worker has almost certainly increased.

Table 9.1 shows that factory jobs in inner Sydney and inner Melbourne fell by about a quarter from 1969 to 1975. This acceleration of losses since the 1960s has resulted from continued decline of manufacturing up to 1974, and then more

TABLE 9.1   *Manufacturing jobs in Sydney and Melbourne 1968-75   (in thousands).*

Area	1968/9	1973/4	1974/5	1968-74 change no.	1968-74 change %	1974-75 change no.	1974-75 change %
Sydney							
Inner[a]	145.5	122.5	109.1	−23.1	−15.9	−13.4	−10.9
Metro.	389.1	387.3	357.9	−1.8	0	−29.4	−7.6
Melbourne							
Inner[b]	84.4	71.9	64.4	−12.5	−14.8	−7.5	−10.4
Metro.	369.8	398.8	370.3	+29.0	+7.8	−28.5	−7.2

[a] Inner Sydney: Sydney, South Sydney, Leichhardt and Marrickville.
[b] Inner Melbourne: Melbourne, Fitzroy, Collingwood and Richmond.
Source: Unpublished data supplied by Godfrey Linge ANU. (The published figures are not comparable over time because firms having fewer than four employees were not included in 1974-75).

losses were caused by the recession and tariff changes. There was probably little movement of these jobs outwards, because there was very little growth elsewhere in the metropolis. In the inner areas more industries declined (clothing, footwear, paper products), more old industrial plants closed as a result of company rationalisation, and there was almost no land cheap enough to attract what little new industry there was. Adelaide had very small losses in inner areas and more growth in outer areas.

The losses of inner-suburban, blue-collar jobs partly explains the high unemployment rates in inner Sydney shown in Table 9.2. The trends were similar in Melbourne; but inner Adelaide, which has fewer low-skilled workers, did not experience any disproportionately large losses of manufacturing jobs compared to other parts of the metropolis. As during the 1961 recession, the inner areas in Sydney and Melbourne had disproportionately large shares of the unemployed probably because these areas house so many low-skilled workers. It is this overall loss of low-skilled jobs, rather than movement to outer areas, which explains the problem of unemployment. Firms that shift to outer areas usually adopt new, capital-intensive techniques which reduce requirements for unskilled labour. Indeed, unemployment in the far outer suburbs, which won most of the small increase in manufacturing jobs that did occur, increased by nearly as much. If there is a problem of unemployment because appropriate jobs are available but not close enough, it probably exists in outer rather than inner areas.

White-collar employment in inner areas will probably continue to grow. The trend towards fewer workers for any given amount of office space should be more than offset by the gradual utilisation of the vast amount of empty office space; few new office blocks will be built anywhere until this space is used.

TABLE 9.2   *Percentage of labourforce unemployed in Sydney, by subregion, 1971 and 1977.*

Sub-region	1971	1977
Inner	1.1	10.2
Outer west	1.1	8.4
Other	.5	4.4
Total	.7	6.0

Source: Unpublished June 1977 figures from the offices of the Commonwealth Employment Service (CES). Labourforce estimates for 1977 were the 1971 Census figures multiplied by the percentage of population change from 1971 to 1976. The figures have errors, caused by people travelling to CES offices away from their residences, changes of office catchments over time and the lack of any areal breakdown on figures for unemployed professionals. They especially underestimate unemployment in the 'other' suburbs, including the North, which have more professional workers. Local Government Areas served by offices in each sub-region are: Inner area — Ashfield, Botany, Drummoyne, Leichhardt, Marrickville, Randwick, South Sydney, Sydney, Woollahra. Outer western areas — Baulkham Hills, Blacktown, Blue Mountains, Camden, Campbelltown, Colo, Fairfield, Holroyd, Parramatta, Penrith, Wollondilly.

Whenever construction of office buildings does recommence, neither land-use controls nor market pressures are likely to divert it to suburban centres. On the other hand, blue-collar jobs will probably continue to decrease in inner areas, although the rate of loss could slow if the economy improves. The inner city should nevertheless continue to have a disporportionate share of whatever low-skilled jobs remain available. Many will be in services related to offices and others may be in transport and storage industries which should be stimulated in Sydney by the development of Port Botany.

The changes of employment raise important policy questions. First, there is the ominous possibility that structural change in the economy will continue to keep unemployment rates high even if the economy generally improves: a permanent class of unemployable people could emerge in the inner suburbs. If this is the case, physical land-use planning can do nothing to create jobs; planners can only influence the location of jobs. Claims to the contrary by consultants to the Melbourne and Metropolitan Board of Works (Little, 1977) are based on poor analysis and a number of questionable assumptions.[2] Their policy recommendations for more centralised growth of jobs, and of residents on high incomes, would exacerbate the economic and urban problems of the poor in both inner and outer areas. To direct job growth into the inner suburbs would not help the unemployed inner-suburban residents, who simply do not have the necessary skills to take the new jobs becoming available. But it would encourage non-residential incursion and gentrification in inner areas, and aggravate journey-to-work problems of residents in outer areas. The answers to problems of slow economic growth and structural change, if there are any, lie in national economic policy, not urban policies.

Another policy question, where planning controls can help, is the relationship between the location of jobs and the demand for inner-suburban housing. So long as the large number of office jobs remain, or even increase in the city centre, there will be a continuing middle-class demand for accommodation in the inner areas. Conversely, the loss of manufacturing jobs from the inner areas has been accompanied by large losses of resident manufacturing workers. However, there is a limit to this substitution of middle-class for working-class residents: the inner areas still have a very large surplus of blue-collar jobs over resident blue-collar workers, who still need low-cost housing. Blue-collar workers continue to form an unusually high proportion of the resident labourforce in inner Sydney and Melbourne. Moreover, many of the inner-suburban poor do not work (Table 10.3). Whatever the employment situation, these people will still need low-cost housing and access to public transport and welfare services.

Summary

Non-residential development in the inner suburbs declined considerably during the 1970s. The number of jobs has probably not increased and relatively few dwellings have been taken by development. Of the incursion that has occurred, a very large proportion has been caused by government action. If the economy improves in the future, it is probable that pressures for city-centre growth, especially for facilities for office-workers, will re-emerge.

Government is increasingly placing limits on non-residential incursion. The current economic climate presents some opportunities for reinforcing and extending these policies. However, the development potential for accommodating more office-workers is still very large and the political obstacles to reducing it are substantial. The decentralisation of government workers, who are the major users of CBD offices, is probably the most feasible way of minimising increases in numbers of office workers in or near the city centres of Sydney and Melbourne. In Adelaide, decentralisation is less needed and less feasible. If office development that does occur in the inner areas of the three cities is firmly restricted to the CBD, this would limit incursion and encourage the use of public transport.

CHAPTER 10

Residential Development and Policies in the 1970s

This concluding chapter shows that, despite the social importance of maintaining cheap accommodation, inner-suburban development of the 1970s has continued to reduce the availability of low-cost housing. Although relatively few old dwellings were lost, prices and rents have risen considerably. The 'slum' problem of the late 1940s has evolved into the 'gentrification' problem of the 1970s. It is unlikely that these losses of the metropolis' cheapest housing, near jobs and urban facilities, have been matched by compensating increases elsewhere in the metropolis or by a lessening of demand for such accommodation. To enable low-income households to adjust to these changes without undue hardship, the chapter recommends income supports, tenant protection and, most importantly, the provision of more, and more appropriate, inner-suburban housing by public housing authorities.

The other major policy concern of this chapter is the increasing imbalance between inner-city jobs and resident workers. Although the number of jobs may not have increased during the 1970s, inner-suburban populations and the resident labour force have declined sharply. More housing is needed and can be encouraged by a variety of actions to encourage further development of flats without demolishing existing houses. One promising possibility is to make use of under-utilised industrial or government land. Relaxation of excessive controls on building flats and on subdivision of existing housing, especially in middle suburbs, could also increase the supply of rental housing near jobs and shops. Both these actions could be important as part of a metropolitan strategy to limit urban sprawl and use of the private car.

Housing Stock and Population Changes

The number of inner-suburban dwellings, like the number of jobs, has stayed more or less constant since 1971. Up to 1976 the number of dwellings rose moderately in inner Adelaide and declined slightly in inner Sydney and moderately in inner Melbourne (Table 10.1). The main reason for this lack of growth, relative to the 1960s, was the sharp reduction of flat-building and probably higher numbers of amalgamations of formerly subdivided houses. Vacancy rates were higher, partly because of Census under-enumeration, but also because of temporary absences of residents, and renovations to dwellings.[1]

153

TABLE 10.1 *Changes in population and dwellings in Sydney, Melbourne and Adelaide, 1971-6   (in thousands).*

	Sydney		Melbourne		Adelaide	
	Inner [a] Stat.Div.		Inner	Stat.Div.	Inner	Stat.Div.
Population						
1971	361.1	2 935.9	307.6	2 503.0	128.3	842.7
1976	319.9	3 021.3	259.6	2 604.2	114.8	900.4
1971-76 change	–41.2	+35.4	–47.9	+101.2	–13.4	+57.7
Total dwellings						
1971	137.0	962.3	114.9	785.7	40.8	265.4
1976	136.1	1 063.7	112.6	888.9	45.3	309.9
1971-76 change	–.9	+101.4	–2.3	+103.2	+4.6	+44.4
Unoccupied dwellings						
1971	11.6	70.2	9.4	51.1	2.8	13.3
1976	15.7	87.2	12.8	72.0	3.8	19.2
1971-76 change	+4.1	+17.0	+3.4	+20.9	+1.1	+5.9

[a] Excludes Paddington, which was in the Woollahra LGA after 1968.
Source: Preliminary results from the 1976 Census with no adjustment for under-enumeration. There are minor discrepancies in the totals caused by rounding.

However, recent surveys by the Real Estate Institute show that accommodation available for rent is in very short supply in inner areas.

With less redevelopment, the number of demolitions of inner-suburban dwellings declined markedly during the 1970s. Of the 2600 dwellings lost in inner Sydney from 1971 to 1976, 760 were lost in 1971 but only 160 in 1975.[2] About three-quarters of these losses were houses; they were spread through most of the inner LGAs except Botany.

After 1971 there were very large population losses in the inner suburbs of all three cities, but particularly in Melbourne and Sydney (Table 10.1), only part of which can be explained by under-enumeration.[3] Higher vacancy rates, are another reason, but the main factor has probably been a considerable reduction of occupancy rates in existing houses, due to population aging, movement of small affluent households into the inner suburbs, and movement of larger, foreign-born families out of the inner suburbs. There were relatively fewer children, more aged people, and almost the same proportion of young adults as in 1971. All these figures have been affected by the declining birth rates and the fall in net overseas migration (APIC, 1977:4).

Gentrification

Despite slow metropolitan growth (Table 10.1), the demand for buying and renting inner-suburban houses has probably increased during the 1970s. The trend for young adults to form group households has been maintained. Many small households of the baby boom generation are still being formed. They continue to be attracted by the access to jobs, to tertiary education and other attractions of the inner suburbs. Moreover, because house prices have until recently been rising faster than wages (Figure 10.1), there are financial reasons why middle-income households would either remain longer in inner-city rental houses, or else buy less expensive houses in the inner city. High interest rates have increased these difficulties.

Since 1971, home improvements have increased and values have continued to rise in inner Sydney. There was a 50 per cent increase in the annual number of alterations and additions from 1970 to 1976 (Figure 7.3). By the mid 1970s, prices for renovated terraces generally exceeded $60 000 in Paddington and averaged $35 000 to $40 000 in Surry Hills, Glebe and Balmain (*Sydney Morning Herald*, 26.11.77). Old, narrow and derelict terrace houses in Woolloomooloo were

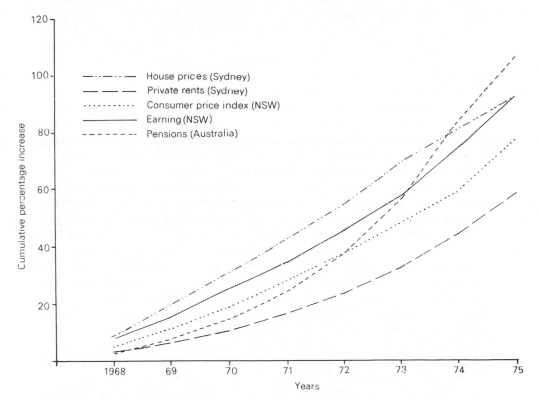

FIGURE 10.1. Incomes and housing costs in Sydney, 1968-75
(Three-year moving averages.)
Sources: House prices from unpublished data collected by Philip Shrapnel & Co. (see note 1, Chapter 7); pensions from annual reports of Department of Social Security; earnings (average male earnings), private rents, and Consumer Price Index from the *New South Wales Yearbook*.

auctioned for up to $40 000 (SMH, 3.6.77). Partly because of the high prices in the popular areas, estate agents report a growing 'spill-over' of young, white-collar workers buying and renovating cheaper houses in less salubrious, industrial areas (*Sydney Telegraph,* 8.8.76). In general, the pattern of rising prices and middle-class popularity is spreading outward.

The prices of old houses located outside the innermost terrace areas have also increased considerably. Semi-detached house in North Sydney are in strong demand, for prices approaching $40 000. In Leichhardt and North Sydney newly constructed terrace housing has been sold at prices from $50 000 to $60 000. In North Sydney, unrenovated terrace houses in areas recently rezoned from commercial to residential use are being sold for $40 000 to $50 000 (Sydney *Daily Mail,* 27.10.77). The exception to the rising prices is Marrickville, where prices have generally risen less rapidly, and may have even fallen slightly during 1977 (*SMH,* 17.9.77), partly because of the rapid decline of southern European immigration in recent years. Although this may indicate some relative 'filtering down' in middle suburbs, the sale prices in Marrickville are still considerably above those in the innermost areas. Despite the relatively fast price rises, inner suburban house prices (excluding Paddington) in 1976 averaged only $33 000, compared to $45 000 for all of Sydney (ABS, 1977b).[4]

The forces behind rising prices have also affected rents. House rents in Balmain are over $20 weekly per bedroom — $65 to $79 for a two- or three-bedroom house; even in industrial Redfern, dilapidated, two-bedroom, terrace houses rented for $40 per week, and renovated ones rented for over $60 per week (*SMH,* 26.11.77). In a reversal of the slum-formation process, rents on unrenovated houses have risen when nearby houses were improved.

In Melbourne, the Centre for Urban Research and Action has studied house sales from 1970 to 1975 in Fitzroy and South Melbourne, LGAs just north and south of the CBD. The Centre's study (1977) reported that white-collar workers comprised almost two-thirds of the owner occupant buyers but less than half the owner-occupant sellers (p. 12). Moreover, these ownership changes have been accelerating rapidly and, in 1975, the proportion of sales from blue-collar to white-collar households was 61 per cent in South Melbourne and 59 per cent in Fitzroy (p. 14). Similarly, sales from immigrants to Australians rose from a fifth to two-thirds in South Melbourne and from a third to half in Fitzroy. Unlike the earlier years, when established migrants sold to more recently arrived compatriots, the migrant working classes were being replaced by the Australian-born middle class. The explanation lies in both the strong middle-class demand and the reduced inflow and moves outward of immigrants.

The invasion by white-collar workers was accompanied by price inflation. From 1970 to 1975, median prices in the inner city rose at twice the rate of the next ring of suburbs to the northwest and by more than in the more affluent southeast (p. 21). By 1975 the location of Melbourne's cheapest houses had shifted from the inner suburbs to the next ring of suburbs in the inner northwest. The population change reflected by these sales was accentuated by the high turnover rates in the buoyant market: up to 16 per cent a year during the 1972 boom (p. 23). In just six years, two out of every five houses in Fitzroy and South Melbourne had been sold at least once (p. 25).

Investors, who comprised a quarter of the buyers (p. 26), have played an important role in the transition from the working classes to the middle classes. In South Melbourne, they bought almost half of those properties sold by blue-collar workers, widows or retired persons;.those that they resold to owner-occupants went mainly to middle-class purchasers. In both LGAs, investors often resold within six months of buying, after only superficial renovations; capital gains on half of these sales exceeded $100 a month during the boom years (p. 36).

The heavy involvement of investors seeking capital gains suggests that owner-occupancy rates may have fallen. In fact, owner-occupants accounted for two-thirds of the sellers but only half of the buyers (p. 26). No figures are available on subsequent house rents but they probably rose (although perhaps more slowly than prices) and most were probably let to middle-class occupants. Investors have not caused gentrification but they almost certainly have contributed to the accelerated turnover and large increases of prices and rents.

In inner Adelaide, median house prices from 1970 to 1976 also rose faster than the metropolitan average, a 221 per cent increase.[5] However, there were considerable differences between inner Adelaide and inner Melbourne and inner Sydney. Because the quality of the inner-area housing in Adelaide is far better than that in Melbourne and Sydney, the prices in 1976 were about equal to the metropolitan averages. There was a net increase of white-collar workers but, unlike the inner areas of the other cities, inner Adelaide also had net increases of skilled blue-collar workers and relatively small losses of migrants; the main losses were of pensioners and non-skilled workers. The small losses of migrants is probably explained by the availability in the inner areas of larger houses, suitable for their growing families. Within inner Adelaide, the increase of white-collar workers was most pronounced in better suburbs like Unley but even poorer suburbs like Thebarton have been improved by the existing residents. The suburb of St Peters had a marked upturn of renovations during the early 1970s (Pugh, 1976:374).

In all three cities, local councils in the inner areas are responding to the demands of the new middle classes. They are improving neighbourhoods for all residents but are also accelerating the displacement of renters on low incomes. Inner-area councils have undertaken a wide variety of improvements such as street closures, tree planting schemes, the provision of small parks, the establishment of 'historic zoning' for residential areas, and other measures that increase the amenity of the areas. The New South Wales government has announced plans to buy more inner-suburban land for use as parks (*Sydney Daily Telegraph,* 27.2.78). Restraints on the building of flats, rezoning of housing areas from non-residential to residential uses, and the abandonment of inner city freeway proposals have had a similar effect.

The City of Sydney reports:

> It is obvious that the protection and conservation of existing residential areas sought under Action Priority 9A will not arrest the continuing decline in the City's population, nor provide for the needs of people on low incomes. Such conservation will assist small, middle-income families and single people in their search for terrace houses to renovate and occupy. Land values and the price of housing will continue to rise. Residents with larger, low-income families will continue to be displaced as renovation proceeds, so will the elderly, the migrants, the transients and other disadvantaged groups. As they leave they will be partially replaced by young people on relatively high incomes (1974*b*:42).

Similarly, The City of Melbourne Strategy Plan (1974) reports that '... [residential] value changes during the past four years will be reinforced by the Strategy Plan' (reported in VCOSS, 1975:67). The new middle classes, investors, and local councils are steadily transforming the quality and occupancy of inner-city housing.

There is every indication that the strong demand for inner suburban houses will continue. All the factors behind the current high levels of demand — the baby boom coming of age, relatively slow rises of real income, concentration of white-collar jobs in or near the CBD, and the distance of the city centre from the urban fringe — are unlikely to diminish. If car travel becomes much more costly there will be even greater demand for inner-suburban housing, particularly by white-collar workers. Nor is there any indication that the middle classes are reluctant to move into some poorer-quality housing which so far has remained unimproved by its lower-income occupants. Rising house prices and rents, and more middle-class invasion, will probably continue.

Few policy recommendations can be made about the gentrification process. It has hastened many improvements of inner areas and met important needs of the new middle classes. Moreover, it would be very difficult to stop the process, even if this were desirable. South Sydney Council tried, without success, to prevent unrelated people from living together, as a means of limiting rent rises and displacement of working-class families (SMH, 12.6.76). It would be equally inappropriate and unsuccessful to neglect inner suburban improvement, on the grounds that it encourages rises in housing costs. Improvement should, however, be concentrated on the worst areas, where the housing is less attractive to higher-income groups. Investment in more welfare services, such as 'meals-on-wheels', rather than in physical improvements to the neighbourhoods, would also help the poor, while having little attraction to high-income groups. The most important point, discussed later in this chapter, is that inequities resulting from gentrification can be compensated for by providing housing programmes for the poor and by lowering housing costs throughout the metropolis.

Development of Flats

In marked contrast to the 1960s, the inner suburbs during the 1970s have not had enough flats built to offset population losses caused by other changes. Table 10.2 shows that the amount and metropolitan share of inner-suburban flat building in Melbourne and Sydney have fallen dramatically. High interest rates, and perhaps a satisfaction of demand, caused much of the metropolitan reduction. The inner areas were further affected by the shortage of vacant or under-utilised sites and the higher values of existing houses. Inner Adelaide had little decline in the amount of flat building, because the demand for flats came later and there were more opportunities for infill. However, residential subdivisions declined markedly and few sites were available in 1976 (Lewis, 1978:5). In the inner suburbs of all three cities, the building of new flats became increasingly difficult.

TABLE 10.2   *Flat-building completions in Sydney, Melbourne and Adelaide, 1971-6 (in thousands of flat units).*

City	1971-2		1975-6		1971-6 Total	
	Inner area	Metro.	Inner area	Metro.	Inner area	Metro.
Sydney	2.2	14.8	.5	5.4	7.8	68.6
Melbourne	2.4	8.8	.5	6.2	7.5	47.1
Adelaide	.8	11.0	.6	10.3	3.3	52.0

Source: ABS (1972-1977*b*).

Existing flats are being improved and prices and rents are rising. A number of old flats are being upgraded and converted to strata titles for sales to owner-occupants, in some cases displacing tenants (CURA, 1977:47). These flats are then either let at higher rents or sold to owner-occupants. The declining number of new inner-area flats, and continued strong competition by young people for near-city locations, arc thc rcasons why inner-area flat rents have recently risen so much faster thatn those elsewhere in the metropolis. In Melbourne, a newspaper survey of rents for unfurnished, one-bedroom flats found that rents in inner suburbs were 6 per cent below the metropolitan average in 1971 but 13 per cent above it in 1975 (CURA, 1977:14).

These market influences behind the decline of flat building and rising rents have been reinforced by strict government controls in all three cities. These regulations have reduced the availability of land and decreased densities at which flats may be built. Action plans by the City of Sydney recommend tighter restrictions on flat building, Leichhardt has virtually prohibited flat development in most areas, and in 1975 the North Sydney Harbour Foreshores interim development order has also reduced the maximum heights permitted and decreased the allowable proportion of sites covered by new blocks of flats. Inner councils have also adopted stringent building regulations. In Melbourne, local councils have similarly excluded flats from many areas, restricted the number of storeys permissable, increased requirements for car parking, prohibited bedsitter and other small flats, and reduced allowable site coverage (CURA, 1977:115-18). Although similar controls have been imposed elsewhere, the effects have been especially significant in inner areas because of their high land costs.

There are many reasons for the marked change in Council attitudes toward flats. The consequences of poor-quality flat development were amply illustrated by the worst development of the 1960s. With building of flats becoming less profitable, house owners may feel that they are more likely to have their property values reduced by nearby flats than to make profitable sales to flat developers. The rising number of articulate, middle-class owners of old houses have led the fight against flats throughout inner city areas.

In Sydney, the Victoria Street development in Potts Point near Kings Cross well illustrates the obstacles confronting inner-suburban development of flats (Smith, 1976). The site was bought for $5.6 million in 1971 and the developer proposed to build three 45-storey towers. To minimise resident opposition, nearly all the 350 displaced tenants were helped to find alternative accommodation and were paid an average of $230 each for relocation expenses. However, eight of them refused to move, and they were supported by a 'green ban' by the Builders Labourers Federation, a National Trust declaration on the old houses, and dozens of squatters and hundreds of protestors. Although the development proposal met all planning requirements and was approved by the City Council, the State Planning Authority (SPA) rejected the proposal as the public controversy grew. Smith (1976) reports that the developer had to get a court order to evict the squatters, had to produce five schemes before gaining building approval from the SPA, and had to agree to demands from the BLF that 10 per cent of the units be made available at 15 per cent discount to buyers nominated by the BLF (Smith, 1976). It took six years, and $4 000 000 in interest payments, before the developer could begin to sell the units, at prices between $40 000 and $60 000.

Despite these difficulties, the City of Sydney in June 1977 had development approval outstanding for projects totalling 4000 new flats and 381 hostel rooms. Most were in three major developments: Victoria Street, Potts Point (650 units); the Palisades, Darlinghurst (950 units), and a complex of three tower blocks proposed for the corner of Market, Sussex and Kent Streets. The Victoria Street project may be followed by others if interest rates decline, if there is clearly a market for them, and if opposition from residents is overcome. However, the units would be very expensive and estate agents are already reporting some difficulty in selling and renting expensive home units in Kings Cross. Except for these major projects in mixed residential/commercial areas, the emphasis in the inner suburbs in all three cities has turned toward building high-quality, less intrusive town houses, usually for sale to owner-occupants, at prices up to $100 000 each in inner Sydney.

As a result of the high cost of building flats, the only source, other than new government housing, of supply for more low-rent dwellings is to subdivide existing buildings. However, many local councils in inner and middle suburbs have completely banned subdivision of existing dwellings or have allowed them only in areas zoned for flats (Housing Industry Association, 1976). In Paddington, resident action groups steadfastly oppose subdivisions of existing houses (City of Sydney Resident Action Group Committee, 1977:26). Marrickville Council affixes the following stamp when approving structural modifications to existing dwellings: 'Subject to the premises not being used or adapted for use as a residential flat building, boarding house, or house let in lodgings'.

Given the continuation of current market and government constraints, it is unlikely that much additional building of flats or subdivision of existing dwellings will take place in the inner suburbs. Primarily as a result of the strict regulations applied by local councils, new flats that are built will be costly and will require the demolition of more houses than before. Unless this situation changes, the City of Sydney and other inner councils are unlikely ever to reach their goal of increasing their resident populations.

More development of flats in inner areas would have the desirable effects of reducing journeys-to-work and making better use of urban infrastructure (water and sewerage facilities and local schools) that is under-utilised in some inner areas (Pak-Poy and Associates, 1973). However, building more inner-suburban flats probably would not lessen competition for inner-area houses. These flats would be more likely to attract residents who otherwise would live in flats outside the inner city rather than in houses within the inner city. The inner-suburban flats will successfully compete in the metropolitan market only if the costs of providing them are not too much more than those in middle suburbs.

More inner-suburban flats could be built, and their costs lowered, if councils would relax stringent building regulations. Although controls are needed to prevent poor-quality flat-building, many councils have overreacted and apparently want to stop development of flats altogether. As part of its programme to increase residential populations, the City of Sydney has reduced the number of parking spaces required per unit in Chippendale and Woolloomooloo, and reduced the proportion of site areas that must be used for open space in Darlinghurst. At the same time, development approval could still be limited to those projects in which the yield of new flats would be high relative to the houses taken. There are areas where relatively high densities could be permitted with few harmful effects on nearby housing. This is also true of middle suburbs, which have more opportunities for infill development which would neither destroy existing dwellings nor overload services. If areas near railway stations, especially, could be zoned and developed for flats, more people could have accessibility comparable with inner-suburban locations with fewer social costs. These developments could consolidate the existing urban areas and minimise urban sprawl, without major redevelopment of inner areas.

To supply more low-cost housing, it also is important that local councils in inner and middle areas allow existing housing to be subdivided or altered for multiple occupancy. As this type of dwelling has largely been lost in the innermost areas, they should be permitted in other areas if there is a demand for them. As with the controls on flats, action at the state level will probably be necessary to overcome local government resistance to this way of housing poor residents in their areas. The South Australian government is currently considering policies that will allow 'granny' flats and subdivisions of dwellings in areas zoned for single-family housing.

Development of flats on inner-area land currently used for non-residential purposes would provide more housing near jobs without loss to existing dwelling stock. In some inner areas, land has already become more valuable for residential than for industrial uses. For example, the eight-hectare 'Yarra Falls' site in Collingwood, on the banks of the River Yarra in Melbourne, is being redeveloped from a textile factory into low- and medium-cost housing. Similarly, the Angliso Meat Works site of about eighteen hectares in Footscray is being considered for mixed commercial residential development.

The City Councils of Melbourne, Sydney and Adelaide have supported such changes, but only the Adelaide City Council has made any progress in this area (Llewellyn-Smith, 1977). Despite the recent decline in the land market, the value of nearly all land near city centres used for non-residential purposes is still far too expensive even for high-cost, high-density flat development. Mixed residential/ commercial development, made possible in Sydney by changes to state regulations on building flats (Schedule 7) in 1965, and since 1971 encouraged by bonuses that allow greater densities on mixed-use developments, have still been notably unsuccessful because of high land prices.

To rezone non-residential areas to residential use would encourage development of flats but it would not become politically feasible unless the value of the land in residential use exceeded the value in industrial or commercial use. These opportunities are likely to be rare in the near future but, if they do emerge, approvals for the rezoning would help to increase residential populations. Plans that promote residential redevelopment, by providing substantial neighbourhood improvements in commercial and industrial localities that are already declining, may be more immediately practicable. The City of Sydney is currently considering such a scheme in Pyrmont. The NSW Land Commission could play a valuable role in acquiring land and funding the improvements.

Government participation is needed to complement land-use controls in making these changes. The City of Sydney has proposed deferred payment for the purchase by private developers of some of its land for building new flats. In February 1978 the New South Wales government announced that its 'surplus' land throughout the metropolis would be sold or leased. If inner-city properties having residential potential were used only for residential purposes, residential populations could be increased. The South Australian government is making an inventory of state land and may also develop similar proposals. Commonwealth properties could also be used for these kinds of developments.

A good deal of publicity has been given to the possibility of converting non-residential buildings to residential uses. In Sydney, minor modifications to local building ordinances (Ordinance 70), which require that converted dwellings meet the standards of new ones, could facilitate these conversions. However, even with these changes, the outlook for such conversions is bleak. Proposals for the conversion of vacant office space to residential use are expensive and impractical. The owners would rather leave them vacant until more profitable commercial users become available. Ideas for the conversion to residential use of the seventeen vast wool stores in Pyrmont would be very expensive, probably more costly than redevelopment.

Consequences for Low-income Households

Rising rents and prices of inner-city housing have had far-reaching implications. Because inner-suburban housing in Sydney and Melbourne had been the cheapest in the metropolis, the changes have reduced the supply of low-cost housing in these cities. The difficulties have been alleviated to the extent that pensions and average earnings have risen faster than rents or prices in general (Figure 10.1). However, with the numbers of the unemployed and single parents rising, so the number of people who depend on pensions has increased. In 1976 the unemployment benefit for a family of four amounted to about only half of average male weekly earnings.

Opportunities for cheap, private housing generally have not become available elsewhere in the cities. Although rents and prices have been rising more slowly in middle than in inner suburbs, housing costs in middle suburbs are still high. If current trends continue, these areas will probably provide an increasing share of the lowest-cost housing in the metropolis. Middle suburbs offer many locational advantages, including the availability of nearby jobs and shops and good bus and rail services. However, it is not clear whether enough low-cost housing will become available to compensate for the changes in inner areas. Moreover, the displacement of poor people from inner to middle locations also involves the social and financial costs of the move itself.

The rising housing costs in the inner suburbs have had quite different effects on low-income owners and low-income renters. Other than by public resumption, owners could not be displaced and, if they chose to, could make profitable sales and move to better housing elsewhere. Much of the movement out of the inner suburbs by migrants in Sydney and Melbourne probably involved such advancement. However, major difficulties are faced by lower-income renters who are potential buyers. They have been increasingly unable to buy even the cheap housing in industrial parts of the inner suburbs, or anywhere else. For example, the number of years of average male earnings (New South Wales) required to buy an average house was 2.7 in Redfern in 1967 but 3.5 in South Sydney in 1976. For a man on average earnings a 20 per cent deposit on an average South Sydney house (typically a small, unrenovated terrace near industrial uses) would require savings equal to seven months of his pretax earnings. His repayments on the outstanding amount, at 9¼ per cent interest on usual loan terms, would exceed a quarter of his income. Purchasing an inner-suburban house is even more difficult for those borrowing at the higher interest rates charged by building societies, for those buying outside cheap areas like South Sydney, and for those on less than average earnings. The high unemployment rates among women, especially factory workers, has aggravated the problems.

The difficulties faced by renters on low incomes in the inner suburbs are considerable. Rents for even the poor houses in industrial Redfern equal a quarter of average earnings and almost half of the unemployment benefit for a family of four. The Smith Family, a major Sydney welfare agency, reports that its clients in inner areas pay an average of 45 per cent of their incomes on housing (*Financial Review,* 20.8.76). A study of applicants for public housing in Adelaide in 1977 found that, of those who live in inner areas or wish to live in them, 40 per cent pay more than 40 per cent of their incomes on housing and 15 per cent pay more than 60 per cent on housing.[6] As a result of these high rents, many of the poor are forced to economise on food, clothing and other necessities.

The competition for inner-suburban housing also presents other problems. The strong demand enables landlords to require large bonds of up to several hundred dollars, to avoid making repairs, and to discriminate against single parents and others whose ability to pay high rents is suspect. The poorest tenants can often adjust only by overcrowding or living in poorly maintainted dwellings. Despite these problems, it seems that many of the poor remain in the inner areas because even less low-cost, private housing is available for rent elsewhere in the metropolis. A continuation of these trends would mean that the inner suburbs would be increasingly segregated into some areas of high quality housing and others having overcrowding, under-maintenance, poor amenities, and yet high rents.

A 1976 survey provides more information on moderate- and low-income households that had recently moved in Melbourne (CURA, 1977:70-85). Tenants forced to move by evictions, houses being sold or increased rents accounted for 15 per cent of the moves from inner and middle suburbs but only 4 per cent of those from outer areas. When the study also counted as displaced those who moved to escape poor housing conditions, or because of marital breakups, the proportions rose to 48 per cent in inner areas, 35 per cent in middle areas, and 8 per cent in outer areas. Using this wider definition of displacement, almost half of the renters and half of the poor were 'displaced'.

The displaced had considerable difficulty finding other accommodation. Among private renters, almost two-thirds reported problems of high rents and high bonds, of finding housing in desired localities, or of discrimination against families with children. Rents for their new dwellings averaged 50 per cent more than their previous rents. Those earning under $100 weekly had smaller rent increases, but half of them reported repair problems in their new dwellings. The costs of moving averaged more than two weeks of earnings. The proportion of those moving who reported problems travelling to jobs and shops from their new residences, was more than two-thirds in outer areas but only a quarter in inner areas.

The number of inner-suburban residents who could potentially face these difficulties is still considerable. Despite rising incomes throughout the earlier post-war period, the inner suburbs still have a disproportionately large share of people on low and moderate incomes. The 1973 Income Survey in Sydney showed that the proportion of 'income units' in poverty or having 'low incomes' (under 150 per cent of the poverty line) were 13 per cent and 17 per cent respectively for the inner suburbs (excluding North Sydney) compared to 8 per cent and 14 per cent for the rest of Sydney. The inner suburbs had especially large shares of those on incomes below 80 per cent of the poverty line. Of the 16 000 poor, inner-suburban income units, more than a third were aged single people, 15 per cent were sick or unemployed, and a quarter were in the 'other' category, which included recently arrived migrants and people who fit two or more categories (Table 10.3). Given that unemployment has risen many fold since the Survey was conducted (see Table 9.2), the number of poor, inner-suburban households has probably increased in recent years. The people most suceptible to being displaced are those with social and sentimental attachments to the area, who lack cars, and who have limited capabilities for finding accommodation or handling the stresses of moving.

The ability of the poor to resist displacement pressures and avoid rent rises depends largely on their housing tenure. Among inner-suburban households in Sydney, only 15 per cent of the poor in general and 25 per cent of those on low incomes are home owners (Table 10.4) Even among aged couples on low incomes, only a quarter are owners. Moreover, only 6 per cent of the poor or

TABLE 10.3 *Disability groups by income levels, inner Sydney, 1973 (thousands of income units).*

Disability group	Low Income Poor	Low Income Total	Middle or High Income	All incomes
Aged single	5.8	10.0	2.7	12.7
Aged couple	-	2.0	3.5	5.5
Single parent	-	.6	3.0	3.6
Single female	-	2.8	7.6	10.4
Large family	-	1.2	1.5	2.7
Sick or unemployed	2.2	2.5	3.1	5.6
Other	4.0	6.9	16.5	23.4
No disability	1.8	9.5	47.1	56.6
Total	15.7	35.5	85.0	120.5

For definitions see the section on Terminology and Data in Chapter 1.
Source: Unpublished data from the 1973 Income Survey. A dash denotes an estimate of less than 1,000.

those on low incomes are in government housing. In fact, the poor and those on low incomes in inner-suburban public housing are outnumbered by middle- and higher-income people. If the 3700 middle-income households vacated their publicly owned dwellings, nearly all the low-income, inner-area residents on the waiting list for public housing could be housed immediately. Whether out of preference or out of ignorance, only 18 per cent of the private tenants on low incomes are on the Housing Commission waiting-list. About four out of every five low-income, inner-suburban residents depend on the private rental market.

TABLE 10.4 *Housing tenure in inner Sydney, by income group 1973 (thousands of income units)*

Tenure	Low income		Middle or	All
	Poor	Total	High income	incomes
Owner				
Full owner	2.1	7.6	14.2	21.8
Buying	-	1.2	12.6	13.8
Total	-	8.8	26.8	35.6
Renter/lodger				
Rent-free	2.2	4.3	5.9	10.2
Housing Comm.	-	2.2	3.7	5.9
Private, on Hous.				
Comm. list	2.5	3.8	2.1	5.9
Private, not on				
Hous. Comm. list	7.1	14.1	36.2	50.3
Boarder	-	2.7	9.9	12.6
Total	-	27.1	57.8	84.9
Total	15.7	35.9	84.6	120.5

Source: Unpublished data from the 1973 Income Survey. See notes in Table 10.3 and the section on data and terminology in Chapter 1.

Public Assistance for Tenants on Low Incomes

The developments in the private housing market that are disadvantaging poor tenants are largely beyond the direct control of government. Public authorities can ameliorate these difficulties by providing alternative accommodation and protection for private tenants. In providing more government housing, the main question is deciding between either redevelopment or acquisition and renovation of existing dwellings.

In New South Wales the Housing Commission (NSWHC) owned only 8 per cent of the inner-suburban dwellings in 1976 and the waiting time for them averaged four years. Although inner-area public housing consists mostly of flats and most of the applicants have children, a high proportion of them prefer or need inner city accommodation. The Commission reports that many of these people have shift work at hours when public transport is unavailable, some make frequent visits to specialised medical facilities available only near the city centre, and most have strong social or emotional ties to the area.

During the 1970s the NSWHC has shifted its emphasis in the inner city from slum clearance to providing more low-cost rental accommodation. However, except for a few smaller blocks of flats in Marrickville, most of its inner-suburban activity since 1971 has involved the loss of relatively dense, existing terrace housing, replaced by 1040 new high-rise units in Waterloo (including 460 units for the aged) and 100 more units for the aged in Redfern. These small (213 square metres) flats for the aged are very expensive: those in Waterloo (built in the mid 1970s on land bought in the early 1970s) cost over $32 000 per unit; seventy-nine new flats to be built in The Rocks will cost $50 000 each, excluding land costs; and proposals for flats in Woolloomooloo have a projected cost of $60 000 each, including land costs. On the other hand, the Commission could build a three-bedroom, brick-veneer house in an outer suburb for a cost in 1976, of only $26 000, including land. The public authorities are facing the dilemma of whether to build more houses in remote locations, or fewer dwellings (mostly flats) in inner areas.

The NSWHC has faced vociferous opposition to proposals for high-rise flats. For example, in 1973 the Builders Labourers Federation applied a 'black ban' against the high-rise flats for aged persons in Waterloo until pensioners asked them to rescind it. The Commission's 1975 Waterloo proposals, which call for the replacement of over 500 existing dwellings with up to 2000 new flats, have been bitterly fought (NSWHC, 1976). Few tenants in the area oppose the development, partly because they are eligible for government housing once displaced. However, most of the residents are owners, many of them from southern Europe. Their opposition to the Commission has been supported by conservationists, unionists, and the South Sydney Council, which fears an overload on community services.

Despite the political and economic difficulties, the Commission is determined to redevelop in Waterloo, remaining firmly opposed to rehabilitation of the area for a number of reasons. First, it emphasizes that only redevelopment can increase the supply of inner-suburban housing; it does not accept that the saving of existing low-cost housing from gentrification or private redevelopment would increase housing for the poor. Second, the Commission states that the existing cottages are too poorly built to justify renovations, estimated to cost up to $20 000 per dwelling, which would make renovation more expensive than redevelopment. It believes that renovated terraces would have lives of only thirty years, compared to fifty for new flats. Finally, the Commission argues that rehabilitated dwellings are more difficult to maintain, and do not facilitate the delivery of social services or the improvement of community services.

In sharp contrast to the view of the NSWHC, the then federal Labor government embarked on several large-scale renovation programmes. The most important of these was the Glebe Estate of 720 dwellings, mostly terrace houses, located directly north of Sydney University (Wagner, 1977). The dwellings were owned by the Church of England on land granted by the government last century. By the early 1970s the houses had badly deteriorated, but improvements would have necessitated rents beyond the capacities of the existing tenants. Rather than create hardship by selling to private developers, the Church sold the dwellings to the Commonwealth government in August 1974, for $17.3 million.

The government's objectives were to avoid displacing the existing tenants, to maintain the low-cost housing and to preserve the historical and aesthetic character of the area. The plan was to renovate the old houses and to build 250 new dwellings in the spaces made available by site consolidation. Existing dwellings would be let to low-income tenants (using Housing Commission eligibility criteria) and some new ones would be let at market rents or sold in order to increase the project's financial return and social diversity. Since the change of federal government in 1975, the rehabilitation programme has slowed considerably through lack of funds, and the new infill housing has been postponed. There are so many people on the waiting list for Glebe housing that no more applications are being accepted.

Contrary to the views of the NSWHC, a detailed cost-benefit study of the Glebe project (Beattie, 1978) suggests that rehabilitation has many advantages over redevelopment. The total costs of buying, renovating and maintaining the estate was estimated to have cost the government $31 million dollars in 1973. The provision of the same number of dwellings by redevelopment would have been more expensive while providing housing less suitable for children.[7] To build a comparable amount of housing in an outer suburb would have cost only $19 million and would have provided larger, single-family houses.

The Glebe study shows that rehabilitation presented substantial social advantages which the Housing Commission had not calculated. If the government had built in an outer area instead of buying the Glebe, the new tenants would have incurred high travel costs and the existing Glebe tenants the costs of displacement and community disruption. Taking these social costs into account almost eliminates cost differences between the options of outer-area development and Glebe rehabilitation. Redevelopment would not have incurred travel costs but would still have caused high costs of displacement. Compared to outer-area development or Glebe redevelopment, Glebe rehabilitation also preserved buildings of considerable significance. Beattie concludes that, considering total costs and benefits to both government and low-income people, rehabilitation was economically desirable.

The other major rehabilitation programme in Sydney is in Woolloomooloo. As opposition to commercial development in the area mounted, the Commonwealth Department of Urban and Regional Development developed a proposal for preserving the area in residential use. Under the 1975 Tripartite agreement, the Commonwealth provided $17 million for property acquisition and services, the City prepared a land-use plan, and the Housing Commission is developing 770 publicly owned dwellings to house about 2500 people. A quarter will be renovated existing dwellings and the remainder will be made up of medium-density infill and redevelopment. There will also be more open space, a new school, more community facilities, and diversion of through traffic. By early 1978, a small number of terraces had been rehabilitated by the Housing Commission. It is hoped that enough private housing can be built elsewhere in the area to house up to 5000 additional people.

In Victoria, inner-suburban redevelopment by the Housing Commission was limited by the passage of the Urban Renewal Act of 1970 and was virtually stopped in 1972 by massive public opposition (Hargreaves, 1975; Braby, 1976). Since then the Commission has avoided inner areas except for some small, medium-density infill, such as the Raglan Street development in South Melbourne, and a few, small rehabilitation projects. In 1974 the Commonwealth provided a $3.5-million loan to the Victorian government for the purchase of an estate of 136 nineteenth-century buildings in Emerald Hill from the Melbourne Family Care Organisation. A restoration programme under the guidance of the Emerald Hill Liaison Committee was in progress in 1977. In 1976, the Victorian government agreed to a three-year pilot project in which the Housing Commission would buy and renovate inner-suburban houses which would then be managed by the Fitzroy-Collingwood Rental Housing Association. By September 1977, twenty properties had been purchased and plans were underway for buying more (McCutcheon, 1977).

The South Australian Housing Trust has done more rehabilitation than any other state housing authority. From 1973 to June 1977, it purchased 923 houses, 400 in inner areas, for rehabilitation and public rental. (SAHT, 1977:30). These renovated dwellings were provided under a 'special rentals' programme designed to serve special-needs groups such as single parents and the physically or mentally handicapped. Because land and building costs in Adelaide are lower than in Sydney or Melbourne, the Trust in 1976 could buy and renovate an inner-area house for $23 000 compared to $28 000 for the land and construction of a new suburban house: by late 1977, the costs for either were about equal at $33 000. In 1977 the Trust bought the old Afton Hotel, and has since purchased two more hotels, to provide housing for pensioners and transients on low incomes. These are leased back to the former management for continued operation.

The redevelopment plans for Hackney came to a dramatic halt in 1972. Resident action group mobilised intense opposition to the plans and the Premier of South Australia abruptly announced that most of the area would be renovated instead (Sandercock, 1975:136-8). Any residents dislocated by the project were personally assisted into comparable housing of their choice (O'Reilly, 1977). A cost benefit analysis of the proposals (Pugh, 1976) concluded that redevelopment in 1973 would have been economically viable but it would have involved substantial social costs. The study concluded that renovation, which provided less but still significant financial returns, was preferable.

The Trust's post war construction in inner areas has consisted of 450 dwellings, mostly three-storey, walk-up structures. Some were infill, some were on sites formerly occupied by poor housing, and a few were built on land formerly used for non-residential purposes. Because both the construction and rehabilitation programmes have been small, the Trust owns only 2 per cent of all the inner-area dwellings, compared to 10 per cent for all of the metropolis. Public housing is only slightly under-represented in the inner suburbs of Sydney, while Melbourne's inner suburbs have a higher proportion of public housing than does the rest of the metropolis (see Table 1.4).

The South Australian Housing Trust also has continued its Housing Improvement and Rent Control programme which, by June 1977, had declared over 9000 homes substandard; many were placed under rent control until improvements were made (SAHT, 1977:44). The programme has led to the improvement of many dwellings but to the demolition or change of use of many others. During the early 1970s, almost as many houses under rent control were removed from the rental market as were improved (Bradbrook, 1977:151). Of the dwellings that were improved, some poor tenants had rent rises that may have forced them to move. The housing improvement programme, together with the Trust renovation programme, are the main strategies for dealing with the 19 000 dwellings (half within seven kilometres of the city centre) estimated in 1971 to need improvement.

Public housing policy is fraught with many difficult decisions. A reasonable goal would be to have inner suburban housing to match the proportion of applications for inner area accommodation on the waiting lists. The higher cost of this policy would mean that the total number of public dwellings would be reduced, but it would avoid the high transport costs and in many cases the social costs of outer area locations imposed on low-income tenants. These problems have been heightened by the housing authorities' policies in Melbourne and Sydney of selling their housing within the established urban areas and building only on the urban fringe. In Sydney, nearly all the new tenants in government houses live forty-eight or more kilometres from the city centre. In Adelaide, this problem is less severe, because the Housing Trust does not sell the old 'double units' (duplexes) located in middle suburbs near jobs.

In providing more government housing in the inner suburbs, widespread clearance is inappropriate, even if it provides many more dwellings at a cost per dwelling similar to the purchase and renovation of existing dwellings. It causes major social disruption and destroys much housing that, although dilapidated and having little renovation potential, still provides an important source of low-cost housing. More high-density development for pensioners and medium-density housing for families, which are especially needed in inner Sydney, can be provided in other ways that take little existing housing. This housing could be built on under-utilised government land or on industrial land in residential areas. Even if these sources of land are unavailable, the authorities still could increase their yield of new dwellings per old dwellings destroyed by emulating private developers: they can develop small blocks of flats on larger parcels on the outer edges of the inner city.

An expansion of the renovation programme in all three inner-city areas would have the substantial advantages identified by the Glebe study. In a situation of increasing gentrification, public acquisition preserves housing for the poor that would otherwise be lost. Renovation also supplies the kind of dwellings most needed by poor families with children. In Melbourne such a programme is also especially needed, because of the relative over-supply of government flats in the inner suburbs. These units have very short waiting lists despite the urgent shortage of private rental accommodation in the inner city.

Purchase and renovation by public authorities can improve the existing inner-suburban housing and keep it available for the poor.[8] Purchases need not be compulsory and existing tenants on low-incomes should be able to stay if they so choose. Under a dispersed programme of public acquisition and rehabilitation, the stigma of living in public housing is reduced and the tenants can gain greater social supports from more capable neighbours. To keep costs down, modest but structurally sound dwellings could be purchased and rehabilitated to a reasonable standard but not restored as historic buildings. If tenants of the rehabilitated dwellings are permitted to buy them, it should be only at full market value and with private financing, so as to enable the Authority to replace the dwellings without further subsidies.

More opportunities in public housing for the inner-suburban households on low incomes can also be provided by changing management policies. The most needy could be better served without altering income requirements if the following groups were given priority on the waiting list:
(1)   inner-suburban tenants who are forced to move or who pay more than a third of their incomes in rent;
(2)   people with special needs for ready access to central health and other facilities;
(3)   families (with children) having inner-city jobs but no car; and
(4)   aged, inner-suburban renters.
The number of openings for new tenants could be increased by assessing rents for public housing at market values, rather than by historic costs, with rebates provided if rents exceeded a quarter of earnings. This policy, which is proposed for the 1978 Commonwealth/State Agreement, would encourage those tenants whose incomes increase to move, or to buy their dwellings; if they were to stay, they would pay enough rent to enable the housing authority to supply more housing. Unless public housing funds are increased several fold, such steps to reduce benefits for people on lower-middle incomes are the only way to increase resources for the poor.

Even with more public housing and different management policies, some needs would remain unsatisfied. A pool of emergency housing is required for those who have exceptional needs yet must wait for public housing. Proposals have been made in South Australia for dwellings owned by a variety of government agencies, such as roads and education departments, to be used for these purposes (Committee of Inquiry into Emergency Housing Needs, 1977). Many of the most disadvantaged inner-city residents lack even the skills necessary to maintain themselves in public housing. Half-way houses and other residential care facilities are a way to serve transients and others who suffer personal as well as financial difficulties. Subsidies for private organisations that provide for these persons could come from expanding funds for the Homeless Persons Assistance Act of 1974. This programme provides Commonwealth Funds to private welfare organisations that supply housing for poor transients.

Local councils can also provide low-cost housing, in some cases receiving subsidies from the Commonwealth government (for aged persons' housing). The City of Adelaide owns some dwellings, and the City of Sydney, under a former Labor Council, built many flats. However, the present Council in Sydney is selling 242 flats of the 1000 that it owns (*Sunday Telegraph,* 12.12.77). Although they are being offered at generous terms many tenants cannot afford them. These sales are directly contrary to the Strategy Plan's goal of maintaining accommodation for the poor. Alderman Denny Linker explains that 'the Council does not believe its ratepayers should have to pay for low-cost housing' (Sydney *Sunday Sun,* 24.5.76).

The majority of the low- and moderate-income households will continue to depend on the private rental market. The lot of these groups can be improved by both raising their incomes and by more rights for tenants. Any policies that minimise income inequalities — the provision of adequate pensions, the implementation of more progressive tax scales, or the protection of low-skilled jobs — would be especially helpful for the inner-suburban poor.

The Housing Allowance Experiment, which the Commonwealth is beginning in 1978, would also benefit the inner suburban poor (CURA, 1977).[9] It may not increase the supply of rental housing, but it should improve the ability of the poor to compete with higher-income groups, to pay smaller proportions of their incomes on their rent, and yet enable them to pay enough in rent to cover the costs of adequate maintenance and limited improvements. If sufficient funds were made available, an allowance could reach many of the needy groups that do not live in public housing. However, these policies should be viewed as complementary rather than as alternatives: public housing works on the supply side and allowances on the demand side.

The third element of assistance for poor tenants is tenancy legislation (Bradbrook, 1975). To use it for lowering rents would restrict supply and disadvantage newcomers to the market. But it can provide more security of tenure by requiring considerable advanced notice for evictions and by establishing a standardised lease and bond conditions which respect the rights of tenants and landlords. It also reduces the chances that housing allowances or other supports will be passed on to landlords without benefiting tenants. The South Australian Residential Tenancy Act of 1978, which is administered by the

Consumer Protection Agency under the Attorney General, provides for two months notice to evict tenants and provides tribunals that make judgements on disputes over rents, bonds or repairs within fourteen days of the complaint being lodged (Duncan, 1977). Similar legislation has recently been passed in New South Wales (*Financial Review,* 14.2.78). Even with more legal protection, organisations such as the Tenants' Union of Victoria are needed to inform tenants of their rights (*SMH,* 27.5.77).

Conclusion

The post-war development of Australia's inner suburbs has been, in many respects, a success story. Unlike the dramatic decline of the American inner city, the old housing near Australian city centres has been improved, mainly by owner-occupants on relatively low incomes. Some of the difficulties caused by the loss of some cheap housing have been offset by rising real incomes for all income groups and considerable increases of both inner-suburban flats and outer-suburban houses. Although there has been less redevelopment in recent years, unemployment and other economic and social problems have increased and poor tenants are facing increasing competition for inner-suburban houses from higher-income groups.

In terms of policy, the notable failures have been the unchecked growth of office jobs and some over-zealous slum clearance. But policies during the 1970s have increasingly been based on the understanding that the inner suburbs can no longer be regarded as slums, and need protection from over-development. Firm land-use controls and the decentralisation of government jobs and public institutions would prevent further incursion and growth of employment in the inner city. If controls on land and building permitted and encouraged further development of flats in inner areas, the journey-to-work problems caused by the considerable centralisation of existing jobs could be minimised. A combined programme of more public purchase and rehabilitation of housing, income supports, and tenancy legislation would improve and retain inner-suburban housing for people of modest means.

The implementation of these policies would require action by all levels of government. Many public policies have been and will be influencing the land use and housing of the inner suburbs, and the economic position of its residents. Too often these policies have been made by individual agencies with little concern for their effects on the inner suburbs or their relationship with the actions of other agencies.

At the national level, the Department of Environment, Housing and Community Development (EHCD) can facilitate the exchange of information on the inner suburbs between state and local agencies. It can make provisions within the Commonwealth/State Housing Agreement for encouraging state housing authorities to expand their inner-suburban renovation programme. The Department can also identify the consequences for the inner suburbs of policies developed by a wide range of other Commonwealth departments. The

Department's recent report on urban renewal (EHCD, 1978), which discusses a wide range of local and state policies for inner areas, represents an important step forward in communication between levels of government.

In coordinating policies for the inner city, state planning agencies, in close cooperation with housing authorities, are best equipped to take the lead. They are concerned with the entire metropolitan area and potentially can influence other state agencies that have major impacts on inner areas. State planning authorities have residual powers over most land uses and are the most appropriate arm of government for making those decisions, such as controlling the size of the CBD, which affect the entire metropolis. Only state action can prevent local councils from serving local interest in ways that aggravate the metropolitan-wide shortage of low-cost housing. If these actions are to be taken, the state planning authorities will require more authority, more resources, and more of a sub-regional emphasis in their organisation. The first step would be to establish comprehensive outline plans for the inner areas based on solid research and agency and public consultations.

In the past, local government has seldom addressed the problem of maintaining low-cost housing. Even the resident action groups, which have done much to limit over-development and improve amenities, often protect the property rights of the more affluent at the expense of the poor. However, local government has the authority to take a more active role in these issues. They might do so if decision-making at the local level were improved. If the LGAs of Sydney and Adelaide were larger, residents affected by city-centre development may better influence it and benefit from its tax revenues. Designation of more equitable ward boundaries in the Cities of Sydney and Melbourne, and full adult suffrage and compulsory voting, could also provide more balanced power between residents and property interests.

The success of these policies, and the governmental reorganisation necessary for their effective implementation, will depend upon political support. The public would more readily accept them if it was widely understood that decentralisation of employment and urban services benefits both inner- and outer-area residents. If the voters knew of the difficulties endured by the inner-suburban poor, there would be more acceptance of the need for compensatory government housing and income programmes. Identifying and publicising these issues has underlined the policy advances made during the early 1970s. Further initiatives are required to assure that the highest costs of urban change will not have to be paid by those Australians who are least able to afford them.

Chapter 1

1. For a brief review of recent American literature on the inner suburbs, see the book review section of the *Journal of the American Institute of Planners,* January 1977.
2. Harrison (1977) and Neutze (1977) provide useful comparisons of Australian cities.
3. For example: Brisbane (Cities Commission, 1975); Newcastle (Crooks Michell Peacock Stewart Pty Ltd, 1976); Fremantle (Newman, 1977); and Hobart (Graham, 1977). Nearly all planning reports by inner-area councils also show concern for issues of redevelopment and incompatible land uses.
4. The map shows that, in 1971, Paddington was in the local government area (LGA) of Woollahra. Unless otherwise noted, it is included in the definition of the inner city used in this study.
5. Oversampling of outer suburbs was corrected by discarding every third record in these areas (Davis, 1977).
6. These were the Botany Interim Development Control Map, January 1974; Leichhardt Planning Scheme, June 1968; Marrickville Planning Scheme, December 1972; North Sydney Planning Scheme, April 1963 (with amendments up to December 1973); and City of Sydney Planning Scheme, December 1970.

Chapter 2

1. Johnston (1971) provides an excellent review of the literature on urban spatial patterns in Australia and North America.
2. Many of the concepts developed in this section are from Hoover (1968) and Richardson (1969).
3. This section draws heavily from Frieden (1964).
4. Cox (1973) presents a more general analysis of governmental involvement in conflict between and within areas.

Chapter 3

1. See Manning (1978) for a detailed analysis of journeys to work in Sydney.
2. These estimates are sensitive to the variable size of the CDs. Corner shops and other local neighbourhood uses were not counted as non-residential activities here because they cause few problems for local residents. Non-conforming land uses could not be identified.

3. The historical material in this section is drawn mostly from McCarty (1974), Jackson (1974), Barrett (1971) and Spearritt (1978).
4. See Kendig (1976a) for a description of the uses of cluster analysis in classifying residential areas. Of the many available clustering techniques, the one chosen for the Sydney data was POLYDIV, a divisive technique best suited for data arrays having many cases but relatively few differentiating variables. The program was developed by the Commonwealth Scientific and Industry Research Organisation (CSIRO) (Lance & Williams, 1975).
5. Unfortunately, data on housing age and the value of owned dwellings were not available. The figures are for occupied dwellings only. In conducting the cluster analysis, CDs having fewer than a hundred people were excluded. For the remaining CDs, those having fewer than fifty houses (or flats) did not take into account the tenure, cost and size of their district's houses (or flats) in allocating them to groups.
6. The 'Terrace' areas were separated into two sub-groups by the cluster analysis. This 'better' half consists mostly of the originally more fashionable localities which are not immediately next to the CBD or industrial areas.
7. These measures slightly underestimate the numbers of low-income earners in the inner city because they exclude certain kinds of people who have high rates of poverty, a higher proportion of which are located in the inner city: boarders, lodgers, aged parents living with children, and all but the first individual in other kinds of shared accommodation. (See the section on Terminology and Data in Chapter 1, page 16.)
8. The difference between the slight over-representation of large families, shown by the Poverty Inquiry data, and significant under-representation, shown by the SATS data, probably results from the inclusion of North Sydney (which has very few children) in the SATS data.
9. Table 10.3 provides more detailed data on poverty rates in inner Sydney. Similar findings for Melbourne are reported by CURA (1977:86-8).
10. Table 5.3 provides detailed figures for foreign-born people in the inner areas of Sydney, Melbourne and Adelaide.

Chapter 4

1. Because the SATS survey did not ask for birthplace, it is not possible to specify the family type of migrants.
2. These poverty figures are for aged single people only, because sample sizes rule out any analysis of poor aged couples in the inner city.
3. The higher-status, more capable older people in outer areas may have more dissatisfaction because of higher expectations.
4. These figures differ radically from those reported by aged people in large American cities. For example, in Los Angeles, the proportions of the aged expressing dissatisfaction at specific neighborhood conditions are 67 per cent at crime, 45 per cent at air pollution, and 41 per cent at noise (Kendig, 1976b:49). These findings probably also apply, if perhaps to a lesser degree, among population groups less sensitive than the aged to neighborhood problems.
5. Aged people, invalids, deserted wives, widows, supporting mothers (all as of June 1971), and unemployment beneficiaries in March 1973.

6. It should be pointed out that, even with these controls for income, there is a residual income effect within the low-income category. As was discussed earlier, the 'low-income' group in the inner city contains a far larger proportion of the impoverished than does the 'low-income' population elsewhere in Sydney.

7. Difficulties result from using average figures for the various comparisons. Accessibility and population characteristics differ widely both within and outside the inner city. The accessibility consequences of moving out of the inner city depends, of course, on the particular place of origin and of destination. Moreover, if inner-city residents were to move away, the increase in their travel costs (measured either in time or by the expense or the mode of travel) would probably be higher than is indicated by the differences between the averages for the inner versus other areas. This is especially true for families moving to public housing on the urban fringe. Their low rates of car ownership mean that many would either have to buy cars or spend very long periods travelling on the poor public transport service available outside inner areas. If they moved out of but continued to work in inner areas (a likely possibility given the centralisation of jobs) their trips would probably be longer than those for the workers already living in outer suburbs, many of whom have local jobs.

8. Several cautionary points should be noted before interpretations are made. As with the previous table, the figures only show the direction, not the size, of the flows. A more significant problem is that the data tends to underestimate numbers moving into inner areas, most of whom are probably at the pre-family state of the life cycle. It is impossible to identify persons who have moved from the inner city and locations outside Sydney, and the coding does not make it possible to distinguish those moving in from outside Sydney from people who did not give their 1966 address. Thus, the positive net flow from rural Australia and overseas countries to the inner areas (many of whom are low-income, single people) is not counted. The data also measures households instead of individuals; thus single persons who marry each other after moving into the inner areas count as two families when they enter but only one family if they leave. These kinds of errors explain why the ratio of the totals moving in and moving out (78:100), seems too low considering that the inner city experienced only a small population loss from 1966 to 1971.

Chapter 5

1. Distortions introduced by rent control are avoided by making comparisons only between 1947 (when all rental units were controlled) and 1971 (when virtually none were controlled). Some of the more rapid rise in inner areas may have been caused by the demolition of the worst rented houses. Public redevelopment certainly took the worst housing, which may explain why, in inner Melbourne where there was more public redevelopment, relative house rents in inner areas rose fastest. However, the best houses were more likely to be converted to owner-occupancy, which was a far more important factor than redevelopment in reducing the stock of rented houses.

2.   Industry of employment is the best measure available of socio-economic change over the post-war years. Data on occupation was unavailable before 1966. Employers as a proportion of the labourforce, a good measure in 1971, was less valid for changes over time because many employers, especially in the inner suburbs, have in earlier years been small businessmen of relatively low status. Industrial classifications, especially in manufacturing, have changed over time. The problem is minimised by comparing relative changes between inner and other areas.
3.   See Maher (1976) for an analysis of the post-war population changes in inner Melbourne.

Chapter 6

1.   From the planning schemes described in Note 6 of Chapter 1.
2.   Office workers are defined slightly differently in each of these three sources. But they generally consist of professionals, administrators, executives, managers, clerks and a few categories of sales personnel.
3.   This figure is considerably less than the total population losses in these areas, because declining occupancy rates (people per room) also caused losses. A rough estimate was made by using some broad assumptions: that the mix of housing types lost during the late 1940s and the 1950s equalled that of the 1960s, and that the occupancy rates in these lost dwellings equalled the average occupancy rates of similar dwellings throughout the City of Sydney (pre-1969 boundaries) in 1961.
4.   Most of this material on the University is from James Colman Pty Ltd (1976), in a report prepared for the South Sydney Council.

Chapter 7

1.   Source: Unpublished data from Philip Shrapnel and Company (various years). This data is from the sale prices of auctioned houses, which excludes rent-control-affected sales (discussed later in the section) and probably exceeds the average of all house sales. The data nonetheless should reflect change over time.
2.   Vacancy rates for inner-suburban dwellings were 2 per cent in 1954 and 4 per cent in 1961. Figures were not available for LGAs in 1947 or for dwellings by type for LGAs in 1954 or 1961.
3.   In South Australia, the Act was gradually relaxed from 1951 onwards and replaced in 1961 with the ineffectual Excessive Rents Act (O'Reilly, 1977).
4.   Because conversions can be calculated only indirectly as the total increase of flats minus new construction, the estimate of conversions is a net figure including both conversions and losses of flats already existing in 1954. The net figure for conversions, if losses could be separated out, would be higher. This problem is especially severe in the City of Sydney, where the losses of flats to non-residential incursion in the innermost areas must have significantly offset the net conversions elsewhere in the City.

Chapter 8

1. Data on vacancy rates by dwelling type are unavailable for 1961. A loss of 1300 occupied houses would have resulted from an increase of vacancies by 2 per cent. The vacancy rate in inner-suburban houses was 6.9 per cent in 1971 (Table 8.3).
2. The Census does not separate new houses by type. These figures assume that all the villa units in inner Sydney in 1971 were built since 1961.
3. The change in the number of occupied dwelling units was converted into change of the number of residential buildings; it was assumed that there was one residential building for each house, one for each boarding house, one for every two shares of houses, and one for every five single rooms.

    The Census data on new houses was provide for each CD, and it was assumed that any old houses lost were caused by flat redevelopment rather than new houses.

    Besides these assumptions, there are several other possible sources of error. First, increases of vacancy rates in houses, which the Census did not identify by CDS, probably resulted in slight over-estimation of incursion. Second, some houses were demolished before 1961 for flats built during the 1960s, and others were taken during the 1960s for flats first occupied after 1971. Third, the small number of old flats demolished for new flat development were not identified.
4. The inner middle suburbs were defined in Sydney as the LGAs of Concord, Drummoyne, Burwood, Ashfield, Canterbury and Rockdale. In Melbourne they include Williamstown, Footscray, Essendon, Brunswick, Northcote, Kew, Hawthorne, Coburg and Preston.

Chapter 9

1. Pensioners can apply for exemptions that postpone rate payments until their properties are sold. However, many are reluctant to encumber their estates in this way.
2. The MMBW consultants' (Little, 1977) claim — that the centralisation of jobs and residents will create more jobs — has a number of difficulties. In their analysis of American cities, they attempt to show that more centralised, faster-growing cities create more service jobs that can substitute for the loss of manufacturing jobs. Their conclusion that rapid population growth creates job opportunities runs directly contrary to the well-established principle that it is job opportunities which cause population growth. In contrast to their hypothesis that centralisation facilitates job growth, the fastest-growing American cities have decentralised land-use arrangements and infrastructure. Moreover, their use of American data is inappropriate: Australia's cities have little sign of the declining city centres and regions, as in the American Northeast (Sternlieb & Hughes, 1975). O'Connor (1977) raises additional methodological and conceptual criticisms of the MMBW consultants' analysis.

    The consultants also argue that the centralisation of high income residents would lead to life-style changes which create a demand for personal services that could be provided by low-income people. There is little doubt that high-income residents in the inner city do have more cosmopolitan life-styles than their suburban counterparts. However, there is no indication that high-income people leading suburban life-styles could be induced into the inner city or, even if they could, that their demand for personal services would increase. The way people live depends more on their personal characteristics than on where they live. Changes of residential environments are usually made to facilitate desired life-styles; residential location does not cause life-style changes.

Chapter 10

1. Chapter 8 analyses the reasons for vacancies in 1971. The reasons for the high rates of vacancies in 1976 are difficult to explain and certainly warrant further investigation.
2. These are unpublished ABS figures from disconnections of electricity supply.
3. Under-enumeration in 1976 was estimated at 5 per cent in inner Melbourne and inner Sydney, compared to nationwide averages of 2.7 per cent in 1976 and 1.3 per cent in 1971. Actual under-enumeration in the inner areas was probably higher, because the groups of LGAs used for making the adjustments were larger than the inner areas used in the study. 'After adjustment' figures are not used in Table 10.1 because adjusted figures are at this time unavailable for 1971.
4. Paddington was excluded because figures were available only for current LGA boundaries.
5. This information was provided by Greg Black, of the South Australian Department of Housing and Urban Development. The figures are from the Valuer-General and will be reported in a forthcoming study by the South Australian Council of Social Services on the inner city (Australian Housing Research Council Project, No. 48). The definition of the inner suburbs in his study includes the LGAs used in this study and some additional, adjoining suburbs. His inner-city area contains about 25 per cent more population than the area in this study.
6. Unpublished data provided by Greg Black. See Note 5 above.
7. Unlike the New South Wales Housing Commission, Beattie does not assume a shorter physical life for renovated terraces than for new flats. This assumption is consistent with the findings of this study that structurally sound, brick structures do not have fixed physical lives. In fact, housing in single occupancy, even if very old, is often better built and less likely to have maintenance problems than is newer, multiple-occupancy housing.
    Another difference between the Beattie study and the N.S.W. Housing Commission was the cost of renovation. The actual renovation costs per dwelling of the Glebe project were well below those estimated by the Housing Commission in Waterloo.
8. Under the Housing Improvement Grants in Britain, subsidies have been given to private home owners at all income levels as a means to improve inner-city housing. Unless it were very carefully controlled, such a programme in Australia could accelerate the rising housing costs and exacerbate the difficulties of tenants on low incomes. Even if it were made available only to owners on low incomes, the programme would not benefit the needy renters and the property, once sold, would no longer house people on low incomes.
9. See Neutze (1978: 105) for a more detailed analysis of the Housing Allowance Experiment.

Abbreviations

ABS	Australian Bureau of Statistics
AGPS	Australian Government Publishing Service
AIUS	Australian Institute of Urban Studies
ANU	Australian National University
APIC	Australian Population and Immigration Council
BLF	Builders Labourer's Federation
CBD	Central Business District
CCC	Cumberland County Council
CD	Collectors District
CPI	Consumer Price Index
CURA	Centre for Urban Research and Action
DMR	Department of Main Roads
EHCD	Department of Environment, Housing and Community Development
LGA	Local Government Authority
MMBW	Melbourne and Metropolitan Board of Works
NSWHC	New South Wales Housing Commission
NSWSPA	New South Wales State Planning Authority
PLI	Plant Location International
SATS	Sydney Area Transport Study
SAHT	South Australian Housing Trust
VCOSS	Victorian Council of Social Services
VHC	Victorian Housing Commission
URU	Urban Research Unit, Australian National University

Alexander, I. (1976), 'The changing role of the city centre', Seminar Paper, URU, Canberra.
— (1977), 'To concentrate or disperse? That is the question', Seminar Paper, URU, Canberra.
— (1978), *Office Location and Public Policy,* Longman, London.
Alonso, W. (1964), *Location and Land Use,* Harvard University Press, Cambridge, Mass.
Anglim, J.Y., Brine, J., Dunstan, G., & Fisher, A. (1975), *Incentives for Inner City Living,* AIUS Publication no. 54, Adelaide.
ABS (1972-1977a), *Value of Building Jobs Completed in Statistical Divisions and Local Government Area's,* Sydney.
— (1972-1977b), *Building Statistics, Number of New Dwellings Completed,* Sydney, Melbourne, and Adelaide.
— (1977a), *Manufacturing Establishments; Small Area Statistics,* Sydney, Melbourne, and Adelaide.
— (1977b), *Sales of Vacant Land and of Houses in the Sydney and Wollongong Areas of New South Wales,* Sydney.
AIUS (1975), *Industrial Land in Sydney,* AIUS Publication no. 51, Canberra.
— (1977), *Manufacturing in the Port Phillip Region,* AIUS Publication no. 66, Canberra.
APIC (1976), *A Decade of Migrant Settlement: Report on the 1973 Immigration Survey,* AGPS, Canberra.
— (1977), *Population Report 1,* AGPS, Canberra.

Balmain's Residents Case (1975), *'Impact of Cargo Trucking on Balmain',* Sydney.
Barrett, B. (1971), *The Inner Suburbs: The Evolution of an Industrial Area,* Melbourne University Press, Melbourne.
Bayne, P.J. (1977), 'Legal perspectives of planning the inner city', paper presented to 48th ANZAAS Congress, Melbourne,
Beattie, D. (1978), 'Economic evaluation of the proposal to acquire and rehabilitate residential property in Glebe' in McMaster, J.C. & Webb, G.R. (eds), *Australian Project Evaluation; Selected Readings,* Australia & New Zealand Book Company, Sydney.
Black, John (1977), *Public Inconvenience; Access and Travel in Seven Sydney Suburbs,* URU, Canberra.
Borrie, W.D. (1964), 'Demographic trends and prospects', paper presented to the Conference on Metropolis in Australia, Social Science Research Council, Canberra.
Braby, R.H. (1976), 'Urban renewal — the Melbourne experience', in McMaster, J.C., & Webb, G.R. (eds), *Australian Urban Economics: A Reader,* Australia & New Zealand Book Company, Sydney.

Bradbrook, A.J. (1975), *Poverty and the Residential Landlord-Tenant Relationship*, — Law and Poverty Series, Commission of Inquiry into Poverty, AGPS, Canberra.
— (1977), 'The role of state government agencies in securing repairs to rented housing', *Melbourne University Law Review*, Vol. II, no. 2.
Burgess, E.W. (1929), 'Urban areas', in Smith, T.V., & White, L.D. (eds), *Chicago: An Experiment in Social Science Research*, University of Chicago Press, Chicago.
— (1964), 'Natural area' in Gould, J., & Kolb, W.C. (eds.), *A Dictionary of the Social Sciences*, Charles C. Thomas, New·York.
Burnley, I.H. (1972), 'European immigration settlement patterns in metropolitan Sydney: 1947-1966' *Australian Geographical Studies*, vol. 10, pp. 61-78.
— & Walker, S.R. (1977), *Population and Social Change in the Inner City of Sydney*, School of Geography, University of New South Wales, Sydney.

CCC (1947), *Expanded Housing Study*, Sydney.
— (1948), *Report on the Planning Scheme for the County of Cumberland, New South Wales*, Sydney.
Cities Commission (1975), *Moreton Region Growth Strategy Investigations: Inner Urban Redevelopment Potential.*
City of Adelaide (1974), *The City of Adelaide Plan and Explanatory Statement, Book 1.*
City of Adelaide Development Committee (1972), *City of Adelaide, Interim Development Control, First Statement of Policy.*
City of Melbourne (1964), *Report on a Planning Scheme for the Central Business Area of the City of Melbourne*, Melbourne.
— (1974), *City of Melbourne Strategy Plan: Final Report.*
City of Sydney (1971), *City of Sydney Strategic Plan.*
— (1974a), *Community Services Interim Report*, Action Study no. 28.
— (1974b), *City of Sydney Strategic Plan, The 1974-77 Statement of Objectives, Policies and Action Priorities.*
— (1976a), *Chippendale: A Plan for Preservation of an Inner City Precinct*, Action Plan 31.
— (1976b), *The West Rocks*, Action Plan 29.
— (1977), *The Sydney City Council's Strategic Plan, Objectives and Action, 1977-80.*
— (1978), *CBD Study*, vol. 1.
City of Sydney Resident Action Group Committee (1977), *Planning for Residential Living in the City of Sydney*, The Council of the City of Sydney.
Clutton, A.T. (1966), 'The New South Wales Government Railways in the role of a real estate developer', Joint Urbanisation Seminar — Urban Redevelopment, URU, Canberra.
Commonwealth Bureau of Roads (1973), *Report on Roads in Australia: 1973*, Melbourne.
Cox, Kevin R. (1973), *Conflict, Power and Politics in the City: A Geographic View, McGraw-Hill, New York.*
Crooks Michell Peacock Stewart Pty Ltd (1976), *Inner City Residential Study — Newcastle City Council.*
Cullingworth, J.B. (1974), *Town and Country Planning in Britain*, George Allen & Unwin Ltd, London.
CURA (1977), *The Displaced: a Study of Housing Conflict in Melbourne's Inner City*, Melbourne.

184

Darcy, L., & Jones, D.L. (1975), 'The size of the homeless men population of Sydney', *Australian Journal of Social Issues*, vol. 10, no. 3.

Davie, M.R. (1938), 'The pattern of urban growth', in Murdoch, G.P. (ed.), *Studies in the Science of Society*, Yale University Press, New Haven.

Davis, J.R. (1977), 'Using the Sydney Area Transportation Study data for social research', *Australian Journal of Statistics*, vol. 19, no. 1.

De Leuw, Cather *et al* (1968), *Report on Metropolitan Adelaide Transportation Study*.

Department of the Environment, UK (1977), *Policy for the Inner Cities*, presented to Parliament by the Secretary of State for the Environment, HMSO, London.

Department of Housing (1968), *Flats: A Survey of Multi-unit Construction in Australia*, Canberra.

Donald, O.D. (1977), 'Health Care Delivery in Sydney: a Question of Equity', unpublished PhD. thesis, URU, Canberra.

Duncan, P. (1977), 'Tenancy Reform in South Australia', *Shelter*, November.

EHCD (1978) *Urban Renewal: A Report on the Consultations of the Urban Renewal Task Force of the Department of Environment, Housing and Community Development*, AGPS, Canberra.

EHCD (1976a), *Aged Persons Housing Survey*, 1974, vols. I & II, AGPS, Canberra.

EHCD Studies Bureau (1976b), *Inner Sydney Vacant Industrial Premises Study*, AGPS, Canberra.

Evans, A.W. (1973), *The Economics of Residential Location*, MacMillan, London.

Firey, W. (1947), *Land Use in Central Boston*, Harvard University Press, Cambridge, Mass.

Fisher, E.M., & Winnick, L. (1951), 'A reformulation of the filtering concept', in Merton, R.K. (ed.), *Social Policy and Social Research in Housing*, Association Press, New York.

Fitzroy Ecumenical Centre (1975), 'Tenants in privately rented accommodation in Fitzroy and Collingwood', Part III, in Commission of Inquiry into Poverty, *Consumer News on Welfare Services and Rented Housing*, AGPS, Canberra.

Form, William H. (1954), 'The place of social structure in the determination of land use: some implications for a theory of urban ecology', *Social Forces*, vol. 32, no. 4, pp. 317-23.

Fricke, F. (1975), 'The noise nuisance', Appendix 7, in *Balmain's Residents Case*.

Frieden, Bernard (1964), *The Future of Old Neighborhoods*, The MIT Press, Cambridge, Mass.

Gardner, M.G. (1975), A letter in *Balmain's Residents Case*.

Graham, R.J. (1977), 'Battery Point: social action and planning for human scale development', paper presented to the 48th ANZAAS Congress, Melbourne.

Grigsby, W.G. (1963), *Housing Markets and Public Policy*, University of Pennsylvania Press, Philadelphia.

Halladay, A.E. (1971), 'Poverty and the Large Family in Sydney, 1968-69: A Study of Living Conditions and Social Policy', unpublished Ph.D. thesis, Department of Sociology, Research School of Social Sciences, ANU, Canberra.

Hargreaves, K. (1975), *This House Not For Sale: Conflicts Between the Housing Commission and Residents of Slum Reclamation Areas,* Report by CURA, Melbourne.

Harris, C.D., & Ullman, E.L. (1945), 'The nature of cities', *Annals of the American Academy of Political and Social Science,* 242, pp. 7-17.

Harrison, P.F. (1972), 'Planning the metropolis — a case study', in R.S. Parker and P.N. Troy (eds), *The Politics of Urban Growth,* ANU Press, Canberra.

— (1974), 'Planning the metropolitan areas', in I.H. Burnley (ed.), *Urbanisation in Australia: the Post-War Experience,* Cambridge University Press, London.

— (1977), 'Major Urban Areas, Commentary to *Atlas of Australian Resources,* 2nd series, Department of National Resources, Canberra.

Henderson, R.F. (1975), *Poverty in Australia: First Main Report,* vol. 1, AGPS, Canberra.

Holdsworth, J. & Brooks, G. (1971), 'Pilot study into displacement through slum reclamation', *Architecture in Australia,* April, pp. 186-90.

Hoover, E.M. (1968), 'The evolving form and organisation of the metropolis', in Perloff, H. & Wingo, L. Jr. (eds), *Issues in Urban Economics,* Resources for the Future Inc., Washington, DC.

— & Vernon, R. (1962), *Anatomy of a Metropolis,* Doubleday Anchor, New York.

Housing Industries Association (1976), *Report on the Necessity of a Uniform Law Permitting Dual Occupancy Dwellings in New South Wales,* Sydney.

Hoyt, H. (1939), *The Structure and Growth of Residential Neighborhoods in American Cities,* Federal Housing Administration, Washington, D.C.

Hume, I. (1975), 'Aspects of Manufacturing in the Adelaide Suburban Area: A Case Study of the Locational Behaviour of Firms in the Selected Areas', unpublished B.A.(Hons.) thesis, Department of Geography, University of Adelaide.

Jackson, R.V. (1974), 'Owner-occupation of houses in Sydney, 1871 to 1891', in Schedvin, C.B., & McCarty, J.B. (eds), *Urbanization in Australia: the Nineteenth Century,* Sydney University Press.

Jackson Teece Chesterman Willis Pty Ltd (1975), *Sydney Teachers College Proposed Redevelopment of College Site at North Newton — Draft Environmental Impact Statement.*

James Colman Pty Ltd (1976), *Darlington and the University of Sydney,* Report to Council of Municipality of South Sydney.

Johnson, K.M. (1972), *People and Property in North Melbourne,* URU, Canberra.

Johnston, R.J. (1971), *Urban Residential Patterns: An Introductory Review,* G. Bell & Sons Ltd, London.

Jones, M.A. (1972), *Housing and Poverty in Australia,* Melbourne University Press, Melbourne.

Kendig, H. (1976a), 'Cluster analysis to classify residential areas: a Los Angeles application', *Journal of the American Institute of Planners,* July, pp. 286-94.

— (1976b), 'Neighborhood conditions of the aged and local government', *The Gerontologist,* April, vol. 16, no. 2.

— (1976c), 'The social impacts of Port Botany', in Butlin, N.G. (ed.), *The Impact of Port Botany,* The Academies of Social Sciences, Humanities and Science, with ANU Press, Canberra.

186

Lance, G.N., & Williams, N.T. (1975), 'POLYDIV: a divisive classificatory program for all-numeric data', *Australian Computer Journal*, 7, pp. 109-12.
Lewis, D. (1977), 'Policies for Adelaide's Central Area', internal working paper, South Australian Department of Housing and Urban Affairs.
— (1978), 'Housing in Adelaide: Inner Area', internal working paper, South Australian Department of Housing and Urban Affairs.
Little, F.M. (1977), *Socio-economic Implications of Urban Development*, MMBW, research report submitted to MMBW.
—, Morozow, O., Rawlings, S.W., & Walker, J.R. (1974), *Social Dysfunction and Relative Poverty in Metropolitan Melbourne*, MMBW, Melbourne.
Llewellyn-Smith, M. (1977), 'Adelaide City Council and Housing', *Shelter*, no. 3, March.
Logan, M.I. (1963), 'Industrial location trends in Sydney region', *Royal Australian Planning Institute Journal*, April.

Maher, C.A. (1976), 'Population change in inner Melbourne 1961-71' paper for Seminar on Residential Change in the Inner Suburbs, URU, Canberra.
Manning, I.G. (1978), *The Journey to Work*, George Allen & Unwin, Sydney.
McCarty, J.W. (1974), 'Australian capital cities in the nineteenth century', in Schedvin, C.B. & McCarty, J.W. (eds), *Urbanisation in Australia: The Nineteenth Century*, Sydney University Press, Sydney.
McCutcheon, A. (1977), 'A Rental Housing Association Begins', *Shelter*, no. 5, November.
McInnes, K.R. (1966), 'The acquisition of the special uses area, Darlington', Joint Urbanisation Seminar — Urban Redevelopment, URU, Canberra.
MMBW (1954), *Melbourne Metropolitan Planning Scheme, 1954 Report.*
— *(1968), The Melbourne Metropolitan Planning Scheme.*
— (1971), *Planning Policies for the Melbourne Metropolitan Region.*
— (1977), *Melbourne's Inner Area — A Position Statement*, Planning Branch, Melbourne.
Moses, L., & Williamson, H.F. (1967), 'The location of economic activity in cities', *Papers and Proceedings of the Seventy-ninth Annual Meeting*, American Economic Association, San Francisco, vol. lvii, no. 2.

NSWHC (1976), *Waterloo Development Proposals; analysis of options and environmental impact statement.*
NSWSPA (1967), *Sydney Region: Growth and Change — Prelude to a Plan.*
New South Wales Urban Transport Advisory Committee (1976), 'Report by Urban Transport Advisory Committee of New South Wales, to the Minister for Transport and Highways and the Minister for Planning and Environment', Sydney.
Neutze, Max (1971a), *People and Property in Bankstown*, URU, Canberra.
— (1971b), *People and Property in Randwick*, URU, Canberra.
— (1972), *People and Property in Redfern*, URU, Canberra.
— (1977), *Urban Development in Australia*, George Allen & Unwin, Sydney.
Newman, P. (1977), 'Fremantle: A case study in inner city population decline — policy and planning implications', paper presented to the 48th ANZAAS Congress, Melbourne.

O'Connor, K. (1977), 'Socio-economic Implications of Urban Development: A Review', working paper no. 5, Department of Geography, Monash University, Melbourne.

Ogilvie, D. (1969), 'The Rehabilitation of Decayed Urban Residential Areas', Department of Town and Country Planning, University of Sydney.

Ogilvy, E. (1977), 'Planning policies in political context — a case study of Melbourne', paper presented to 48th ANZAAS Congress, Melbourne.

O'Reilly, L. (1977), 'The evolution of housing in Adelaide', paper presented to the 48th ANZAAS Conference, Melbourne.

Pak-Poy, P.G. & Associates (1973), *Inner Suburban — Outer Suburban: A Comparison of Costs,* AIUS, Canberra.

— & Sherrard, H.M. (1966), 'Transportation in relation to urban redevelopment', Joint Urbanization Seminar — Urban Redevelopment, URU, Canberra.

Park, R.E., Burgess, E.W., & McKenzie, R.D. (1925), *The City,* Publications of the American Sociological Society, 21, University of Chicago Press, Chicago.

Patterson, J., Yenckyn, D., & Gunn, G. (1976), *A Mansion or No House,* Hawthorn Press, Melbourne.

Piatkowska, O. (1974), 'Population characteristics and needs of the Redfern House Catchment Area', unpublished paper, Redfern House, Sydney.

PLI (1976), 'Inner Sydney Industrial Land Market', report prepared for the Department of Urban and Regional Development, Sydney.

Pugh, C. (1976), 'Older urban residential areas and the development of economic analysis: a comparative study', in McMaster, J.C., & Webb, G.R. (eds), *Australian Urban Economics: A Reader,* Australia & New Zealand Book Company, Sydney.

Quinn, Robyn (1974), 'Beaconsfield Report', unpublished report for the Beaconsfield Group of the Australian Assistance Plan.

Ratcliff, R.U. (1949), *Urban Land Economics,* McGraw-Hill, New York. *'Report of the Committee of Inquiry into Emergency Housing'* (1977), unpublished report submitted to the Premier's Department, September 1977, Adelaide.

Richardson, H.W. (1969), *Regional Economics: Location Theory, Urban Structure and Regional Change,* Praeger Publishers, New York.

Roseth, J. (1969), 'Revival of an Old Residential Area', unpublished Ph.D. thesis, Faculty of Architecture, University of Sydney.

Ryder, W. (1976), 'From dust to smog', in Butlin, N.G. (ed.), *Sydney's Environmental Amenity 1970-75,* the Academies of Social Sciences, Humanities and Science, with ANU Press, Canberra.

—, with Joy, C. (1976): 'Waste generation and pollution', in Butlin, N.G. (ed.), *The Impact of Port Botany,* The Academies of Social Sciences, Humanities and Science, with ANU Press, Canberra.

SAHT (1977), *South Australian Housing Trust Annual Report,* submitted to the Minister for Planning.

Sandercock, L.K. (1975), *Cities for Sale,* Melbourne University Press, Melbourne.

Smith, V. (1976), 'The battle of Victoria Street', *Architecture in Australia,* June/July.

South Australian Town Planning Committee (1962), *Report and Plan for the Development of the Metropolitan Area of Adelaide.*

South Sydney Community Aid Environment Committee (1974), 'Environmental Quality in South Sydney', unpublished.

Spearritt, P. (1974), 'Sydney's "slums" — middle-class reformers and the Labor response', *Labour History*, no. 26, pp. 65-81.

— (1978), *Sydney Since the Twenties*, Hale & Iremonger, Sydney.

Sternlieb, G. & Hughes, J.W. (eds) (1975), *Post-Industrial America: Metropolitan Decline and Inter-regional Job Shifts*, Center for Urban Policy Research, Rutgers University, New Brunswick, New Jersey.

— & Burchell, R.W. (1973), *Residential Abandonment; the Tenement Landlord Revisited*, Centre for Urban Policy Research, Rutgers University, New Brunswick, New Jersey.

Stevenson, M., & O'Neil, J. (1967), *High Living: A Study of Family Life in Flats*, Melbourne University Press, Melbourne.

Suttles, Gerald D. (1972), *The Social Construction of Communities*, University of Chicago Press, Chicago.

Sutton, A.J., & Richmond, D.T. (1975), *Walk Up or High Rise; Residents Views on Public Housing*, NSWHC, Sydney.

SATS (1974), Report (vols. I-III), Sydney.

Troy, P.N. (1971), *Environmental Quality in Four Sydney Suburban Areas*, URU, Canberra.

— (1972), *Environmental Quality in Four Melbourne Suburban Areas*, URU, Canberra.

URU (1973), *Urban Development in Melbourne*, AIUS, Canberra.

Vandermark, E. (1974), 'Urban renewal', in Burnley, I.H. (ed.), *Urbanisation in Australia: the Post-War Experience*, Cambridge University Press, London.

— & Harrison, P.F. (1972), *Development Activities in Four Sydney Suburban Areas*, URU, Canberra.

VCOSS (1975), *Towards an Inner Urban Strategy?*, Melbourne.

Vinson, T. & Homel, R. (1976), *Indicators of Cummunity Well-Being*, AGPS, Canberra.

Wagner, C. (1977), 'Sydney's Glebe Project: An Essay in Urban Rehabilitation', *Royal Australian Planning Institute Journal*, 15, no. 1, pp. 1-24.

Whiteman, L.A. (1966), 'Education: implication for educational services of city redevelopment', Joint Urbanization Seminar — Urban Redevelopment, URU, Canberra.

Woodruff, A.M. & Ecker-Racz, L.L. (1969), 'Property taxes and land-use patterns in Australia and New Zealand', in *Land and Building Taxes*, Becker, A.P. (ed.), University of Wisconsin Press, Madison.

INDEX

189